THE TITLE OF THIS BOOK

The word "heliotropium" is the Latin name for an ancient plant which had the unique habit of turning to face the sun at all times. The plant's name is derived from two Greek words: *helio,* meaning "sun," and *tropos,* meaning "turn." The Roman writer Pliny wrote of this plant, "I have often spoken of the wonderful property of the heliotrope, which turns itself round with the sun, even on a cloudy day, so great is its love of that luminary. But at night it closes its azure flower, as if from missing its rays."

Thus the heliotrope excellently represents the attitude of the faithful soul toward the Will of God, which is represented by the sun. This sun must ever be gazed upon by us with fixed and unshrinking eye, in whatever direction its course may bend; and this one thing must we ever resolve in our mind: *"As it pleases God, so does it please me.* The Will of God alone is to me the rule of life and death. As it hath pleased the Lord so shall it be done. Blessed be the Name of the Lord." *(See pages 75 and 76).*

THE HELIOTROPIUM

VOLVNTAS DIVINA.

SYMBOLVM HVMANÆ VOLVNTATIS

HELIOTROPIVM
seu
CONFORMATIO
humanæ voluntatis cum
divina;

Libris quinque. explicata
coram

Ser.mo vtriusq; Bavariæ Duce
S.R.I. Archidapifero,
Electore :

MAXIMILIANO
et Ser.mâ *coniuge*

ELIZABETHA:
Eisdem Ser.mis Prīcipib°
inscripta & dedicata,
AB
HIEREMIA DREXELIO
è Societate IESV.

IHS

COLONIÆ AGRIPP.
Sumptibus Cornelii ab
Egmond et Sociorum.
M DC XXX.

Voluntas divina.

Voluntas humana.

Title-page of the Latin edition, Cologne, 1630

HELIOTROPIUM

Conformity of the Human Will
to the Divine

By
FATHER
JEREMIAS DREXELIUS

Edited by
FERDINAND E. BOGNER

*"The Lord gave, and the Lord hath
taken away . . . blessed be the name of
the Lord."*

—Job 1:21

TAN BOOKS AND PUBLISHERS, INC.
Rockford, Illinois 61105

Nihil Obstat: Remigius Lafort, D.D.
                      Censor

Imprimatur: ✠ John Cardinal Farley
                      Archbishop of New York

Library of Congress Catalog Card No.: 84-51597

ISBN 0-89555-245-0

Cover Illus.: Boumard Fils, Paris, 5380.

TAN BOOKS AND PUBLISHERS, INC.
P.O. Box 424
Rockford, Illinois 61105
1984

PREFACE

IN offering "The Heliotropium" to the public we are not presenting a new book. It was first published in Latin in 1627. An English translation, the basis of the present edition, appeared in 1862.

The author, Jeremias Drexelius, was the most distinguished ascetical writer of Germany in the seventeenth century. Born at Augsburg, Aug. 15, 1581, he entered the Society of Jesus at the age of seventeen years, became teacher of rhetoric, and afterwards court preacher at Munich—a position which he held for twenty-three years. He was a valued friend and adviser of the Elector Maximilian I. By the people he was esteemed as a saint. He died April 19, 1638.

The writings of Drexelius, without doubt, excel, in almost every respect, all other contemporary works of the same kind. Their popularity is attested by their wide sale. Of one treatise alone 20,400 copies were disposed of in Munich before the year 1642; while the total sale of his various writings reached the astounding figure of 170,700 copies. There were subsequently many reprints, besides translations into several foreign languages.

A great many, no doubt, will imagine that this book is a difficult one to read, to follow, and to understand, owing to the deep problem of which it treats. Quite the contrary is the case. The language is simple and pleasing, the statements are logically and forcefully placed, and interest is sustained throughout.

The volume is divided into five parts or books. A glance at the following summary will acquaint the reader with their contents:—

Book I brings home to us the necessity of seeing God's Will in everything. Understanding this well, we are taught in Book II how to unite our will, which always remains free, to God's Will. The Third Book explains how we receive many benefits by uniting our will to God's. Whatever might hinder this union is clearly pointed out in Book IV. Numerous aids, helping us to attain to this true union with God, are suggested in Book V.

Going carefully over the pages of this book, I found in them a wealth of material suitable for the present day. The one great problem in life, which is not understood as it should be, by the vast majority, is the question of the Divine Will. Of all the mistakes made by men, the failure to recognize God's Will is, undoubtedly, the saddest and greatest. The keynote to happiness and peace of mind is the realization that this Will means everything. Doctrines of all kinds are being preached and taught. Our sympathy is quickly enlisted in the various methods of bringing help to man's troubled mind. But all the while we lose sight of the fact that the Finger of God rules and dominates all things. When this becomes plain, then, and only then, will the heart of man find its long-sought rest.

Before turning the book over to the publishers, I made a thorough trial of its principles and illustrations, in my work in the confessional and in giving counsel, so often sought from the priest. It bore fruit, and I am convinced that such a work should be more widely known. My brother priests, especially, will, I am sure, be glad to know of it. There are many other good works on the same subject, it is true, all teaching the same truth, but not in so simple and convincing a manner. In this work a difficult theological problem has been placed within easy grasp of the ordinary reader.

The contents of this volume will prove a source of true spiritual joy to the reader. The confessor will find it invaluable in his direction of souls. The priest knows how difficult it is for the majority of people to see God's Will in the event of death, sickness, or other calamity. God's Will is the solution to such difficulties when they arise—the only answer to rash, impetuous questioning—a sweet and soothing answer! People struggling in the world need to realize this. They are anxious to know it. I feel, therefore, that the zealous priest will welcome "The Heliotropium." These pages will help Religious to see their life of cross and trial in the light of peace and comfort. No one, in fact, can tire of perusing the volume as spiritual reading. FERDINAND E. BOGNER.

CONTENTS

BOOK I

CONCERNING THE RECOGNITION OF THE DIVINE WILL

CHAPTER I

BOOK II

CONCERNING THE CONFORMITY OF THE HUMAN WILL TO THE DIVINE

BOOK III

CONCERNING THE BENEFITS ARISING FROM THE CONFORMITY OF THE HUMAN WILL TO THE DIVINE

Chapter II

Chapter III

Chapter IV

Chapter V

Chapter VI

BOOK IV

CONCERNING THE HINDRANCES TO CONFORMITY OF THE HUMAN WILL WITH THE DIVINE

Chapter I

Chapter II

Chapter III

Chapter IV

Chapter V

Chapter VI

BOOK V

CONCERNING THE AIDS IN CONFORMING THE HUMAN WILL
TO THE DIVINE

Chapter I

Chapter X

Chapter XI

THE HELIOTROPIUM

BOOK I

CONCERNING THE RECOGNITION OF THE DIVINE WILL

"Lord, what wilt Thou have me do?" *Acts* ix. 6.

THE HELIOTROPIUM

Book I

CHAPTER I

A TWOFOLD FOUNDATION IS LAID, AND IT IS SHOWN
THAT ALL PUNISHMENTS PROCEED FROM THE
HAND OF GOD

I

OF all the doctrine which Christ delivered in so many and such divine discourses this was the sum,—that man should absolutely and entirely conform himself to the Divine Will, in particulars as well as in generals. And this our Saviour most fully taught, both by precept and example, and gave Himself as a Pattern for our imitation. In order the more completely to set forth this teaching of our Lord, I propose, according to the custom of Theologians, to lay a twofold foundation. The first,—that the entire measure of our spiritual growth lies in the conformity and agreement of the human will with the Divine, so that in proportion as the one is more genuine, the other will be more luxuriant.

Now that a Christian man's entire perfection consists in Love (charity) is sufficiently evident, for the Holy Scriptures are full of testimonies to this. "Thou shalt love the Lord thy God with thy whole heart, and with thy whole soul, and with thy whole mind. This is the greatest and the first commandment." (*Matt.* XXII, 37.) "And now there remain faith, hope, charity, these three; but the greater of these is charity." (I *Cor.* XIII. 13.) "But above all these things have charity, which is the bond of perfection." (*Col.* III. 14.) "Now the end of the commandment is charity." (I *Tim.* I. 5.)

But that exercise of charity which is by far the noblest, and the one to be most often repeated, is this very conformity with the Will of God in all things. To have the same likes and dislikes is firm friendship, according to the judgment of S. Jerome and all wise men.

The second foundation is,—that nothing whatever is done in the world (sin only excepted) without the Will of God. No power belongs to Fortune, whether she smile or frown. These are but the dreams of heathen, who used to feign that the changes of human life were disposed by some goddess or other. S. Augustine, ridiculing this idea, says (*De Civit.* IV. 18) :—"How then is the goddess Fortune sometimes good, and sometimes bad? Is it that when she is bad she is no longer a goddess, but is changed into some malignant demon?"

Christian wisdom treats all idea of Fortune with contempt.

"Good things and evil, life and death, poverty and riches, are from God." (*Ecclus.* XI. 14.)

But this truth, which is most clearly witnessed to in the Sacred Writings, must be unfolded a little more fully.

2. In this way Theologians teach that all evils in the world (sin excepted) are from God. In all sin there are two things to be considered,—the guilt and the punishment. Now God is the Author of the *punishment* which attaches to sin, but in no way of the *guilt*. So that, if we take away the guilt, there is no evil belonging to the punishment which is not caused by God, or is not pleasing to Him. The evils then of punishment, like the evils of nature, originate in the Divine Will. We mean by evils of nature, hunger, thirst, disease, grief, and the like, things which very often have no connection with sin. And so God truly (and, as they say in the schools, effectively and positively) *wills* all the evils of punishment and nature for reasons of perfect justice, but only *permits* sin or guilt.

So that the latter is called His Permitting Will, the former His Ordaining Will. All, therefore, that we call evil proceeds from the Will of God. Thus Theologians teach; and this foundation must be laid as deeply as possible in the soul, for it is of the utmost importance humbly to receive, and ever to hold, as an infallible truth, that the first cause of all punishments and evils is the Divine Will, always excepting guilt, as I have said already.

Having carefully laid this foundation, we arrive at the following conclusion:—Since whatever is done in the world happens through the Permission or Command of God, it is our duty to receive everything as from the Hand of God, so conforming our will to His most holy Will, through all things, and in all things, as to ascribe nothing to accident, chance, or fortune. These are but monstrous conceptions of the ancients, and are not for an instant to be endured among Christians. And it is not only to fortune or chance that nothing is to be ascribed, but neither to the negligence or persevering care of man, as prime causes. Vain and idle are such complaints as,—"This or that happened to me because this or that man hated me, or managed my affairs badly, or did my business carelessly. Things would certainly have turned out differently if he had only been well disposed towards me, and had entered into the business with all his heart, and had not spared his pains." This kind of philosophy is vain and foolish. But true, wise, and holy is this,—"The Lord has done it all." For, as I have already said, good and evil things are from God.

3. And here very many persons deceive themselves through miserable ignorance, for they persuade themselves that only those evils which arise from *natural causes,*—such as floods, earthquakes, landslips, barrenness, scarcity of corn, damage caused by the weather, troubles arising from disease, death, and the like,—are inflicted by God, since in this case there very often is

no sin which can be connected with the punishment; but that those evils which derive their origin from *vice and human wickedness* (as, for example, calumny, deceit, theft, treachery, wrong, rapine, oppression, war, murder) are not from God, and do not proceed from His Providence, but from the wickedness and perverse will of those who devise such things as these against others. And hence those complaints so frequently in people's mouths of late years:—"This scarcity of corn is not God's doing. It is caused by men immoderately greedy of gain, and not by God." Such ways of speaking are mad and impious; they are utterly unworthy of a Christian man, and should be banished to the shades below the earth.

But in order to make my meaning as clear as possible, I will illustrate it by an example. Take the case of a man who wishes his neighbour to be stripped of all his goods, and who, in order to put this abominable design into execution, creeps secretly into the house of the man he hates, sets fire to it, and immediately hurries away. Presently, when the house is in flames, he runs to the spot with others, as if with the intention of helping to put out the fire, when all the while it is quite different: for, if occasion serves, he does not try to keep the flames under, but collects spoils for himself, and secretly removes from the fire plunder to increase his own property. All such designs as these, regarded by themselves, without perversity of will, and all such actions as these, considered *"in genere entis"* (as the Schoolmen say) have God as their Au thor. God brings these things about, just as He brings about other things in creatures void of reason. For as these last can neither move, nor do anything without God, so cannot the incendiary either enter a house, or leave it again, or scatter fire in it, without God. But it does not follow that these several acts are evil in themselves, for they may also be compatible with virtue, but the will of the incendiary is evil; it is a most wicked design which that abandoned man has followed, and of this God is not the Author and Cause, although He has *permitted* this design to be carried into execution. He might indeed have hindered it, if it had so pleased Him. Since, however, God by His Own just Judgment did not hinder that wicked design, He permitted it. The causes of His Permission I shall give further on.

4. The same line of reasoning holds good also in reference to other sins; and this may, perhaps, appear the clearer from the following example. Take the case of a man who is lame in consequence of a wound which he has received; he attempts to walk, it is true, but he moves over the ground with greater pain, and with a more awkward gait than a sound man. Now the cause of motion in the foot is the natural impelling force, but the cause of lameness is the wound, not the moving power of the soul. And just in like manner God is the Cause of that act which any one performs when sinning, but the cause of error and sin in this act is man's free will. God supplies help to the act, but not to that wandering and departure from

law and rectitude. Although, therefore, God is not, and cannot be, the Author of sin—for "Thy eyes are too pure to behold evil, and thou canst not look on iniquity" (*Hab.* I. 13); . . . "Thou hast loved justice, and hated iniquity" (*Ps.* XLIV. 8)—yet it is, nevertheless, most certain that all the evil of punishment arising from second causes, whether rational or irrational (in whatever way, or for whatever reason it may happen), proceeds entirely from the Hand of God, and from His most benign Disposal and Providence. It is God, my good friend, it is God, I say, Who guided the hand of him who struck you. It is God Who moved the tongue of him who slandered you. It is God Who supplied strength to him who wickedly trampled you under foot. God Himself, speaking of Himself by the mouth of Isaias, declares (chap. XLV. 7) :—"I form the light, and create darkness; I make peace, *and create evil;* I, the Lord that do all these things." And how completely does the Prophet Amos confirm this, when he says (chap III. 6),—"Shall there be evil in a city, which the Lord hath not done?" Just as if he had said, there is no evil which God does not do, by *permitting* the evil of guilt, and by *ordaining* and working out the evil of punishment.

Thus God, intending to punish the adultery and murder of king David by the sin of his incestuous son Absalom, says (2 *Kings* XII. 11, 12) :—"Behold, I will raise up evil against thee out of thy own house, and I will take thy wives before thy eyes, and give them to thy neighbour, and he shall lie with thy wives in the sight of this sun. For thou didst it secretly: but I will do this thing in the sight of all Israel, and in the sight of the sun." Admirably has S. Augustine said:—"In this way God instructs good men by means of evil ones." Thus it is that the Divine Justice makes wicked kings and princes its instruments, as well for exercising the patience of good men, as for chastising the forwardness of bad. Examples of this are ready at hand from every age, in cases where God works out His Own Good pleasure through the wicked designs of others, and by means of the injustice of others displays His Own just Judgments. And just as a father seizes a rod, and strikes his child, but a little while afterwards throws the rod into the fire, and becomes reconciled to the child, so God threatens by Isaias, and says (chap. x, 5, 6):—"Woe to the Assyrian, he is the rod and the staff of My anger, and My indignation is in their hands. I will send him to a deceitful nation, and I will give him a charge against the people of My wrath, to take away the spoils, and to lay hold on the prey, and to tread them down like the mire of the streets. But he shall not take it so, and his heart shall not think so; but his heart shall be set to destroy, and to cut off nations not a few." How plainly does God declare Himself to be the Author of such great evils! "My indignation," He says, "is in their hands. The rod of My fury is the king of Assyria, for punishing the abominable wickedness of the Jews. I have sent him that he should carry away spoils, and should

bring down the surpassingly insolent and inflated
minds of those who have cast aside their faith, and
worshipped the idols of the Gentiles with a mad service. But the king of Assyria himself will have far
different thoughts, and will not come to chastise, but
to slay, and utterly destroy them. But when I have
chastened My people by the Assyrians, then woe to
this rod! woe to the Assyrians! for as the instrument of My anger will I cast them into the fire."
The same may also be observed in other Divine chas-
tisements.

Titus, the Roman Emperor, when he had shut up
Jerusalem with the closest siege, determined upon
making the circuit of the walls, and examining everything with his own eyes. When he saw the trenches
full of dead bodies, and a deep stream of corruption
flowing from the decaying corpses, he groaned aloud,
and raising his hands and eyes towards Heaven, called
God to witness that it was not his work. (JOSEPH.
de Bell. Jud. l. VI. c. 14.)

5. But it may be objected—if this is the case, if
the Will of God is the origin of all evils, why do we
strive against it? Why do we attack disease with
medicines? Why do we oppose armed battalions to
the enemy? Why do we not at once open our gates
and welcome destruction within our walls? Why do
we not follow the example of that most holy Bishop
Lupus, and address all our misfortunes in the same
words as he did Attila, "Welcome, thou flail of God?"
It is good, my friend, not to be wiser than we ought,

but "to think soberly." (*Rom.* XII. 3.) That war and
deaths of all kinds are from God, it is clear enough.
But the conclusion drawn from this, viz., that therefore we must not resist an enemy, and must not grap-
ple with disease, is bad. For the will of *sign* (*voluntas signi*), I use the language of Theologians, is one
thing, and the will of *good-pleasure* (*voluntas bene-
placiti*) is another. Now concerning the will of sign,
made known to us by laws, it is sufficiently clear for
the most part, but concerning the will of good-pleasure it is not so, and we cannot at once tell how far it
extends. But more of this further on. For the present let us take disease as an example. From whatever
cause it arises, without the smallest doubt it proceeds
from the Divine Will. Since, however, the sick man
does not know how long God wills that he should be
afflicted with sickness, he may very properly strive
against it, and use any lawful remedy for recovering
his health. But when he has tried all remedies, and
has made no progress, nor recovered his health, let
him feel fully persuaded that it is the Divine Will
that he should be afflicted with a still more grievous
and protracted sickness. This is the right way, then,
to reason. God wills that you, my sick friend, should
be ill; but because you know not whether He also
wills that you should never be cured, you may, for that
reason, lawfully use remedies. If, however, He wills
that the disease should continue, He will withdraw
all efficacy from the medicines, so that you may not
be cured.

And the same is to be said about enemies. God often willed that the children of Israel should be attacked, lest they should fall into sluggish ways; but as long as it did not appear that He willed that they should also be overcome, so long might they resist the enemy. It would have been otherwise if God had warned them, as He did by the Prophet Jeremias, that they should surrender themselves as servants to King Nabuchodonosor. In the same way, too, if a fire which has broken out cannot be extinguished by any amount of labour, it is a plain proof that God willed not merely that the house should catch fire, but that it should be burnt down, either to try His friends, or punish His enemies. And the same is to be observed in all other cases.

Then again, as it sometimes happens that a father puts a wooden sword into his son's hand, and says:— "Come, my boy, defend yourself against me; let us see what progress you have made with your fencing-master." In this case it is not the son who is opposed to his father, but the fencer to an adversary; and just in the same way when any one desires that a fire should be extinguished, or an enemy destroyed, or a disease subdued, he does not resist the Divine Will which approves the punishment, but the guilt, which God hates. For a house is set on fire either to inflict an injury, or from envy. To resist guilt of this kind is permitted to every one. And so he who tries to drive away disease constitutes himself an adversary, not of the Divine Will, but of human offence;

for there is scarcely any disease which has not been occasioned by some intemperance in living. Whoever then grapples with disease does not strive against God, but against intemperance, or certainly against its result. So also he who resists an enemy with arms does not make himself an adversary of the Divine Will, but of him who has begun the unjust war. In such cases as this it is by no means forbidden to defend oneself and one's goods, unless on other grounds it appears that the defence will be displeasing to God.

6. But why should it be thought strange that Divine Providence and Justice should use wicked men as its instruments, when even devils themselves fulfil this office? "It happens," says S. Gregory (*Mor.* II. 14), "by a wonderful dispensation of piety, that, through the very means by which the malignant enemy tempts the heart in order to destroy it, the merciful Creator disciplines it that it may live." It is said of Saul,—"the day after the evil spirit from God came upon Saul." (1 *Kings* XVIII. 10.) But how could that spirit be *evil,* if it was from God? How could it be of God, if it was evil? And this the same history explains, when it says—"An evil spirit from the Lord troubled him." (1 *Kings* XVI. 14.) It was an evil spirit in consequence of the desire of his own perverse will, but it was a spirit of the Lord, because sent from the Lord to torment him. S. Augustine, Bishop of Hippo (in *Ps.* XXXI. Exp. ii. 25), throws much light on this; nor will it be amiss to quote his

words at length. "What is right in heart?" he inquires. "Not resisting God. Attend, my beloved, and
understand the right heart. I speak briefly, but yet
a thing of all the most to be commended. Between
a heart right, and a heart not right, there is this difference:—Whatever man, let him suffer what he may
against his will, afflictions, sorrows, labours, humilia-
tions, attributeth them not but to the just will
of God (let this be well observed), not charging him
with foolishness, as though He knoweth not what he
doth, because he scourgeth such an one, and spareth
another; he indeed is right in heart. But perverse in
heart, and froward, and distorted are they, who, whatever evils they suffer, say that they suffer them unjustly, charging Him with injustice through Whose
Will they suffer; or, because they dare not charge
Him with injustice, take from Him His government.
Because God, saith one, cannot do injustice, but it
is unjust that I suffer, and such an one suffer not; for
I grant that I am a sinner, yet surely there are some
worse, who rejoice, while I suffer tribulation; because, then, this is unjust, that even some worse than
I should rejoice, while I suffer tribulation who am
either just, or less a sinner than they, and it is
certain unto me that this is unjust, and it is certain
unto me that God doth not injustice; therefore God
governeth not the things of men, nor is there any care
for us with Him. They then who are not right in
heart (that is, who are distorted in heart) have three
conclusions. Either there is no God; for, 'the fool

hath said in his heart there is no God.' (*Ps.* XIII. 1.)
Or, God is unjust, Who is pleased at these things,
and Who doeth these things. Or, God governeth not
human things, and there is no care for all men with
Him. In these three conclusions there is great impiety." And then a little further on the same Father
continues:—"So that is the right heart, brethren. Let
every man to whomsoever anything happens say, 'The
Lord gave, and the Lord hath taken away.' (*Job* I.
21.) Lo, this is a right heart, 'As it hath pleased
the Lord, so is it done. Blessed be the name of the
Lord.' He said not, 'The Lord gave, and the Devil
hath taken away.' Attend, therefore, beloved, lest
haply you should say, the Devil did this for me. Unto
thy God alone refer thy scourge, for not even the
Devil doth anything against thee, unless He permit
Who hath power above, either for punishment, or for
discipline: for the punishment of the ungodly, for
the discipline of His sons. For 'He scourgeth every
son whom He receiveth.' (*Heb.* XII. 6.) Neither must
thou hope to be without a scourge, unless haply thou
wish to be disinherited; for 'He scourgeth every son
whom He receiveth.' What, *every* son? Where then
wouldest thou hide thyself? Every one; and none
will be excepted; none without a scourge. What?
even to all? Would you hear how truly He saith *all?*
Even the Only-Begotten, without sin, was yet not without a scourge." This is, indeed, a noble piece of instruction, and thoroughly worthy of Augustine. But
since, according to that Father's meaning, neither devil

nor man has power against any one, except by the Permission of God, I must now briefly mention what sort of things God permits; for what reason, and on what grounds He permits them.

CHAPTER II

HERE the greater part of men fall into the most
miserable error, since with them the Divine Permission scarcely differs from human, inasmuch as it
rests in idleness, doing nothing, and does not restrain
those who wish to act, even though it can. From this
one error countless evils spring. In consequence of
this we rush one upon another, and, as though we
were the artificers of every misfortune and the authors
of every evil, we mutually assail one another with
tongue, and hands, and teeth, as if God all the while
were an indifferent Spectator of our quarrels, and allowed the most grievous acts of injustice when He
could prevent them. This is the very seed-plot of all
disorders, and for the purpose of uprooting it I proceed to lay down three points to be considered in
every Divine Permission. The first is the Will of permitting. The second, the Cause of permission. The
third, the Will which co-operates with that which is
permitted.

1. The better to understand this I must repeat that
there are *two kinds* of evils. The first comprising

those things which cause vexation, pain, loss, disgrace, such as poverty, imprisonment, disease, banishment, death, which are not to be called evils so much as bitter medicines administered by the Divine Hand. The second comprising those things which are properly called evils, as sin. The former kind God truly wills, either for the punishment of the wicked (as S. Augustine says, see above chap. 1. 6), or for the correction of His children. The latter God cannot be said to *will*, but to *permit*. For since God truly wills all things which truly exist (for by His Will all things are, and without it nothing exists), sin (which is improperly said to exist) He cannot will, but permits. But since God most clearly foresees all things that will be, He could easily prevent whatever He wills to prevent. Since, however, He does not prevent numberless things, we must conclude that God by His Own most just Will, from Eternity willed, and so decreed, to permit them. God, then, suffers anything to be done, not through being unwilling, but through willing it. Men, indeed, permit many things which they are either unable to prevent, or which they certainly would prefer not to be done. But not so the Supreme Ruler of all things. There is, therefore, in God a *Will of permitting*, which I have set down as the first point under the head of Permission. And now the question arises, why God should will to permit sin, or what is the cause in God of this Permission.

2. Never certainly would such infinite Goodness

permit so great wickedness in the world, unless it could thence produce greater good, and turn to salvation things which were devised for destruction. God permitted the jealousy of his brethren to exercise its malice against innocent Joseph; but with how great good was this Permission, not merely to his parents and brethren, but to the whole land of Egypt! God permitted guiltless David to be harassed with the most cruel injuries by wicked Saul, but it was to the greatest advantage of David himself and the entire kingdom of Israel. God permitted Daniel, most unjustly accused, to be cast into the den of lions, but it was to his own great good and that of many others. But why do I mention such as these? God permitted His Own Son to be crucified by murderers, but His Permission was for the ineffable good of the whole human race. And so from every Divine Permission there flow the greatest increase to the Divine Glory, and the richest blessings to the human race. Hence the Goodness of God and His Mercy, hence His Bounty and Power, hence His Providence, hence his Wisdom and Justice shine forth in a way which is altogether wonderful. Hence it is that the courage of many grows, the contest thickens, rewards are multiplied, and crowns of victory are increased.

And how worthy of wonder does Divine Providence show itself in these daily Permissions! For what great thing is it if you have produced good from good? but it is great indeed if you produce good from evil. Any one can be a pilot in a calm sea, as the saying is. (SENEC. *Ep.* 85.) It requires no great skill, when the wind is favourable, the ship stout, the sea calm, the stars shining brightly, and the rowers well-used to their work, to reach the harbour already in sight; but when the winds are raging, the ship dismantled, the sky thundering, pirates lurking around, the rowers unskilled in their work, and the stars hidden from sight, still to reach the wished-for harbour, this in truth is a feat to be admired in a pilot. And such is God in His Permissions. By means of seeming contraries He conducts to a happy end. By means of so many sins of men he advances His Own Glory. In such an accumulation of wickedness He causes His Own dear ones to shine the more conspicuously. Under God's guidance, acts of fraud turn to the advantage of the person who has been deceived; vexations and injuries add strength to the vexed; the wickedness of so many abandoned men strengthens the piety of others, and preserves them from perishing; and where many are thought to be utterly swallowed up they emerge again. The dungeon and chains opened for Joseph the way to an exalted throne of dignity; the envy of his brethren was of more service to him than the kindness of all the world besides. The treachery of Saul conferred on David a kingly crown. The den of lions raised Daniel higher than any courtiers or kings could have done. From the Cross Christ passed to Paradise; from Olivet He ascended to the Throne with the Father. But if God did not permit sins, and did not ordain what He permitted, and did not by His Ordinance turn them into good, we should have difficulty in recognizing the avenging Justice of God. But in this way we are taught lessons of deeper wisdom, and are constrained to confess a most wonderful order and connection of causes, by which so many blessings emerge at length from evils of such magnitude. There are, therefore, manifold causes for the Divine Permission. And this was the second point.

3. The third point is the Will of God *co-operating* in everything which He permits. God decreed from eternity not only what in the course of time He would permit, nor only the most just causes of His Permission, but He also had, and still has, a Will which co-operates in all His Permissions. In the schools of Theologians it is a point most clearly laid down, that God is the Helper of all those things which really are done and exist. Nothing exists anywhere without the help of the First and Chief Cause.

Since, then, God from eternity decreed to permit all those things which He does permit, and this for the most just reasons; and furthermore since He makes Himself a Helper in His Permissions, why do we assail Heaven and men with so many and such foolish complaints? Why do we so often rail at the Providence and most just Permissions of God? Why do we not rather ascribe all events to the Divine Decree, feeling sure that most just and weighty grounds of Divine Permission are lying underneath, and that an end of the deepest moment is proposed, against which it ill beseems us to struggle? Good and evil wills alike serve God; and among their various ends they all come to this, which, if I may so call it, is the End of ends.

Without question the holiest men have ever held it as the most certain truth that all things happened to them as if God were the Doer of them; because turning away the eyes of their mind from the thought of another's sin, they constantly viewed the Permissions of God as the actual and efficient causes of whatever happened. For God is so Good that on no account would he permit evil, unless he knew that from it He could produce greater good. S. Augustine speaks most admirably to the point (*Ench.* tom. III. c. 27 et 11):—"God has judged it better," he says, "to work good out of evil, than to allow no evil. For since He is supremely Good, He would in no way allow any evil to be in His Works, unless He were as Omnipotent as Good, so as to be able to bring good even out of evil." Excellently, too, does Theophilus Bernardinus speak (*De Persev.* l. XI. c. 4):—"God," he says, "winds Himself in among our errors and sins in a most penetrating way, not indeed as approving and participating in them, but as turning us away from them and correcting them, since out of evil things He brings forth the more good, just as if it was fire out of water." And here we must reflect, as the same writer admonishes us, that all who hurt us (in whatever way the injury is done) support a two-fold character. One in which they have *wicked intentions* towards us, and devise no common mischief against us; the other, in which they *are able to effect* what they have devised, and are the instrument of the Divine Justice which punishes us. If they only acted out the first character, viz., of malicious people, they would not hurt us at all; but because they support the other also, they do the work of God, Who justly punishes us, even though they act in ignorance of His designs. In this way Nabuchodonosor was a servant of God; and so, too, Attila, Totila, and Tamerlane, the scourge of God. Thus also Vespasian and his son, for the love of glory, and to increase their dominion, endeavoured to destroy the Jews; but they erred. In reality they were the executioners and ministers of the Divine Vengeance against that impious nation. The Jews could not digest their happiness without the help of these Imperial warm baths. But that we may follow out this line of reasoning more closely, let me ask a few questions.

3. I direct my questions to you, my Christian friend, to you particularly who so frequently disturb heaven and earth with your complaints. Be kind enough to tell me what you find fault with in the man who has injured you? Is it only with his *will* of injuring you, or only with his *power,* or both? With *both,* you will say. But I will instruct you not to find fault with either. Not with the will of injuring, for this without the power is vain, and has never done you any harm at all. Not with the power of injuring, for this is from God, and is just and right. You know that "there is

DIVINE WILL

no power but from God." (*Rom.* XIII. 1.) Why do
you then complain that one is able to do to you what
God permits him to do? A great injury is done to me,
you will say. But what sort of injury is it, let me
ask? God punishes your sins, exercises your patience,
multiplies your reward, and is an injury done to you?
Yes, but, you say, I am filled with indignation at this
wicked man, and his will which is so thoroughly corrupt. But you persist in looking at *man,* while I
wish you to look at *God* alone. However corrupt
the human will may be, what has it been able to do?
What has it done? You do not grieve on this account,
because he *willed* to injure you, but because he actually
did injure you, or was *able* to injure you. But why,
I would ask, and how could he do this? Whence did
he derive the power? And why had he the power?
Was it not from the Divine Power and Permission?
And if it is Divine, is it not also just, laudable, and
holy? Therefore, either hold your peace, or else direct your complaints against the Divine Permission,
and engrave this on your mind, that God never would
permit that the wicked will of another should devise
any evil against you, if it were not for your good, provided that you yourself do not become a hindrance.
"And who is he that can hurt you, if you be zealous
of good?" (1 *Pet.* III. 13.) S. Augustine (in *Ps.* LXI.
21) says, most admirably:—"Fear not the enemy; so
much he doeth as he hath received power to do. Him
fear thou that hath the chief power. Him fear that
doeth as much as He willeth, and that doeth nothing

[25]

unjustly, and whatever He shall have done is just. We might suppose something or other to be unjust: but inasmuch as God hath done it, believe it to be just. Therefore, thou sayest, if any one slay an innocent man, doth he justly or unjustly? Unjustly, certainly. Wherefore doth God permit this? Thou desirest to dispute before that thou doest anything, in consideration whereof thou mayest be worthy to dispute, why God hath permitted this. The Counsel of God to tell to thee, O man, I am not able. This thing, however, I say, both that the man hath done unjustly that hath slain an innocent person, and that it would not have been done unless God permitted it; and though the man hath done unjustly, yet God hath not unjustly permitted this."

And in the same way he speaks of the death of our Lord:—"Accordingly, my brethren, both Judas, the foul traitor to Christ, and the persecutors of Christ, malignant all, ungodly all, unjust all, are to be condemned all; and, nevertheless, the Father hath not spared His Own proper Son, but for the sake of us all He hath delivered Him up. (*Rom.* VIII. 32.) Order if thou art able; distinguish these things if thou art able. Render to God thy vows which thy lips have uttered. See what the unjust hath here done, what the Just One. The one hath willed, the Other hath permitted: the one unjustly hath willed, the Other justly hath permitted. Let unjust will be condemned, just Permission be glorified. Do not therefore wonder; God permitteth, and in judgment permitteth. He permitteth, and in number, weight, and measure He permitteth. With Him is not iniquity. Do thou only belong to Him."

This then is the shortest way to attain tranquillity,— not to regard the *man* who inflicts an injury, but *God* Who permits it. It was the custom of the Saints to think, not of him who for any reason might do them a wrong, but of Him who did not hinder the wrong-doer. Thus they accounted even injuries to be blessings; "for the doers of injustice," they said, "are those who make us blessed; but those who speak of us as blessed, deceive us." And so, with eyes ever fixed upon God, they rested on the Divine Will in everything, and waited to receive all things from God.

But understand from this that no man's sin merits pardon the more because God brings forth the greater good from it;—for man affords the occasion of good alone, not the cause; and even the occasion he does not afford of himself, but through the abundance of the Divine Goodness. If some wicked person has set fire to the cottage of a poor man, he has not on this account committed the less sin, because the poor man has borne his loss patiently, or some prince has erected in its place a ten times better house. Another person's virtue and a happy circumstance do not wipe out the guilt of the incendiary; and so sin does not acquire any excellence because it has afforded opportunity for doing good. But that we may understand this the better, we must now consider how secret are the Judgments of God.

CHAPTER III

AND here that saying of the Prophet must constantly be repeated,—"O Lord, Thy Judgments are a great deep." (*Ps.* xxxv. 6.) Great, great beyond all measure! From ancient times the two servants of the king of Egypt, the butler and the baker, pointed out this "deep," as it were with a finger. Both served the same king, both fell into disgrace, both were thrown into prison and bonds, and for no light reason, for with both was king Pharao angry; both of them also he remembered during his feast; to both he might have granted the favour of life, without prejudice to his justice; or both he might have condemned to death. And yet he sentenced the one to a punishment of shame, while he restored the other to his former office. The baker he hanged, and exposed him as food for the birds; the butler he restored to favour, and at last admitted him again to serve at the royal table. And such are the Judgments of God, Who banishes some from His Presence through Justice, but admits others to it through Grace. His Judgments are a great deep! "Who is able to declare His works?

For who shall search out His glorious acts?"
(*Ecclus.* XVIII. 4.)

1. How secret were the Judgments of God about
Nabuchodonosor, and that Pharao which knew not
Joseph! (*Exod.* I. 8.) S. Augustine (*De Prædest. et
Grat.* 15) well says concerning them:—"Nabuchodonosor, having been scourged after his numberless in-
iquities, merited repentance which brought forth good
fruit; while on the other hand Pharao was made more
obdurate by the very scourges and perished.   Both
were kings and wicked ones; both were admonished
by scourges; and what, I pray, made their ends so different?   One of them, when he felt the hand of God,
bewailed his sin, and came to his senses; the other, refusing to acknowledge the Will of God, continued in
his sins and perished."   And so it is that the same
medicine, compounded by the same hand, affects two
persons, who are labouring under the very same disease, in an entirely different way, and leads one to
health, the other to the grave.   Thus the two thieves
who were crucified with Christ were equally guilty, and
were punished in the same way by the self-same death,
and yet after death they shared habitations as different
as it was possible to be!   The Judgments of God are
a great deep!

That excellent king Asa, who "did that which was
good and pleasing in the sight of his God, and destroyed the altars of foreign worship, and the high
places, and broke the statues, and cut down the groves"
(*2 Par.* XIV, 2, 3), he, I say, who was the best of

kings, yet at the end of his reign corrupted his earlier praise. For a long time he bore himself illustriously, for thirty years he might have been considered a pattern for the most excellent princes; but at length, trusting in the king of Syria more than in God, he threw into prison the prophet Hanani who rebuked him for what he had done, slew many of the people, and, being afflicted with a painful disease in his feet, trusted more to the skill of physicians than to the Divine aid. Alas! how little did his end answer to his beginning! How was that holy king changed from himself! And, on the other hand, Manasses, a most wicked king, who disfigured the whole of his life with infamy through his evil deeds, at length came to himself, and crowned his bad beginning with a noble end. Thy Judgments, O my God, are a great deep,—too deep to fathom!

2. What objects of wonder are Saul and David! Both of them at the beginning were deserving of praise; both fell into grievous sins, to the scandal of the whole kingdom; for this both were punished, but with what a different effect! Saul, a man of obstinate impiety, perished most miserably; David turned his punishment into healing discipline, and thereby became a man after God's Own Heart. And here it is impiety to ask *"why* is this?" That "why" came from the school of the devil. Many have been ruined by that querulous "why" and "wherefore." "Why hath God commanded you?" (*Gen.* III. 1) asked at the beginning the subtlest of serpents. To whom they ought to have replied,—"We know that God has commanded

but *why* He has commanded is not for us to inquire. It is the Will of the Lord, and the grounds of this Will are not to be investigated by us." "For who hath known the mind of the Lord? Or who hath been His counsellor? Or who hath first given to Him, and recompense shall be made him? For of Him, and by Him, and in Him are all things." (*Rom.* xi. 34-36.) But perhaps some one will say,—"Yet it may be lawful to require some reason for this or that command." From whom? from God—to Whom alone that which He pleases is lawful, and Whom nothing pleases but that which is lawful?

How wonderful also is it that the Samaritans with the utmost readiness believe our Lord's words, and pray Him to remain with them, while the Gerasens are unbelieving, and pray Him to depart from them! The faithless Jews cannot be induced by words, or deeds, or by any wonders and miracles to believe in the Truth. Thy Judgments, O Lord, are a great deep!

Julian of Alexandria (*Euseb.* 6, 34; *Niceph.* 3, 30), a holy Martyr, being deprived of the use of his feet, was carried in a chair to the judgment-seat by two servants. One of them, renouncing his faith and his master, apostatized most disgracefully; the other, Eunus by name, remained faithful to God and his master; and so both of them, having been placed on camels, and scourged through the whole city of Alexandria, were at length thrown together into a fire, and ended their life most holily. When Besa, a soldier, saw them, and, through pity for the innocent, tried to restrain the violence of the wonted crowd, he was accused before the judge and beheaded. In truth he received the reward intended for that traitor. Thy Judgments, O Lord, are a great deep!

"O Lord, how great are Thy works; Thy thoughts are exceeding deep. The senseless man shall not know; nor will the fool understand these things." (*Ps.* xci. 6, 7.) Truly Thou art a God that hideth Thyself! In the year 1117, when the whole of Italy was disturbed by earthquakes, it is related that some of the nobles of Milan were sitting in a tower, engaged in business of the state, when a voice was heard outside, which called one of them by name to come out. At first he hesitated, and doubted who called, and who it was that was called; and so he sat still, and waited for a repetition of the summons, when behold! a stranger presented himself at the door, and begged him to come out. He had scarcely gone a few steps from the place when the tower fell, and buried them all! Now why should this man alone, and none of the rest, have been preserved from death? The Judgments of God are a great deep! Who can fail to see that in this case the miracles of old time were repeated? Thus it was that an angel led out Lot and his family from the destruction of Sodom. Thus likewise a thousand others, amid the multitude of those who perished, have been saved from destruction.

In the year 1597, there lived at Monreale, in Sicily, a man abandoned to an evil life, who had been often admonished that he should give up his impure life.

Still the wretched man persisted in his wickedness, and after the last warning was stabbed in the lap of the wretched companion of his sin. Another man, of similar habits, who for many years had lived in impurity, when he heard of this sad death, determined to grow wise through another man's sin, and reconciled himself to God. And what can I here exclaim again, but this same, Thy Judgments, O Lord, are past finding out!

3. And it was this which hurried away S. Paul into such great wonder. To those twins, Esau and Jacob, when they were not as yet born, and had done no good or evil, it was said,—"Jacob I have loved, but Esau I have hated. What shall we say then? Is there injustice with God? God forbid. O man, who art thou that repliest against God? Shall the thing formed say to Him that formed it, why hast Thou made me thus? Or hath not the potter power over the clay, of the same lump, to make one vessel unto honour, and another unto dishonour?" (*Rom.* ix. 13, 14, 20, 21.) The goldsmith fashions his silver and gold, the potter the clay, according to his will, although between the potter and the clay there is not even the shadow of such a relationship as exists between God and man, the vilest worm of earth. Who therefore will say to God, "Why dost Thou so?" (*Job* ix. 12.)

Dorotheus (*Serm. de Occult. Dei Jud.*) relates that a ship full of slaves for sale once upon a time arrived at a certain city. Now there was in that place a virgin of most saintly life, and who was entirely devoted to

[33]

the care of her soul. She was exceedingly pleased that an opportunity was afforded her of purchasing from the ship a little maid whom she might train, under her own immediate guidance, while she was still of a teachable age, to sanctity of life. And, fortunately, the captain had two little damsels, one of whom the lady bought at a high price. She had hardly left the ship when there arrived a woman of profligate manners, who acted plays with a dancing-girl; and she having bid for the other little maid, when she heard that she might be obtained for a trifling sum, bought her and carried her away. Alas! wretched little one, who hast fallen to a mistress as wicked as the other has to a good one! And who can here search out the depth of the Divine Judgment? Both of these little maids were of an innocent age, both were offered for sale, both were ignorant of the lot which awaited them, both, like a new vase, would preserve the odour of that which they earliest imbibed; and yet the one, from being trained in manners becoming a maiden, without difficulty became accustomed to the practice of virtue from her tenderest years, and in this way worthy of the companionship of Angels; while the other, being instructed by that Fury in every kind of wantonness and profligacy, and imitating too successfully the abandoned manners of her mistress, became a noble prey for the Devil. And yet she would have been different, if she had had a different mistress. But, "Thy Judgments, O Lord, are a great deep!"

The experience also of S. Gregory the Great, in his

own family, is much the same (*Hom.* 38 *in Evang.*
tom. I. 1644.) This most holy man had three aunts
on his father's side, Æmiliana, Tarsilla, and Gordiana,
all of whom devoted themselves to Christ, and the
Society of Holy Virgins. The first two preserved the
vow of virginity with the utmost fidelity, and finished
their life by a most blessed end. But the third, Gordiana, would listen to no admonitions, and so, greedily
devouring the baits of sin, burst at length from all restraint, left the Society, and married a farm-bailiff.
"O Lord, Thy Judgments are a great deep!" Let no
one try to fathom them! "Behold, God is great, exceeding our knowledge. Who can search out His
ways?" (*Job* xxxvi. 23, 26.) King David is very
cautious here,—"I am become," he says, "as a beast before Thee." (*Ps.* LXXII. 21.) Into Thy Judgments,
O my God, I do not pry; I behave as Thy beast. It is
the part of a beast to obey the command of his master,
not to discuss his orders. And what wonder is it that
a man who had not been educated in the Schools, but
who had passed the earliest days of his youth in tend-
ing a flock, should think thus of himself, when the very
Seraphim, those most glorious spirits, do the same?
For, when question was in heaven concerning the re-
jection of the Jews, the Seraphim covered their face
and feet with two wings each (*Isai.* VI. 2), confessing
that they could not by their knowledge attain to such a
height, as worthily to extol the wonderful works of
God; that the Divine Judgments surpass all power of
understanding; and that they are therefore content

to know that the Deity is thrice holy,—holy in Itself, holy in Its Judgments, holy in Its Works. If, then, the most glorious Angels thus adore the secret Judgments of God, how much more ought we, who are utterly insignificant men of earth, to exclaim,—"The Lord is faithful in all His words, and holy in all His works?" (*Ps.* CXLIV. 17.) And here let that most admirable saying of S. Augustine (*Cont. Jul.* III. 18) be a comfort to every one:—"God is able to save some without any good deserts, because He is Good. He cannot condemn any without evil deserts, because He is Just."

4. We behold wonderful revolutions in the world, continual changes, events altogether unexpected, and sometimes we say,—"Pray let us see how the thing will end." After a time we do see, and are astonished, muttering to ourselves some such freezing exclamation as "I could not have thought it!" But we know not, miserable creatures that we are, what will follow; and however things may turn out, the reason of them is not to be asked,—"For My thoughts are not your thoughts, nor your ways My ways, saith the Lord. For as the heavens are exalted above the earth, so are My ways exalted above your ways, and My thoughts above your thoughts." (*Isai.* LV. 8, 9.) To inquire the *reason* of the secret Counsel of God is nothing else, according to S. Gregory, than to wax wanton against His Ordinance. It becomes us to say at all times with Blessed Paul,—"O the depth of the riches of the Wisdom and of the Knowledge of God! How incomprehensible are

His Judgments, and how unsearchable His ways!"
(*Rom.* xi. 33.) In this life there are many things
which we shall never rightly search out. Let it suffice us to know that God is not unjust, and that at the
last day there will not be one who will not be constrained to say,—"Righteous art Thou, O Lord, and
true is Thy Judgment." King David, indeed, tried his
utmost to search out the secret Judgments of God. "I
studied," he says, "that I might know this thing."
(*Ps.* LXXII. 16.) But at length, not finding any end
to his search,—"It is a labour in my sight," he confesses, "until I go into the sanctuary of God." This
knowledge of secret things must be postponed for a
better world.

Let us, therefore, also fold the wings of a curious
mind. The regular flow and ebb of the sea has exercised all the learning of philosophers, and how can we
fathom the most profound recesses of the Divine Judgments? Who can find out why one was born in Tur-
key, and another among Christians? Why the Gospel
of Christ has come so late into many countries, and
meanwhile so many thousands of men have perished
while the same Gospel has early been spread in other
provinces? What is the reason why one country is
throughout its entire length infected with heresy, while
another flourishes in entire freedom from all contami-
nation of it? Why does the Divine Vengeance pass
by some, while it falls upon others? Why are some
innocent people overthrown, and why do the sins of
ancestors descend to their posterity? Why were so

many expeditions of kings and emperors undertaken
in vain for the recovery of the Holy Land? Let us
shrink from asking why God gave to Adam place for
repentance, but not to Lucifer. Why Christ showed
mercy on Peter, but not on Iscariot. Why one person
dies in the cradle, another in old age. Why one per-
ishes in depravity, though he has not been depraved
for long, while another recovers himself from depravity, though he has for a long time wallowed in vice.
Why one is rolling in riches, while another has neither
bread nor money. What meanest thou, O wandering
mind, by this curious inquiry? Do you desire to touch
that heavenly fire of the Divine Judgment? You will
be melted with the heat. Do you wish to scale the
citadel of Providence? You will fall. Just as moths
and other tiny insects ever and anon in the evening fly
round the light of a candle till they are burnt, so the
human mind disports itself around that hidden flame
We have the eyes of bats for this sun. We are only
human; we understand not the secret Counsels of God
"The works of the Highest only are wonderful, and
His works are hidden." (*Ecclus.* XI. 4.) There never
was a man who could at the same time read a book
written within and without. That book of the Divine
Judgments is written within full of Predestination,
without of Providence. The Eternal, all-wise God
has "ordered all things in measure, and number, and
weight; and who shall resist the strength of His Arm?"
(*Wisdom* XI. 21, 22.) Let us rest assured of this,
that the Cause before all causes is THE WILL OF GOD.

and he who seeks a different cause than this is ignorant
of the strength and power of the Divine Nature; for
it is necessary that every cause should in a certain way
be prior to, and greater than, its own effect; but nothing is prior to, nothing is greater than, God and His
Will. Of this, therefore, there is no cause. And
what more do you now desire? God has permitted,
God has willed, God has done! The Will of God is,
as Salvian rightly and piously says, Supreme Justice.
It is the most consummate wisdom quietly to acquiesce
in the Decrees of the Divine Will and Providence.

CHAPTER IV

HOW THE WILL OF GOD MAY BE RECOGNIZED IN ALL THINGS

IT requires a varying mode of treatment in the management of a nursery full of children, a school full of pupils, a house full of servants, a monastery full of Religious, and a plain full of soldiers, and yet the way of ruling is the same in all—viz. by obedience, which constrains differing wills to unite in one.

A general will not command well unless he is able, either with his mouth or hand, to carry about all his soldiers with him, that is to say, either with his voice or signal to enforce obedience to every order. Things are then managed well, and the discipline is uniform and regular when in a house the master of the family, in a school the tutor, in a monastery the abbot, in a camp the general, leads about with him all who belong to him, either with his tongue or his hand; that is to say, when he governs with a word or a sign, and constrains them to go wherever he wishes.

But as it is fitting that a soldier should wait for an order either from the tongue or hand of his general, holding himself in readiness to execute whatever command is given him, in the same way also it is right that the Christian should so hang, as it were, on the Tongue or Hand of God, that whatever He wills, says, commands, or in whatever direction He gives a sign, he should immediately will the same, and that he should instantly go in that direction, yea, run, or rather fly. We should all of us exclaim,—"In the head of the Book it is written of me that I should do Thy Will, O my God! I have desired it, and Thy law in the midst of my heart." (*Ps.* xxxix. 8, 9.) Yea, of my memory, my understanding, my will. Thy Will, O my God, is to me the summing up of all laws!

When Saul had been struck down to the earth by Christ, his first question was,—"Lord, what wilt Thou have me to do?" (*Acts* ix. 6.) And let this be the never-ceasing question of all good men, "Lord, what wilt Thou have me to do?" Show me, O my good Jesus, by a word or sign, what is Thy Will, and I go, I obey, I do whatsoever Thou willest me to do.

This question, therefore, must now be answered before all others—viz. in what way the Will of God is to be recognized in all things? And here I will furnish some rules by means of which the Divine Will may easily be discovered.

FIRST RULE

WHATEVER leads away from God is contrary to the Will of God. Whatever attracts towards God is in accordance with the Divine Will. "For this is the Will of God, your sanctification." (1 *Thess.* iv. 3.)

Therefore, if any one detect any such thing in himself as to be constrained to confess that this business, this society, this trade, this way of living, does not make me more holy, but I am being led away from God, though gradually and by easy steps, it follows that neither that business, nor that society, nor that trade, nor that way of living, is according to the Divine Will.

SECOND RULE

THE Will of God is most clearly revealed to us by the law of God and of the Church. In all doubtful cases, therefore, we must not merely inquire what the laws of God and the Church require, but what is more or less conformable to them. Christ long ago pointed out this most excellent interpreter of the Divine Will to that rich young man who asked what was the shortest road to eternal life, when He said,—"Thou knowest the commandments." (*Luke* XVIII. 20.) Of a truth nothing is better than to have regard to the commandments of the Lord. Abraham points out this messenger between God and men, charged with the Divine Will, when he says to the rich man,— "They have Moses and the prophets; let them hear them." (*Luke* XVI. 29.) Blessed Paul also says,— "Be not conformed to this world, but be reformed in the newness of your mind, that you may prove what is the good, and the acceptable, and the perfect Will of God." (*Rom.* XII. 2.) The "good" Will of God is contained in the Decalogue—the "acceptable" in the evangelical counsels—the "perfect" defines that His Will should be done on earth as it is in heaven.

THIRD RULE

IT is commanded by blessed Paul,—"In all things give thanks; for this is the Will of God in Christ Jesus concerning you all." (1 *Thess.* v. 18.) And here, first of all, it is most noteworthy that *"in all things"* we must give thanks, even when things are most full of trouble and adverse. S. Chrysostom (*in loc.*) has well said:—"Have you suffered some evil? If you choose, it is not evil. Give thanks to God, and thou hast already changed the evil into good. This is the part of a philosophic mind." The ancient Germans used to train their children in such an excellent way, that if ever they injured their finger in the fire, they immediately said, "Thanks be to God." It is a short but noble precept. Whatever then, my Christian friend, either presses upon you or afflicts you, say a hundred times, say a thousand times, "Thanks be to God." S. Paul adds,—"Extinguish not the Spirit." Let there be a place for Its Divine Inspirations. God not unfrequently unfolds His Will by means of secret addresses, which are then safely believed to be really Divine, when the Glory of God alone is proposed as the thing to be followed. But S. Paul further adds,— "Despise not prophecies." Hence it is by no means right that commentaries on God's Book, holy sermons in church, or admonitions of faithful men, should be despised by him who desires to conform himself to the Divine Will. He who is not willing to hear them, is not willing to understand the Will of God. Last of all, S. Paul commands,—"From all appearance of evil refrain yourselves." As good bankers know false coin either by the ring, or the stamp and inscription, and refuse it, so let us avoid, as contrary to the Divine Will, whatever carries on its face the appearance of even the faintest shadow of sin.

FOURTH RULE

BESIDES the laws of God and the Church, there are other interpreters also of the Divine Will, chiefly in doubtful matters. Among them are to be reckoned the magistrate, as well civil as religious, and all such as lawfully bear rule over others; to which are to be added parish priests, spiritual pastors and masters. When Saul was now prepared to obey the Divine Will, and had asked,—"Lord, what wilt Thou have me to do?"—the Lord did not burden him with precepts, nor did He suddenly infuse into him all knowledge, but sending him as a disciple to Ananias, said,—"Arise, and go into the city, and there it shall be told thee what thou must do." (*Acts* ix. 6, 7.) Ananias was to Paul what Peter was to Cornelius, a most faithful interpreter of the Divine Will.

Thus it pleases God that His Will should be unfolded to man by man. And hence those admonitions which are so frequent,—"Seek counsel always of a wise man." (*Tobias* IV. 18.) "Do thou nothing without counsel, and thou shalt not repent when thou hast done." (*Ecclus.* XXXII. 24.) "Be continually with a holy man, whomsoever thou shalt know to observe the fear of God, whose soul is according to thy own soul: and who, when thou shalt stumble in the dark, will be sorry for thee. And establish within thyself a heart of good counsel; for there is no other thing of more worth to thee than it. The soul of a holy man discovereth sometimes true things, more than seven watchmen that sit in a high place to watch. But above all these things pray to the Most High, that He may direct thy way in truth." (*Ecclus.* XXXVII. 15-19.) In all matters, therefore, where there is doubt concerning the Divine Will, from no one must counsel be sought rather than from those to whom we have entrusted our conscience. And here it may generally be affirmed that the entire will of spiritual masters, or superiors, or those in any way set over us, is the Will of God, sin alone being excepted. Whatever, then, the director of any one, or superiors, or those placed in authority have ordered must be received in no other way than as a certain indication of the Divine Will. And here blessed Paul sets us an example. Writing to the Galatians (II. 1), he says:—"Then after fourteen years I went up again to Jerusalem with Barnabas." And what was the cause of so long a journey? "I conferred with them the Gospel." (II. 2.) Lo! he who for so many years had been the evangelizer of the whole world, now submitted his teaching to inquiry, just as if he were the least esteemed of the disciples, and constituted the elder Apostles as his judges, so that whatever they should decree concerning his doctrine, and approve by common consent, or disapprove of, or add to, or take from, he would accept as that it should be so believed and taught. It is more wonderful that he adds,—"And I went up according to *revelation.*" (II. 2.) Could not He Who revealed to Paul that this journey was to be undertaken, have just as well revealed what He would effect by it? In good truth God wills that *man should be taught by man.* S. Paul went to Jerusalem for the purpose of interrogating the Apostles about his doctrine, not because he himself stood in any doubt of it, but because others did; and for their confirmation it seemed most prudent to interrogate the elder Apostles. Therefore,— "See and ask for the old paths, which is the good way, and walk ye in it, and you shall find refreshment for your souls." (*Jer.* VI. 16.)

FIFTH RULE

But if neither time nor place allow of seeking advice, let a man reason with himself, and by an easy process he will be able in this way to unravel every doubt concerning knowledge of the Divine Will. Let him carefully consider which of two things, about which he is doubtful, is the more pleasing to his own will, which is the more gratifying to his carnal appetite, and which is the more desirable in his own estimation. When he has ascertained this, which is easily done, and has seriously resolved with himself to conform his actions as closely as possible to the Divine Will, then he will safely choose that which is the less pleasing to his will, which is the less gratifying to his carnal appetite, and which has about it less splendour and show. For the other choice, which is in accordance with the inclination of our own will, or fleshly feelings and thoughts, ought fairly to be held in strong suspicion by every one, and be thought to be closely allied to error; but this, which struggles against one's inclination, may be believed to be, for the most part, the safer:—"While thou dost not," says Isaias, "thy own ways, and thy own will is not found, to speak a word." (LVIII. 13.) A man who has a troublesome and sluggish digestion may easily be convinced in this way;—that which you most eagerly desire is the least wholesome for you. Melons, cucumbers, mushrooms, snails, iced drinks, undressed fruits and vegetables, and food of this kind, things which irritate the stomach, do the utmost harm, but at the same time they are very often heaped into the stomach greedily. So in the matter before us; very often that which is pleasing and sweet to the senses of the body is harmful to the spirit; that which pleases the human will is displeasing to God. "Mortify, therefore, your members which are upon the earth; fornication, uncleanness, lust, evil concupiscence, and covetousness, which is the service of idols; for which things the wrath of God cometh upon the children of unbelief." (*Col.* III. 5, 6.) Therefore,—"Go not after thy lusts, but turn away from thy own will," the son of Sirach admonishes you (*Ecclus.* XVIII. 30), that you may conform yourself to the Will of God.

But if the matter be one of entire indifference, as, for instance, if two beggars meet you, both of them in the same state of destitution, but yet your alms are not enough to divide between the two, give to which you please, with the intention of fulfilling the Divine Will, and you will not do amiss. But if the indifferent thing be one of greater moment, you must have recourse to reflection and prayer. Then if, when considering the propriety of undertaking some one or more things, it is not quite clear what the Divine Will is, do not let any of them be undertaken hastily, until it appear in some way or other that they will not be contrary to the Divine Will. In every deliberation of this kind Reason and Conscience can effect very much; and no bad counsellors are they in a doubtful case, for when they are disposed to examine a thing with care they will easily pronounce what is best to be done. But it may happen that a man of tender conscience may fall into a labyrinth where the spirit and flesh struggle together in such a way, as that he begins to fear lest perhaps he is opposing himself to the Divine Will. And here let the same thing be a solace to him which often is to a preacher. An afternoon preacher (to explain what I mean) sees nearly all of his hearers sleeping. He is greatly vexed at the sight of so many drooping heads, but it seems better than if the same number of people were shamelessly to engage in idle talk. And so long as two or three do not sleep, he says to himself, that is enough for me, and is a sufficient reason why I should go on. One must stand for thousands. And so let the other man thus reason with himself, however he may be disturbed. Only let those two eyes, the *Reason* and the *Will*, be watchful, only let them carefully observe the Will of God, and I care nothing about other things, for I shall stand firm and unshaken; and although I cannot follow the indications of the Divine Will very closely, yet I will do my best to follow them.

SIXTH RULE

IN order to discover the Divine Will it is of the utmost avail to ask with Paul,—"Lord, what wilt Thou have me to do?" It was the custom of the saints, in all doubtful cares and perplexities, to take refuge in the safeguard of prayer, as of old Moses and Aaron did in the Tabernacle of the Testimony. And as when the clouds collect in such dense masses that the sky begins to thunder, bells are rung in towers to scatter them; so, as often as the sun of the Divine Will is withdrawn from our eyes, and we know not what is to be done, the best thing is to beat heaven with our prayers. Thus Saul, when overtaken by that sudden tempest in the midst of the open country, cried out,—"Lord, what wilt Thou have me to do?" And it is the most fitting time for repeating this little prayer over and over again, when we approach the heavenly feast; then should we redouble our fervour as we exclaim,—"Lord, what wilt Thou have me to do?" Yes, every day in the most solemn part of Holy Mass, at the awful moment of the Consecration, let this be the most ardent of all our prayers,—"Lord, what wilt Thou have me to do?" for it is highly desirable that a form of heavenly aspiration should be used by devout people every day during celebration. Jacob Lainez was accustomed to say every day at the end of the Consecration, after the words of the centurion,—"Lord, I am not worthy"—while he held Christ in his hands.— "May that which I have promised please Thee, O Lord?" And so, in cases of every kind, we ought to pray, while the heavenly Bread is being broken,— "Lord, as Thou willest, so do I also will; that which I have rightly promised I recall not." This daily oblation of self to the Divine Will is the most excellent preparation for the last conflict in death.

But if a person has for a long time asked something of God, and has not yet obtained his desire, let him rest assured that the Father, who is supreme in Goodness, wills not that that should be obtained from Him which His son has for so long a time sought, or that the most Benignant Father wills that the patience of His child who asks should be exercised so as to obtain a greater reward. There can be no doubt but that God in His infinite mercy frequently defers the help that has been sought, in order that He may the more abundantly reward more persevering prayers, and more enduring patience. These of a truth must not unfrequently be wrested from many, just as money is

from misers. God would demand from us fewer prayers and less patience, if He did not in this way urge the
slothful forward. And so it is often very much to
our profit to have obtained nothing by our daily prayers; for oftentimes the benefit of prayers which are so
long delayed is greater than it would have been if they
had been granted. And it is this which may well
bring great comfort to everyone that he has made
many prayers, and not a few.

How did King David fast, and weep, and pray,
prostrate on the earth before he knew the Will of God
concerning his little child who was at the point of
death; but when he heard that he was dead, he discovered that the Will of God had ordained that he should
die, and so he "arose from the ground, and washed
and anointed himself, and when he had changed his
apparel, he went into the house of the Lord, and worshipped." (2 *Kings* XII. 20.) Our Lord, after a
threefold prayer at the Mount of Olives, being now
certain about His Father's Will, said,—"Sleep ye now,
and take your rest: behold the hour is at hand."
(*Matt.* XXVI. 45.) And so, even when prayer is rejected, its refusal is received with quietude and calmness of mind, if only for this reason, that it is now
evident what Almighty God wills to be done. Heli
the priest, when Samuel related what vengeance God
would take both upon himself and his sons, made only
this reply,—"It is the Lord, let Him do what is good in
His sight" (1 *Kings* III. 18) ; just as if he had said,—
"You have told me, Samuel, what is painful for me to

hear; but, because I am now certain concerning the
Divine Will, I cheerfully receive what you have said,
however distasteful it may be, and recognize a proof
of God's Ordinance. I and my sons deserve to be
punished, and we shall suffer punishment since it so
seems good to the Divine Will, against which it is impiety to struggle. Let the Good God do whatever is
pleasing to His most holy Will; we are servants, and
He is the Lord; we offend in many ways, and it is a
master's prerogative to punish faults." When the people of Cæsarea were endeavouring with their tears to
stay Paul as he was setting out for Jerusalem, he said
to them, with the utmost earnestness,—"What do you
mean weeping and afflicting my heart? For I am
ready not only to be bound, but to die also at Jerusalem, for the name of the Lord Jesus. And when we
could not persuade him, we ceased, saying, the Will
of the Lord be done." (*Acts* xxi. 13, 14.) This is
true serenity of soul, when we find that our prayers are
fruitless, to desire this one thing alone, that *the Will
of the Lord be done*.

SEVENTH RULE

No one discovers the Divine Will with greater certainty than he who with entire sincerity desires to conform himself to it in all things. This desire is, in
truth, the thread for unravelling the mazes of all
labyrinths. All uncertainty about the Divine Will is
removed, if, when one is ignorant as to what God wills,

or which of two lawful things He would rather have done, he is yet so disposed in mind as to say, with perfect sincerity of intention,—"If I knew, O Lord, what Thou willedst to be done by me in this matter, I would immediately do it." After this protestation has been made, let him unhesitatingly do what he will, and cease to disturb himself, for he will not easily offend against the Divine Will. Such a son as this the All-loving Father will not desert, nor will He suffer him to wander far from His Will. If there is no man at hand by whom He may instruct him, He will send an angel, as He did to Joseph, when he was deliberating as to what was best to be done in a weighty matter. Thus also an angel was sent to the three kings from the East, after they had worshipped the Divine Infant in his manger-cradle, to warn them to beware of the treachery of Herod, and to return to their own country by another way. And so to Agar, the handmaid of Abraham. And to numberless others in the same way, either an angel has been sent as a defence against error, or, instead of an angel some faithful man. So true is it that He does not deny a knowledge of His Will to such as truly seek it. "The spirit of Wisdom is benevolent" (*Wisdom* I. 6), and bestows itself without grudging upon all. God is nigh unto all them who seek for Him in sincerity, and reveals His Will, by a way of teaching as wonderful as it is sweet, to all those who with true submission are followers of Him. We best learn to *know* the Will of God *by doing it*.

CHAPTER V

OF HOW MANY KINDS THE WILL OF GOD IS, AND IN WHAT THINGS CHIEFLY IT REQUIRES THAT OURS SHOULD BE CONFORMED TO IT

S. CYPRIAN, bishop of Carthage, a man of the greatest eloquence and holiness of life, as well as a most valiant martyr, has made a kind of summary of what the Divine Will demands from its followers. They are words worthy of Cyprian, and they should be engraven in gold. And would that they were inscribed on all the churches and houses of Christians! Would that they were engraved also on their hearts, as a comprehensive account of Christian life and perfection!

"The Will of God," he says (*De Orat. Dom.* 10), "is what Christ has done and taught. It is humility in conduct, steadfastness in faith, scrupulousness in our words, rectitude in our deeds, mercy in our works, governance in our habits; it is innocence of injuriousness, and patience under it, preserving peace with the brethren, loving God with all our heart, loving Him as our Father, and fearing Him as our God; accounting Christ before all things, because He accounted nothing before us, clinging inseparably to His love, being stationed with fortitude and faith at His Cross, and when the battle comes for His Name and honour, maintaining in words that constancy which makes confession, in torture that confidence which joins battle, and in death that patience which receives the crown. This it is to endeavour to be co-heir with Christ; this it is to perform the commandment of God, and fulfil the will of the Father."

1. And of these we must specially store in our inmost mind the following,—innocence of injuriousness, patience under it, preserving peace with the brethren, and loving God with all our heart. We wretched mortals often deceive ourselves here most grievously; we acknowledge the Will of God with the readiest affection when it rewards us, and loads us with benefits; but when it chastises us we turn away from it, as if it were not the Will of God at all: but as if men, animated with the most malignant feelings, had conspired against our welfare and name, so that they might either destroy us altogether, or grievously harass us, and this as if God either knew nothing about it, or certainly did not command it.

This is downright blindness and madness. Are we to imagine that pleasant things only, and those which suit us are sent from heaven? Nay, but sorrowful things also, and things which tend to our discomfort; nor is anything at all in this vast machine carried on, or disturbed, or thrown out of gear (sin only excepted), of which the cause and origin is not from that First Cause. Jeremias, in his lamentation, says,—

"Who is he that hath commanded a thing to be done, when the Lord commandeth it not? Shall not both evil and good proceed out of the mouth of the Highest? Why hath a living man murmured, a man suffering for his sins?" (*Lam.* III. 37-39.) How senseless and perverse is that man who believes that there is anything which God does not either send, or at least does not permit! Cassian (*Coll.* III. 20) puts it most clearly:— "It behooves us," he says, "to believe with unshaken faith that nothing at all is done in the world without God; for we must confess that all things are done either by His Will or Permission."

The ancients fabled certain giants who attempted to thrust down the gods from their abode. Let us have done with fables; ye, O querulous ones, ye are those giants; for if all evils which afflict us here are not only permitted by God, but also sent upon us by Him, what are you doing when you chase and fight against them, but doing all that lies in your power to snatch away His sceptre and power in ruling? All created things willingly obey, and submit themselves to that Supreme Law; while man alone, the noblest of all creatures, kicks against his Maker, and resists His Will. Why do we show our anger to so little purpose? Deaths of all kinds are from God, yes all, I repeat, all of them. If an earthquake has in one direction swallowed up some cities, it is from the Providence of God. If in another place a pestilence has mown down many thousands, it is from the same. If there is slaughter, war, tyranny, in this or that quarter, it is from the same. But, not to dwell on public calamities, if your enemy plunders you of part of your goods, if another assails your fair name, and a third injures you in other ways, it is all of God, Who not only permits, but also sends it upon you by His Divine Wisdom, that you may fully understand that all these things are sent upon you from Heaven. The Divine Will, therefore, not merely demands of us that we should be as averse to inflicting injury upon others, as if we were *able* to inflict none, but it also requires that we should so endure injuries inflicted by others, as to preserve peace with all men, even though they may not wish to preserve it with us.

But that we may more fully understand the mystery of the Divine Will, let me briefly explain that which I have already referred to above.

2. According to Theologians there is a twofold Will of God. One of *Sign* whereby God commands, forbids, permits, persuades, or works anything; and this He declares by His laws and precepts. The other of *Good-pleasure,* whereby it is decreed what He wills in all respects to be done, either with condition or without it. He has willed to bestow eternal felicity on angels and men, but on the condition that they do not resist His Will. Other things God wills without any condition being attached. Thus, as He has willed to create the heaven and the earth, so He wills that the order and the government of the universe, whereby He disposes of all things with most consummate Wisdom, should be perpetual. And this Will of God no

one can resist; it is subject to no laws; it does nothing
at another's command; it obeys none. God Himself
declares this by Isaias, when He says,—"My counsel
shall stand, and all my will shall be done." (*Isai.* XLVI.
10.) "So shall My Word be which shall go forth
from My Mouth; it shall not return to Me void, but
it shall do whatsoever I please." (*Isai.* LV. 11.) But
we, miserable servants that we are, whether we will
or not, must bear whatever God has decreed concerning us. We are all of us coupled to manifold troubles.
With some the chain is of gold and loose; with others
it is of vile metal and pinching. But what does it
matter? The same bond surrounds us all, and even
the binders themselves are bound. Life is altogether
servitude; yea, and life is altogether punishment. We
must, therefore, accustom ourselves to this condition
of existence, and complain of it as little as possible.
And here it is a great comfort to know that God wills
it so; that it thus seems good to Him, and that there
is no one who can resist the Divine Will. Queen
Esther proclaimed this when she said,—"O Lord, almighty King, all things are in Thy power, and there
is none that can resist Thy will." (*Esth.* XIII. 9.)
And this S. Augustine also sets forth most excellently—"These are," he says, "the great works of the
Lord, wonderfully designed to fulfil all His Will, and
designed with such a depth of wisdom, that, when
the angelic and human creation had sinned (that is,
had done not what He, but what they, willed), even
by that same will of the creature, whereby that which

the Creator willed not was done, He fulfilled that which He willed, turning to a good account even the evil, as being Himself supremely good." Although, therefore, the wicked fight against the Divine Will, yet by their means God performs His Own Will, and turns their most perverse will to the best account. It is clear from what has been said that though God wills salvation for all, yet all will not attain to it, because they do not fulfil the condition which is required, being rebellious against the Divine Commands. And of these our Saviour prophesied with severity when he said,—"Not every one that saith to Me, Lord, Lord, shall enter into the Kingdom of Heaven; but he that doth the Will of My Father who is in heaven." (*Matt.* VII. 21.) A wise man early transfuses his whole self into the Divine Will.

3. And this being so, we can do nothing better or more profitable than absolutely submit and conform our own will to the Divine, and say with Heli the priest,—"It is the Lord; let Him do what is good in His sight" (1 *Kings* III. 18); with Joab,—"The Lord will do what is good in His sight" (2 *Kings* x. 12); with King David,—"But if He shall say to me, thou pleaseth me not; I am ready, let Him do that which is good before Him" (2 *Kings* xv. 26); with Judas Machabeus,—"As it shall be the Will of God in heaven, so be it done" (1 *Mach.* III. 60); with Christ our Saviour,—"My Father, if it be possible, let this chalice pass from Me; nevertheless, not as I will, but as Thou wilt." (*Matt.* XXVI. 39.) For if the Son was so obedi-

[59]

ent, as perfectly to fulfil the Will of the Father—for, "I came down from heaven," he says, "not to do My Own Will, but the Will of Him that sent Me" (*John* VI. 38)—if this was required of the Son, how much less does it become servants to refuse to recognize His commands. Let us think it perfectly just that whatever from eternity has pleased God, should please man also. The soldier in camp, when he hears the signal for marching, collects his baggage; but when he hears the trumpet-call for battle, he lays it down, and takes up his arms, being prepared with mind, hand, and eye, to execute every order of his general. And so let it be with ourselves; and in this our warfare let us follow our Leader cheerfully and with a firm step, wherever He may call us. Whatever happens, let us bear it, not only patiently, but cheerfully, and let us rest assured that difficulties of all seasons are according to the Law of Nature. And as a brave soldier endures wounds, counts his scars, and, though pierced through with spears, still loves the general for whom he falls, so let us keep in mind that old precept—"FOLLOW GOD."

I have now pointed out how we are to arrive at a knowledge of the Divine Will. But it is not enough to know it; we must more closely unite our own will to it. But wherein this union consists I will set forth in the following Book.

BOOK II

CONCERNING THE CONFORMITY OF THE HUMAN WILL TO THE DIVINE

"Not my will, but Thine, be done." *Luke* XXII. 42.

THE HELIOTROPIUM

Book II

CHAPTER I

THE COMMENCEMENT OF CONFORMING THE HUMAN WILL TO THE DIVINE

THERE was once upon a time an eminent Divine who for eight years besought God with unwearied prayers to show him a man by whom he might be taught the most direct way to heaven. One day, when he was possessed of an unconquerable desire to converse with such a man, and wished for nothing so much as to see a teacher of truth so hidden, he thought that he heard a voice coming to him from heaven, which gave him this command:—"Go to the porch of the church, and you will find the man you seek."

Accordingly he went into the street, and at the door of the church he found a beggar whose legs were covered with ulcers running with corruption, and whose clothes were scarcely worth threepence. The Divine wished him good day. To whom the beggar replied, —"I do not remember that I ever had a bad one." Whereupon the man of letters, as if to amend his former salutation, said,—"Well, then, God send you good fortune." "But I never had any bad fortune," answered the beggar. The Divine was astonished at this reply, but repeated his wish, in case he might have made a mistake in what he heard, only in somewhat different words:—"Say you so? I pray, then, that you may be happy." But again the beggar replied,— "I never was unhappy." The Divine, thinking that the beggar was playing upon words merely for the sake of talking, answered, in order to try the man's wit,—"I desire that whatever you wish may happen to you." "And here, also," he replied, "I have nothing to complain of. All things turn out according to my wishes, although I do not attribute my success to fortune."

Upon this the man of letters, saluting him afresh, and taking his leave, said:—"May God preserve you, my good man, since you hate fortune! But tell me, I pray, are you alone happy among mortals who suffer calamity? If so, Job speaks safely when he declares,—'Man born of a woman, living for a short time, is filled with many miseries.' (*Job* XIV. I.) And how comes it that you alone have escaped all evil days? I do not fully understand your feelings." To this the beggar replied,—"It is so, sir, as I have said. When you wished me a 'good day,' I denied that I had ever had a bad one. I am perfectly contented with the lot which God has assigned me in this world. Not to want happiness is my happiness. Those bugbears, Fortune and Misfortune, hurt him only who wills, or at least fears, to be hurt by them. Never do I offer my prayers to Fortune, but to my Heavenly Father Who disposes the events of all things. And so I say I never was unhappy, inasmuch as all things turn out according to my wishes. If I suffer hunger, I praise my most provident Father for it. If cold pinches me, if the rain pours down upon me, or if the sky inflicts upon me any other injury, I praise God just the same. When I am a laughing-stock to others, I no less praise God. For sure I am that God is the Author of all these things, and that whatever God does must be the best. Therefore, whatever God either gives, or allows to happen, whether it be pleasant or disagreeable, sweet or bitter, I esteem alike, for all such things I joyfully receive as from the hand of a most loving Father; and this one thing I will—what God wills. And so all things happen as I will. Miserable is the man who believes that Fortune has any power against him; and truly unhappy is he who dreams of some imaginary unhappiness in this world. This is true happiness in this life, to cleave as closely as possible to the Divine Will. The Will of God, His most excellent, His most perfect Will, which cannot be made more perfect, and cannot be evil, judges concerning all things, but nothing concerning it. To follow this Will I bestow all my care. To this one solicitude I devote myself with all my might, so that whatever God wills, this I also may never refuse to will. And, therefore, I by no means consider myself unhappy, since I have so entirely transfused my own will into the Divine, that with me there is no other *will or not will* than as God wills or wills not."

"But do you really mean what you say?" asked the Divine; "tell me, I pray, whether you would feel the same if God had decreed to cast you down to hell?" To which the beggar at once replied,—"If He should cast me down to hell? But know that I have two arms of wondrous strength, and with these I should hold him tightly in an embrace that nothing could sever. One arm is the lowliest humility shown by the oblation of self, the other, purest charity shown by the love of God. With these arms I would so entwine myself round God, that wherever He might banish me, thither would I draw Him with me. And far more desirable, in truth, would it be to be out of heaven with God, than in heaven without Him." The Divine was astonished at this reply, and began to think with himself that this was the shortest path to God.

But he felt anxious to make further inquiry, and to draw forth into sight the wisdom which dwelt in such an ill-assorted habitation; and so he asked,— "Whence have you come hither?" "I came from God," replied the beggar. To whom again the Divine,—"And where did you find God?" "Where I forsook all created things." Again the Divine asked, —"But where did you leave God?" "In men of pure minds and goodwill," replied the poor man. "Who are you?" said the Divine. "Whoever I am," he replied, "I am so thoroughly contented with my lot that

I would not change it for the riches of all kings. Every one who knows how to rule himself is a king." "Am I, then, to understand that you are a king?" said the other. "Where is your kingdom?" "There," said the beggar, and at the same time pointed with his finger towards heaven. "He is a king to whom that kingdom on high is transferred by sure deeds of covenant." At last the Divine, intending to bring his questions to an end, said,—"Who has taught you this? Who has instilled these feelings into you?" To which the other replied,—"I will tell you, Sir. For whole days I do not speak, and then I give myself up entirely to prayer or holy thoughts, and this is my only anxiety, to be as closely united as possible to God. Union and familiar acquaintance with God and the Divine Will teach all this."

The Theologian wished to ask more questions, but thinking it would be better to postpone this to another time, took his leave for the present. As he went away, full of thought, he said to himself,—"Lo! thou hast found one who will teach thee the shortest way to God! How truly does S. Augustine (*Conf.* viii. 8) say,—'The unlearned start up and take heaven by violence, and we with our learning, and without heart, lo! where we wallow in flesh and blood!' And so Christ, when giving thanks says,—'I confess to thee, O Father, Lord of Heaven and earth, because Thou hast hid these things from the wise and prudent, and has revealed them unto babes.' (*Matt.* xi. 25.) Beneath a filthy garment, forsooth, great wisdom often lies concealed. And who would think of seeking for such Divine learning in a man of so mean an appearance? Who would believe that so much of the Spirit was hidden under such unlettered simplicity? Lo! those two arms of unconquerable strength, *Oblation of Self* and *Love of God,* draw God whithersoever this poor man wills! With these arms God permits Himself to be closely bound; other embraces He refuses."

CHAPTER II

WHAT KIND OF HUMAN WILL IS MOST SUITABLE TO THIS CONFORMITY WITH THE WILL OF GOD

IN order that young maidens might be sought for king Assuerus, the most comely that could be found were gathered together from all provinces of the kingdom to Sufa the palace; and a year was to be spent by them on nothing else but the adornment of their body. And what purifications with unguents, and with sweet odours, and with other things, were there not! How much care and expense were lavished on adorning the person! So great a thing was it esteemed to find favour in the eyes of the king! And should not the human will, destitute of all preparatory adornment, fear to rush, like a country-woman fresh from the fields, into the embrace of the Supreme King? Let the will of man know that it can then only find favour in the Divine Eyes, if it tries, not merely to remove from itself even the smallest blemishes, but likewise to furnish itself with such adornments as may attract the Divine Will to union with itself. And, therefore, for the sake of preserving a proper arrangement, and avoiding obscurity, I propose so to treat the subject as to apply to the Will different names by way of titles, so that it may learn from these what sort of preparation is needed for this conformity to the Divine Will. When a master is going to receive a new servant into his house, he makes many stipulations, and says to him,—"I wish that my servant should not be a tale-bearer, nor given to finery, nor a gambler, nor quarrelsome, nor a drunkard; but it is all important that he should be active, honest, and obedient." And if it is the privilege of a master to lay down rules of this kind for his servants, why should not God have the same right, when about to admit the human will into friendship with Himself? Therefore let the will of man know that it must now live according to different laws, and chiefly these that follow:—

1. *Let the Will be pure.* This is above all things needful, for the Heavenly Spouse is of such purity that He both hates and banishes from His Presence everything that defiles. It is necessary, therefore, that the will which is to be united to Him should also hate every kind of impurity. And it must do this so thoroughly as not merely not to encourage avarice, not to indulge in luxury, not to give way to anger, but even if it feels the smallest leaning and affection towards these polluting habits, at once to expel them bravely, and not merely be unwilling to think of what is impure, but also willing to meditate upon everything that is the contrary.

But my business is not to speak of those things which are clear to every one. Another vice there is, of wondrous subtlety, but at the same time of the utmost quickness in its operation,—Envy. From this let the will be pure, and let it keep itself from all contagion of this pest. Let the will which desires to be conformed to the Divine Will be altogether free from jealousy. Let it not be affected with envy at another's happiness, nor be oppressed at the envy of its own; for he who is truly united to God sees others abounding in Grace and worldly riches, and yet does not envy them, but, turning to God, says,—"Dost Thou will, O Lord, that this or that man should be raised to wealth and honours, while I am left to pine away in contempt? I do not strive against Thee, O my God, nor do I ask of Thee a reason for it. Thy one and only Will is to me cause enough, and abundantly sufficient reason. For most sure am I that unless Thou didst permit it, and it were not for my good, no one would obtain from Thee that which, when Thou grantest it, is obtained with no trouble, and perchance with few words. But in other things also I know that it is by Thy Permission, O my Lord, that one man thus assails me, another deals with me thus, and another thus disturbs me. Never, so far as I know, have I injured them. But in Thy Will I find answer enough for this. Thou hast permitted it, Thou hast ordered it. Be they, then, Semeis to me, and let me be David, if it thus seem good to Thee, O my God!"

S. Ignatius, the holy bishop of Antioch and martyr, exclaimed,—"I am Christ's corn, and must be ground by the teeth of wild beasts that I may be found to be pure bread." And thus, in truth, God prepares us as Lord's bread for his table. What have we, then, to complain of against men? They are the millstones which grind us the wheat which is spread upon them. And that we may cause this thought to sink down deeply into our soul it will be advisable every hour several times to raise our heart towards God by repeating such little prayers as,—"Blessed be God for ever! Lord, what wilt thou have me to do? Thy Will be done!" This is the first step in the preparation of the human will—that it should be pure from blemishes, especially from all grudging and envy. But besides this there must be,—

2. *A Patient Will.* When any one is harassed by adversity let him seek all his help from patience, and say with calmness,—"Whatever I suffer is all from God; but is sent upon me from God by means of this occasion, this man, or this cause; and I am as sure of this as I know I am alive." And here very many come to a standstill, from not having such a firm faith in God as to feel certain that adverse things and all untoward events come from Him, just as much as prosperity and the successes which they have most ardently wished for. If we held this as certain, which in itself is perfectly certain, we should not be so prone to bear things with impatience or objection, nor should we so often need to be urged forward with these words,—"O ye of little faith." But that adversity of all kinds, by whomsoever brought about, comes down to us from God, Christ declares when he says,—"Are

not two sparrows sold for a farthing? And not one
of them shall fall on the ground without your Father.
But the very hairs of your head are all numbered.
Fear not, therefore, better are you than many sparrows." (*Matt.* x. 29-31.) Does God, then, fall to
the ground with an insignificant sparrow? Certainly
the Will of God does, and why not God Himself?
Who, as He works without ceasing in all created
things, swims likewise with the fish, flies with the bird,
crawls with the serpent, and walks with the four-footed
animal. God forsakes not what He has made. Although, therefore, so many thousands of larks are so
often caught at the same time in nets, yet none of
these, no, not even the smallest, is taken without the
Will of God,—"*Not one of them* shall fall on the
ground without your Father." But, as far as concerns
the all-provident Will of God, the same rule applies
to the eagle, and the sparrow, and man. If, therefore, not one of the smallest birds falls into the fowl-
er's net without the Will of God, do you think that
you, O man, who were made in the Image of your
Creator, an heir of the Kingdom, are harassed by any
adversity, or afflicted with any injury, loss, or grief,
unless God specially wills it? But that we might understand this more fully, and might never rashly say
that God shows this care towards things with life only,
our Saviour added,—"The hairs of your head are all
numbered." Who could ever count the number of
his hairs? And yet God numbers the hairs not only
of one man but of all men, and without His Will not

a single one can be taken away. Whenever, then, in seasons of adversity we cast away our patience, or utter imprecations against others, or fasten the blame on this or that person, and scatter our reproaches broadcast, we display a very great want of faith. Through a deceptive piety, in sooth, we shrink from making God the Author of those things which we call evils. S. John was the only one who recognized Christ on the sea, while the other disciples knew Him not, and exclaimed,—"It is the Lord." (*John* XXI. 7.) And so there are very many persons who amid the waves of troubles do not acknowledge that God is the cause of the sea being stormy, but are beyond measure exasperated against those whom they consider enemies, and say,—"That is a paltry fellow; this is an idle rascal; that is a rogue; this a night prowler; this is a perfect monster of wickedness who devised mischief against me; through that most abandoned of men this blame has fallen upon me." But far differently is the PATIENT WILL accustomed to speak,—"All this evil," it confesses, *"is from God.* Most justly does God chastise me. It is the Lord, let Him do what is good in His sight." (1 *Kings* III. 18.)

3. *A Cheerful Will.* This disposes a man to be perfectly contented as well with food as with all other things which he daily receives from the Hand of God. Such a man as this says,—"Whatever Thou givest me, O my God, is enough, even though it oftentimes seems too little for my greediness; nor have I in any way deserved it. Thou art too bountiful towards me.

I feel that I am undeserving even of the air I breathe."

He who desires to conform himself to the Divine Will is accustomed never to complain. No one will ever hear from him such lamentations as—"I can scarcely earn my livelihood, while others fare luxuriously, and yet do not toil half as much as I do. They sow little, and yet reap abundant crops." Well indeed did the Bard of Venusium long ago ask the question (HOR. *Sat.* I. 1):—"How comes it, Mæcenas, that no one lives contented with the lot which either reason has assigned him, or chance has placed in his way, but praises those who are engaged in pursuits different from his own?" This is the reason, my good Poet, this is the reason, that we so slowly acquiesce in the Divine Will,—our covetousness hurries us first in one direction, then in another, and often to distant objects, nor is there any limit to our desires; but when we do not obtain what we have set our affections on, we give ourselves up to lamentations and murmurings. That is but a narrow mind which earthly things so much delight.

Let the Heliotrope be constantly before our eyes, of which Pliny elegantly writes (*Nat. Hist.* XXII. 21):— "I have often spoken of the wonderful property of the Heliotrope, which turns itself round with the sun, even on a cloudy day; so great is its love of that luminary. But at night it closes its azure flower, as if from missing its rays." Observe, my friend, that the Heliotrope even of a cloudy day turns itself round with the sun, through love of it. The Will of God

[75]

is our sun. It is not indeed always shining upon us in a cloudless sky; stormy days, accompanied with rain, and wind, and hail, are mingled with fair-weather days. There is no Christian who does not very often experience this heaviness of the atmosphere and stormy seasons.

But let us, like the Heliotrope, turn ourselves round with our sun, the Divine Will, even on cloudy days, so great let our love of that our luminary be. And it is certain that no tranquillity will ever fall to our lot, but numberless things will disquiet us on all sides; we shall be satisfied with nothing, we shall never be contented with our lot, everything will seem to be wanting, although everything is present; we shall never be free from fear, and shall frequently be overcome with weariness, disturbed in mind, timid and irresolute, full of complaints and jealousy; in a word, we shall always be unhappy, as long as we have not turned ourselves round, like the Heliotrope, to this sun, viz. the Divine Will. This sun must ever be gazed upon by us with fixed and unshrinking eye, in whatever direction its course may bend; and this one thing must we ever resolve in our mind,—*"As it pleases God, so does it please me.* The Will of God alone is to me the rule of life and death. As it hath pleased the Lord so is it done, and so shall it be done. Blessed be the Name of the Lord." Now, indeed, our sun is hidden by a cloud, but soon it will show its bright face through this mist of sorrow. Look at the course of ages, and see how variously things turn out!

How often are there cloudy days after a fair sunrise, and how often do fine days follow upon cloudy mornings! Let us, then, dispose our minds in such a way as that before every event we should wish for nothing more than to follow the Divine Will. Once upon a time a certain learned Jew, who, it must be confessed, was ready enough with words, when intending to devote himself to Christ, said—"Master, I will follow Thee whithersoever Thou shalt go." (*Matt.* VIII. 19.) And so let us, being perfectly ready to obey every indication of the Divine Will, both in word and deed, follow it whithersoever it may go.

4. *A Persevering, Long-suffering Will.* We impair nearly all our virtues through want of Perseverance. The children of Israel being tired out with the stay of Moses on the Mount, turned to idols, and made a golden calf for a god, excusing themselves by his long absence. Thus also those two travellers when going to Emmaus said,—"Besides all this, to-day is the third day since these things were done." (*Luke* XXIV. 21.) It is, indeed, the third day, but is the third day yet passed? Is there no time left for Him to rise again from the dead? Is your patience so entirely worn out?

If this third day had passed, and if the fourth or fifth had come, you might be thought to have reason to despair; but since you have not yet reached the evening of this third day, why do you so rashly despair of your rising Lord?

In our prayers we are only too impetuous, and unless that which we ask is immediately granted we plunge all our hope into impatience, or even into despair. But it is far otherwise with God:—"The Lord is compassionate and merciful; *long-suffering,* and plenteous in mercy" (*Ps.* CII. 8); "Neither will God have a soul to perish, but recalleth, meaning that he that is cast off should not altogether perish." (2 *Kings* XIV. 14.) A miser before he spends a piece of money turns it over twice or three times in his hand, and so God, who is slow to punish, "recalleth" as it were, before He smites any one with a sentence of judgment, and casts him down to hell.

But we, who are both of small faith and scanty hope, if twice or thrice we have asked for anything from God, and have not obtained our request, cast away all our trust, like beggars, who, if they have several times sought for alms before a house with clamour and knocking, but have not been attended to, say,—"No one is at home." Knock, ye idle ones, knock! this door is opened to those who knock. In other things what resolute perseverance do we often show! Some seek for an office for a number of years, and very often in vain. With what consummate patience is a rich inheritance waited for! And that the heir may not feel the delay too keenly he comforts himself with the reflection that time quickly passes. And yet we fix limits to the Divine Decree, and prescribe to it a time! The helping Hand of God delays too long for us in disease; and we cry out:—"When wilt Thou come, O Lord? Why dost Thou delay?

Why dost Thou put off assistance? How long must Thou be entreated? For how many years have I been crying, and yet Thou hearest not! Unless Thou, O Lord, dost succour me this year I will cease to pray, and think it useless." And in this we certainly are not unlike the citizens of Bethulia, who said to Ozias and the chief of the city:—"God be judge between us and thee, for thou hast done evil against us, in that thou wouldst not speak peaceably with the Assyrians, and for this cause God hath sold us into their hands. And therefore there is no one to help us, while we are cast down before their eyes in thirst, and sad destruction. And now assemble ye all that are in the city, that we may of our own accord yield ourselves all up to the people of Holofernes." (*Judith* VII. 13· 15.) O ye faint-hearted ones! Must your city, then, be surrendered in despair to the enemy? And is there no help to be looked for from Heaven? But Ozias the priest did little to revive the patience of the citizens which had already died out, when, in the midst of his tears, he said,—"Be of good courage, my brethren, and let us wait these five days for mercy from the Lord. For perhaps He will put a stop to His indignation, and will give glory to His own name. But if after five days be past there come no aid, we will do the things which you have spoken." (*Judith* VII. 23, 24.) But O thou priest Ozias, thy wisdom was not deeper than that of the multitude! Was it your part to measure out a time for God, and to appoint a day for Him to send help? Was not all per-

[79]

severing trust not merely dead among you, but also buried? But Judith, that woman of noblest spirit, could not endure this, and having sent for the elders she said,—"What is this word, by which Ozias hath consented to give up the city to the Assyrians, if within five days there come no aid to us? And who are you that tempt the Lord? This is not a word that may draw down mercy, but rather that may stir up wrath, and enkindle indignation. You have set a time for the mercy of the Lord, and you have appointed Him a day, according to your pleasure." (*Judith* VIII. 10-13.) And what then, O Judith, do you advise to be done? "Let us ask the Lord with tears, that *according to His Will,* so He would shew His mercy to us." (*Judith* VIII. 17.)

In such a way, then, the *Persevering Will* unites man to God, that however much he may be afflicted, he exclaims,—"According to Thy Will, O Lord, do Thou deal with me in Thy Mercy. Although I have cried to Thee, O Lord, for ten, twenty, thirty, or fifty years, yet will I not cease to cry. I place no limits to Thee: and although I were sure that I should not be heard by Thee at all, yet unswerving faith teaches me that I shall not be sent away from Thee empty. If Thou deniest what is asked, Thou wilt give better things. Therefore, if Thou makest any delay, I will wait for Thee, because Thou wilt surely come, and wilt not be slack." (*Hab.* II. 3.)

5. *An Ardent Will.* This means not merely to will or not will that which God wills or wills not, but

solely on account of His not willing or willing, to reject the former and to accept the latter with ardent desire, and to have no other reason for doing one thing, and leaving another undone, than the Divine Good-pleasure. If one were to question a man possessed of such a will as to why he does not will one thing but does will another, he will reply that he has no other reason than that he finds that God does not will the one, and does will the other. "I love," says S. Bernard, "because I love, and I love that I may love, for He Who is loved is Love." S. Augustine counsels us that we ought to feel that as God has willed that all things should exist on account of Himself, so we also should will that neither we ourselves nor anything else should exist, except on account of God and His Will.

When the Old Law was still in force, God willed that every article dedicated to the Altar and Tabernacle should be wrapped in a violet covering, and that when so concealed it should be borne by Levites. The command runs thus:—"All the vessels wherewith they minister in the sanctuary, they shall wrap up in a cloth of violet, and shall spread over it a cover of violet skins, and put in the bars." (*Numb.* IV. 12.) And this was done for the reason which is added—that "they shall not touch the vessels of the sanctuary, lest they die." (Ver. 15.) The bearers of the holy vessels, therefore, saw none of those things which they carried, but only felt the weight of them, for the covering of violet concealed everything from their eyes.

And just in the same way every one who has wholly dedicated himself to God is most sweetly ignorant, and does not so much as desire to know why this or that is permitted or commanded by God. Whatever the burden may be, he takes it on willing shoulders. It is enough for him to see that burden concealed by the violet veil, that is to say, clothed with the Divine Will.

6. *An All-productive Will.* By an all-productive Will, I mean that, which, like the most fruitful soil, brings forth all kinds of the holiest desires, and consecrates them as its first-fruits to the Divine Will. Here the lofty soul, and one which longs for heaven, rises upwards; here sighs full of love, and overflowing aspirations soar on high, such as—"O my God, how do I desire not only to endure great sufferings for Thee, but also to die for Thy sake, even by a painful death!" By means of such heavenward flights of soul God and man are united so closely in nearly all things, that, from this sweet agreement and consent, the most delightful communion of designs, and intimate friendship, arise between them, till at length man can say in regard to all the events of life,—"Yea, Father: for so hath it seemed good in Thy sight." (*Matt.* XI. 26.) "If we have received good things at the Hand of God, why should we not receive evil?" (*Job* II. 10.) And thus with unruffled calmness he receives all things, painful or pleasant alike, as from the Hand of God. And here it is wonderful to think how much light shone upon the old Philosophers.

Epictetus (*Ench.* 15), one of their number, gives almost Divine advice when he says,—"Never speak of having *lost* anything; but of having *restored* it. Has your little child died? He is only given back. Is your estate torn from you? But is not that also restored? Yes; but it was an unprincipled man who seized it, you say. And what does it matter to you by whose agency He Who gave it takes it back? As long as He allows the use of it to you, have a care for it as a thing which belongs to some one else, just as a traveller has of his lodging." And thus let the man who desires to be as closely united to God as possible reason with himself in reference to anything that is taken away; let him not regard the person who takes it from him, but God Who recalls His own. Let him, therefore, repeat without ceasing these words of Christ's—"Yea, Father; for so hath it seemed good in Thy sight." Yea, my father; yea!

And here, good reader, attend, I pray you, to a short explanation of these Divine words. The Heavenly Father, addressing the Son of old by Isaias the Prophet, said,—"I have given Thee for a Covenant of the people, for a Light of the Gentiles." (*Isaias* XLII. 6.) Just as if He had said,—"It is too little for Me that Thou shouldest bring the remnant of Israel to Me; but I will that heathen nations also should be taught by Thee." And these words of the Father preceded our Lord's birth of the Virgin by eight hundred years.

This Decree, then, of the Father, proclaimed so

many years before His Birth, the Son most cheerfully embraced, and answered that He willed the same as His Father. Therefore, S. Matthew (XI. 25) says:— "At that time Jesus *answered* and said." And to whom did He make answer, when there was none who asked a question? He answered His Eternal Father Who so many ages before had addressed the Son. And behold how joyfully the Son embraces the Will of the Father, and says:—"Yea, Father; for so hath it seemed good in Thy sight." "Whatever Thou hast commanded shall be fulfilled by Me." But as the Heavenly Father spoke to the Son by Isaias so many years before He was born, and the Son made answer to Him, so God has from eternity spoken to each one of us; He has most distinctly and accurately ordained at what time each man should be born, and at what time he should die. He has provided every kind of help for obtaining happiness; He has foreseen what each man would think, say, and do throughout the whole course of his life and in what way he would receive the proffered help. Since, then, God has in this way addressed us so benignantly from all eternity, is it not most fitting that we also, each in his own time, should answer with Christ,—"Yea, Father; yea, my Father, since thus, and thus, and thus it seemed good in Thy sight, yea, Father?" And let us repeat, "Yea, Father," every hour, oftentimes renewing our desire; and let us continue this with unwearying perseverance, even to our latest breath. But more of this hereafter.

CHAPTER III

IN WHAT WAY THE WILL OF MAN IS TO BE CONFORMED TO THE WILL OF GOD

I HAVE spoken of the preparation which must precede this union of Wills, and also what sort of human will may be thought to be best adapted to conformity with the Divine. And now I must proceed to show how the will of man is to be conformed to the Will of God in fact.

1. S. Thomas Aquinas says most admirably that all actions allied to virtue are on this account approved by God, if they are performed with the intention that the Divine Will may be obeyed; for there is no merit in spending even life and blood, unless it be according to the Pleasure of the Divine Will. Pœmen, a holy man, constantly admonishes of this, and says:—"Never set up your own will against the Divine; but let your own will ever be most closely united to the Divine." But if this union is real, it is a thoroughly sincere agreement in all things with the Divine Will, which so instructs man that his constant exclamations are,— "As God wills, so do I will. When it pleases God, then it pleases me also."

Ruth, who is deserving of all praise, when addressing Naomi her mother-in-law, said:—"Whithersoever thou shalt go, I will go: and where thou shalt dwell, I also will dwell. Thy people shall be my people, and thy God my God. The land that shall receive thee dying, in the same will I die: and there will I be buried. The Lord do so and so to me, and add more also; if aught but death part me and thee." (*Ruth* I. 16, 17.) A man who is united in will to God thinks and speaks in the same way as of old Eliseus, when bidden to tarry at Bethel, said to Elias,—"As the Lord liveth, and as thy soul liveth, I will not leave thee." (4 *Kings* II. 2.) And this he repeated three times, intending to cleave as an inseparable companion to his master. Josaphat answered King Joram when he sought for aid from him,—"He that is mine is thine; my people, thy people; and my horses, thy horses." (4 *Kings* III. 7.) And in this way let us be joined to God with the closest affection, as Ruth was with Naomi, as Eliseus was with Elias, as Josaphat was with Joram. Let us say with strong faith,— "Thy Will, O my God, is my will; Thy Heart is my heart; I am entirely devoted to Thy Will, O my God." And this union of his own will with the Divine let each person diligently cultivate in everything—in affairs of business, in duties, in labour of all kinds, in sickness, and in death itself, ever acquiescing most completely in the Divine Decree, and having nothing more constantly in his mouth or heart than "Thy Will be done." For as all virtues shone forth more brilliantly during the agony of Christ, so especially

His fervour in prayer. In the hour of His sorest need He exclaimed,—"Father, if Thou wilt, remove this chalice from Me: but yet not My Will, but Thine, be done." (*Luke* XXII. 42.) There is not a better, nor a shorter, nor a more perfect form of prayer, nor one more pleasing to God and useful to man, than this:— "Not my Will, but Thine, be done." "Not as I will, but as Thou wilt." Let the Will of God be done, even though the world should fall! S. Gertrude was accustomed to repeat three hundred and sixty-three times,—"O my most loving JESUS, Thy Will be done." Cassian (*Coll.* IX. 20) asks,—"What does it mean to say, 'Thy Will be done on earth as it is in heaven,' but that men may become like Angels, and as the Will of God is fulfilled by them in heaven, so all those who are on earth should do not their own will but His alone. No one, however, will be able to say this with sincerity but he alone who believes that God disposes for our good all things which are seen, whether they be adverse or prosperous, and that He is more provident and anxious for the welfare and salvation of His Own people, than we are for ourselves." And so, according to the meaning of Cassian, he who thus conforms his own will to the Divine dwells already in the entrance-hall of Heaven; for in Heaven assuredly the countless millions of the Blessed have but one will. And so Arsenius aptly replied to Marcus the Abbot, when he asked,—"Why do you not come back to visit us, Father?" "I prefer," he said, "to hold intercourse with those who live above us, since they have all the same will, while among men there are almost as many wills as there is variety of countenance." He, however, who both in adversity and prosperity fashions himself according to the Divine Will, can well understand what the Psalmist meant in the verse,—"Behold, how good and how pleasant it is for brethren to dwell together in unity!" (*Ps.* cxxxii. 1.) And who are the "brethren" meant? Christ and the righteous man; for the Supreme King is not ashamed to own this feeling of brotherhood.

2. Of old, the Preacher, when about to speak on a weighty matter, said,—"The eyes of a wise man are in his head." (*Eccles.* ii. 14.) But have fools, then, their eyes in their feet, or elsewhere besides their heads? The explanation of S. Gregory is:—"He who fixes every look on God, and on the Will of God, is truly wise. However many eyes he has, he carries them fixed 'in his head.' "

Epictetus, that planet among philosophers in the age of Nero, Domitian, and Marcus Antoninus, lived wholly above fortune. An old woman was his only attendant; a single earthenware lamp (the whole of his furniture) sufficed for those divine meditations of his. And this lamp was sold at his death for a thousand drachmas, that is to say, for a hundred gold Philips, in honour of the memory of so great a man. Lucian, who ridiculed all other philosophers, esteemed him alone. This Epictetus, I say, besides his Dissertations, wrote also an *Enchiridion* which is well worthy of immortality. This treatise contains so much of the spirit of religion, and of hidden wisdom, that you might think that it had been written by a man thoroughly imbued with Christian feeling. This little book will, at the Day of Judgment, put many a Christian to the blush for having written such filthy productions, and having lived conformably to his writings. But to return. This Epictetus, then, who reduced all philosophy to these two great heads, *Sustain* and *Abstain;* he, I repeat, philosophizes with almost divine wisdom about following God's Will with all one's power. And here let me quote his words (EPICT. *Diss.* III. 26) :— "My desire," he says, "I have yielded to God so as to obey Him. Does He will that I should be afflicted with a fever? I will it myself also. Does He will that I should become possessed of something? I myself also will it. Does He not will it? Then I do not will it. Does He will that I should die? Then I will to die. Who can hinder me, or force me, contrary to my determination?" And are you not sad, O rebellious Christian, do you not blush when you hear such words? And why do we, miserable mortals that we are, fight against the Divine Will? We are enclosed on all sides: if we refuse to be led, we shall be dragged, or forced along. Seneca (*Ep.* 75), speaking of perfect liberty, says:—"Do you inquire what it is? Not to fear men, nor the Gods; not to wish for what is disgraceful, or what is in excess of propriety. To have complete mastery over oneself. It is a priceless blessing to become one's own." But no one can become his own who does not in the first place become God's in such a way as that he either wills, or wills not, all things with God. "The soul which desires to be master of itself must be entirely withdrawn from all external objects towards itself. Let it remove itself as far as possible from things which concern others, and devote its care to itself. Let it not feel losses, and let it put a favourable interpretation even on adverse things." (SEN. *De Tranquil.* 14.) This soul begins to be its own; this is true liberty. And so S. Augustine (*De Civ.* IV. 3) says:—"The good man, even though he is a servant, is free: the wicked man, even though he is a king, is a servant. He has as many masters as he has vices."

3. That most valiant hero, Judas Machabeus, in order to inflame his soldiers against the enemy, cried out,—"Gird yourselves, and be valiant men, and be ready against the morning, that you may fight with these nations. Nevertheless, as it shall be the Will of God in heaven, so be it done." (1 *Mach.* III. 58, 60.) Joab, too, when about to engage in a very hazardous battle, said to Abisai, his brother,—"Be of good courage, and let us fight for our people, and for the city of our God; and the Lord will do what is good in His sight." (2 *Kings* X. 12.) It is of the utmost importance so to discipline the mind in all things as for it to ascribe every event to Divine Providence. For it not unfrequently happens that men who are learned, wise, warlike, and holy, act both with bravery and skill, and yet without success; but this is no less to be ascribed to the Providence of God than the most

prosperous event. And, for this reason, the Preacher says,—"I saw that under the sun the race is not to the swift, nor the battle to the strong, nor bread to the wise, nor riches to the learned, nor favour to the skillful; but time and chance in all." (*Eccles.* IX. 11.) He calls that "chance" which seems to us to be such, but not to God. It is no uncommon thing, in truth, that an intelligent and industrious man should be disappointed of his hope; and this we esteem an evil chance. But S. Thomas Aquinas rightly affirms that it may be gathered from the words of the Preacher that nothing exists by chance, or without the Will and Foreknowledge of the First Cause. For chances are found in things amenable to time, and subject to human knowledge; but the Divine Power and Providence has foreknown all things from all eternity: it rules all things as the world rolls on, and directs them towards fixed and certain ends, whilst it has assigned a proper time to everything, and a due variety to human efforts, that even in this way those who are unmindful of Divine Providence may learn, from unexpected chances and adverse events, not to ascribe too much to their own powers, and assure themselves that all things depend on the Divine Pleasure. What then is Fortune, which was so much worshipped by the ancients? It is a fickle, but an empty, apparition from the lower world.

That Divinity which disposes all things for mortals, adverse and prosperous alike, according to its Will, is none other than the Providence of God. God, by means of His Holy Will and Providence, causes human affairs to revolve like a wheel in motion. Those conditions of men which are dark and uncertain He regulates Himself. "I am the Lord, and there is none else; there is no God besides Me. I form the light, and create darkness: I make peace, and create evil; I the Lord that do all these things." (*Isaias* XLV. 5, 6.) Among the ancients Fortune was of two colours, for they moulded her statue with a double face, the one in front being white and shining, while the hinder one was black, as became one in whose will rested the power of good and evil. But this is only the trifling of children. "Good things and evil, life and death, poverty and riches, are from God." (*Ecclus.* XI. 14.) Seneca (*De Tranquil.* XV) speaks to the point, when he argues with himself, and then disposes of his own objections:—"There follows a consideration," he says, "which is not unreasonably wont to sadden one, and to lead to solitude,—viz. when the deaths of good men are surrounded with so much that is evil. For example, Socrates is compelled to die in prison, Rutilius to live in exile, Pompey and Cicero to be assassinated, and so on. And, after this, what can one expect for himself, when he sees the best of men suffering the worst evils?" But listen to his answer. "What then is to be done? See how each of them bore his troubles: and if they were brave, then desire to imitate their courage; but if they died in a cowardly way, and like women, why, then nothing died. Either they are worthy to have their courage approved by you, or unworthy to have their cowardice imitated." And this is the self-same complaint about the prosperity of the wicked, and the troubles of the just, as well as of the early and painful death of the Saints, which is made by Job, David, Jeremias, Habacuc, and the other Prophets. But here Chance and Fortune have nothing which they can call their own. All such things are most wisely disposed, within certain fixed limits, by an All-Provident God.

4. When the children of Israel were about to attack the Benjamites, on account of their shameful deed, they consulted God as to who should go up first to the battle. "And the Lord answered them: Let Juda be your leader." (*Judges* xx. 18.) Joyful at the receipt of this response, and now all but certain of victory, they advanced against the Benjamites with a vast army, and with good courage, and yet they were most disgracefully routed, and lost twenty-two thousand of their men, who were slain in one battle. And a second time they consulted the Lord, intending to hazard another battle, and this time not without long prayer and fasting, for they went up and wept before the Lord even until even. And again the answer was,—"Go up against them and join battle." They obeyed, and because they were now going forth to battle by the direct command of God, they promised themselves a most successful issue, and commenced the fight with thoughts fully bent on victory, and yet they were again routed and slain by the Benjamites as before, eighteen thousand men of Israel having fallen in the battle. And how was this? Twice did God

command His people to fight, and yet in neither battle did they gain the victory, but lost forty thousand chosen men. Who can understand these commands of God? But a third time, "All the children of Israel came to the House of God, and sat and wept, before the Lord, and they fasted that day till the evening, and offered to Him holocausts and victims of peace-offerings. And they consulted the Lord, and said, Shall we go out any more to fight against the children of Benjamin, our brethren, or shall we cease? And the Lord said to them, Go up; for to-morrow I will deliver them into your hands." (*Judges* xx. 26-28.) And here it was easy for cowardice to have argued,—"Twice already has the Lord induced us to fight, but each time with a most disastrous result; who, therefore, will rush any more to destruction? Let him fight who will, it is safest to remain quietly at home." But their trust in God prevailed, and this bade them have recourse to arms afresh, with a prosperous issue at last, for twenty-five thousand of the Benjamites were slain. And here there are two things very worthy of observation. First, the hidden Judgments of God, which are not to be examined into by any mortal. Secondly, persevering trust in God, concerning which I shall speak further at the proper place. And in all these things we must look with unflinching and steadfast eye at the Will of God alone. Let no one be disturbed if an unfavourable result follows upon a good cause, or if the most excellent beginnings turn to an unlucky end. Disease attacks the most temperate, consumption the strongest, punishment falls on the most innocent, excitement on the most retired. And here we must acquiesce in the Will of God alone. In other things it may be lawful to say "still further," but in this, "no further," "for it is God who worketh in you both to will and to accomplish, according to His good Will." (*Phil.* ii. 13.)

5. Pelagius, an ancient writer, relates how that one Joseph asked Pastor the Abbot the following question:—"Tell me, Father, how can I become a monk?" To whom he replied,—"If you desire to find rest in this world and the next, say upon all occasions, Who am I that I should prefer my own will or judgment to the Divine? Then take care whom you judge, for God has His Own saints here in every condition of life." Most wholesome counsel indeed! God of a truth receives laws from no one, and renders to no one an account of His actions. Here, therefore, let the wisdom of all men keep a profound silence, and let it everywhere adore at a distance the indications of the Divine Will, because God will do whatever He wills, and His words are full of power, and no one can say to Him, Why doest Thou thus?

As it is usual in cities to regulate all clocks by one chief clock, so it is most fitting that we should regulate our little time-pieces, or, in other words, each his own will, according to that Supreme and Heavenly Horologe of infinite magnitude, that is to say, according to the Divine Will.

But, in order that we may fully see how the human will is to be united to the Divine, behold a most illustrious example of such a union. Francis Borgia, Duke of Gandia, passed two-and-twenty years with his wife Leonora in wonderful happiness. But when she fell sick, because he saw that he was about to be deprived of half of himself, he devoted himself very earnestly to prayer (inviting also the intercession of good men), as well as alms and fasting. Upon one occasion he entered his chamber alone, when all witnesses had been removed, and earnestly besought God with plentiful tears that He would grant that his wife should recover her health and live, when behold! he distinctly heard a voice within, as he himself related afterwards, which said,—"If you desire that your wife should live longer, let it be as you will; but it is not good for you." And being troubled at this, he doubted not but that it was the Voice of God, and that he was being silently rebuked for asking that of which he was ignorant. And so, bursting into tears again, he poured forth these words from his inmost heart,—"Whence is it, O Lord my God, that Thou committest to my will that which is in Thy Power alone? It is of the highest consequence to me to follow Thy Will in all things. For who knows better than Thou, O my God, what would come from my request? And, therefore, Thy will be done; and not merely concerning my wife, but concerning my children also and myself do Thou ordain, I pray, whatever is pleasing to Thee. Thy Will be done." It was noticed at that time that the disease of his wife remained at such a critical point that the physicians were doubtful whether she would grow better or worse, but that after this prayer it began to be past all hope.

6. And thus in all circumstances, however perplexing, our own will is to be conformed to the Divine. And behold another example of this conformity, much more remarkable than the former! King David, the son of Jesse, had united his will to the Divine by so close a bond of agreement, that God declared, as if congratulating Himself on such a man,—"I have found David the son of Jesse, a man after My Own Heart, who shall do all My Wills." (*Acts* xiii. 22.) "I have *found*," He says, as if He had sought anxiously, and had waited a long time, until He had found him. And this commendation, awarded by God to the king at Hebron, surpassed all his other titles of honour.

Christ, Who was perfectly obedient to His Father in all things, has encouraged us to this virtue by His Own example:—"Because I came down from heaven," He says, "not to do My Own Will, but the Will of Him that sent Me." (*John* vi. 38.) And,—"My meat is to do the Will of Him that sent Me, that I may perfect His work." (*John* iv. 34.) And lest perchance any one should complain,—"He spares His son, but a servant He spares not;" behold! the Son is before us! And see what commands the Father is about to lay upon Him! Not even the lowest of servants would perform commands of the same kind! Upon which one of you, O ye wilful ones, has He enjoined such toil as upon the Son? Whom has He ever exposed to such mockings, and false accusations, and sufferings, as the Son, Who was obedient to the Father, even to the Hall of Pilate, even to the cruel Pillar of Scourging, even to the Hill of Golgotha, even to the most shameful Cross and most painful Death, even to the Sepulchre which was not His Own, even to the Prison of departed souls? For this, He proclaims, I came down from heaven, that I might submit Myself most perfectly to this Will of My Father. What, then, shall servants do, if the Son did this? And so our Lord, summing up all His precepts under one head, says,—"Not every one that saith to me, Lord, Lord, shall enter into the kingdom of heaven, but he that *doth the Will* of My Father Who is in heaven." (*Matt.* VII. 21.)

He who has so disciplined himself as most thoroughly to yield himself to the Divine Will begins already to dwell on the summit of a mountain inaccessible to danger, and has beneath his feet clouds, and storms, and lightnings, and every disturbance of the elements, and all the changes of this mortal life; and there he is placed beyond the reach of all fear, except it be that he fear this alone,—that he be not united closely enough to the Divine Will, and so he exclaims without ceasing,—"Thy will be done on Earth, as it is in Heaven!"

CHAPTER IV

WITH WHAT INTENTION WE MUST USE THE PRAYER,—
"THY WILL BE DONE ON EARTH, AS IT IS IN
HEAVEN!"

WHEN the disciples besought their Divine Master
—"Lord, teach us to pray, as John also taught
his disciples" (*Luke* xi. 1), He assented, and "said to
them, when you pray, say, 'Our Father who art in
Heaven, Hallowed be Thy Name; Thy Kingdom
come; Thy Will be done on earth, as it is in Heaven,'"
&c. But how hard is this prayer, O my God! There
is too much dissimilarity between those blessed spirits
in heaven and us exiles in this vale which is so pro-
ductive of wormwood. To those blessed ones above
all things happen according to their wish, nor is there
anything which cannot please them; but in our case,
we, who are still banished from heaven, can scarcely
find anything which does entirely please us.

There is disgust and loathing everywhere, and
scarcely even a few things, and these only very seldom, turn out according to our wishes; while there
are numberless things which displease us every day,
and excite our anger. But in heaven it is most pleasant, as it is also most easy, to attune oneself to the

Divine Will, for there no adversity disturbs; but here a thousand vexations harass us: we are weighed down with cares; there is scarcely the smallest time for recovering breath; conflict follows upon conflict; our misfortunes are linked together; and a continuous chain of calamities scarcely allows us time to pray without distraction. As, therefore, the full and the hungry do not sing on equal terms, nor do they who have just risen from a sumptuous feast, and they who have kept a long fast, dance on equal terms, so neither can we pray with the same readiness as the blessed,— "Thy Will be done on Earth, as it is in Heaven." Our condition and theirs are too different for this; but remove us thither, O Lord, and we will equally with them unite our desires and acts to Thine. But may God forgive such words, my Christian friends! We are but the idlest of mendicants, and not as ready as might be, even with our tongue. How quickly, alas! do we succumb before things which certainly are not so very difficult; a gentle breeze overthrows us; we shrink from whatever cannot be accomplished agreeably. Christ, O ye timid ones, taught us to do nothing which might not be done. This at least let us do, and strive with all our might to fulfil the Divine Will on earth, as the angels do in Heaven. If in reality we are able to do less, let us at least be liberal in our wishes. S. Cyprian (*De Hab. Virg.* 23) says, excellently,—"Christ taught us to pray, 'Thy will be done on Earth, as it is in Heaven;' and this, not that God should do what He Himself wills, but that we should be able to do what He wills." Whoever, therefore, wishes to follow the example of prayer which Christ sets him, must not repeat the words indistinctly beneath his breath, but should say out fearlessly,—"Thy Will be done on Earth as it is in Heaven." But let him attend carefully to what I am about to add; and let him pray that he may have the power to fulfil the Divine Will—

1. (1) *With perfect Purity of Intention.* Thy Will be done! For this I have determined to follow, not for the sake of gain, nor because Thou hast fenced me in with blessings, as Satan slanderously said of Job (*Job* i. 10); nor yet from fear of punishment, lest I should be banished into hell; but with a single eye I regard Thy Will alone. I will because Thou willest, O my God.

(2) *Lovingly.* Thy will be done! This is my only care, that what I do may be pleasing to Thee, and that even in this way the name of Thy Majesty may be made known by me, a most unprofitable servant. Thy pleasure, O my God, I esteem so highly, that I should think it reward enough *to have pleased Thee;* and so I agree with Chrysostom when he affirms,— "You know not of a truth what it means to please God, if you seek for any other reward."

(3) *Readily.* Thy Will be done! Slowly to will is the part of one who wills not. Most acceptable are those acts of obedience which are prompt, ready, and where there is no delay. It is a sign of one who does a thing willingly, to do it quickly. Favour is taken

away from an act of kindness in proportion as there is an increase of delay; therefore,—"My heart is ready, O God, my heart is ready!" (*Ps.* CVII. 1), to perform all Thy Will.

(4) *Cheerfully.* Some things we do quickly enough, but not with sufficient good-will. "Not with sadness or of necessity," says S. Paul, "for God loveth a cheerful giver." (2 *Cor.* IX. 7.) He who has set the Will of God before himself as his end and aim, if trouble or sorrow intervene he swallows them without difficulty; for he is longing for such dainties as to be able to say,—"My meat is to do the Will of Him That sent me;" therefore,—"Thy Will be done on Earth, as it is in Heaven!"

(5) *Perfectly.* Thy Will be done! Not even the smallest indication of it being omitted. A man who is really anxious to yield himself to the Divine Will does not seek for exceptional cases, nor does he use such language as,—"I will, O Lord, but not yet; I obey, O Lord, only command not that particular thing; I will wash, and even kiss, the feet of all men, only let me not be compelled to perform this office to mine enemy; I will endure being despised, only let me not be put to shame in public; I am prepared for all things, if Thou wilt only not require that particular thing from me." But not so the man who really loves the Divine Will. He makes no exceptions; he withdraws himself from no blows. On the other hand, he rather says,—"Dost Thou will, O my Lord, that I should suffer more, and still more bitter things? Behold me!

I am ready, I am prepared. Lay upon me heavier commands; chastise me more severely; only Thy Will be done!"

(6) *Perseveringly.* Thy Will be done! After the first, after the second, the third, and the fourth decade of my life Thy Will be done; and be it done for ever. "I have inclined my heart to do Thy justifications for ever, for the reward." (*Ps.* cxviii. 112.) Dost Thou will, O Lord, that I should suffer something for a hundred or a thousand years? If Thou willest, I will. And this is the way to recite the Lord's Prayer with devout intention. These are the wings of the seraphim by which we are borne on high to a knowledge of the Divine Will.

2. And here we must specially observe that the blessed in heaven rejoice more fully in the performance of the Divine Will than in the greatness of their own glory. And so they are all most perfectly contented with their own reward, and none is displeased because he has less than another. For they who see God are not merely conformed to the Divine Will, but are also absorbed in it, and are transformed into it, so as henceforward to will the Will of God alone; and they rejoice more that it is the Will of God that they should be blessed, than that they enjoy this blessedness. And upon this conformity of the human will with the Divine there follows a most excellent effect of love, which may be called not so much conformity, as actual union of the human will with the Divine; and this so influences the blessed that with all their

powers, and with the utmost possible ardour, they desire that God should be as He is, as Wise and Powerful, as Merciful and Just, as worthy of all fulness of Honour and Glory and Majesty. Just as a son who has been well brought up does not grudge happiness to his father any more than to himself, and desires that his parent should be honoured as much as himself, or even more than himself; so the blessed rejoice in the blessedness which God enjoys, as much as they do in their own. And hence those songs in heaven so full of joy,—"Alleluia; Salvation, and Glory, and Power is to our God; for true and just are His Judgments. Alleluia; for the Lord our God the Almighty hath reigned. Let us be glad, and rejoice, and give glory to Him." (*Apoc.* xix. 1, 2, 6, 7.)

And this, which I will not call conformity to, but union with, the Divine Will amongst the blessed, we too can imitate in our prayers in this way. Let the understanding contemplate, like a most attentive spectator, God's Power, Eternity, Wisdom, Beauty, and infinite Blessedness; but let the will rejoice that God is Infinite Good, the Fount of all riches, Who wants nothing, Who can do all things, Who is liberal towards all, Who is present in everything. Theologians hold that this is the greatest and most perfect act of Divine love; for as no love can be greater than that wherewith God loves Himself, so our love also cannot be better than by daily being made more conformable to that Divine love. It is a saying of philosophers, that to love is nothing else than to desire good for some one. And if this principle is established, it follows that the more good we desire for any one, the more we love him. But we cannot wish any greater good to God than what He is Himself, the most boundless Good of all goods; and so we cannot love God more ardently than by wishing Him all His Own good. And, therefore, in this way especially the Will of God will be done on earth, as it is in heaven.

3. And they whose wills are thus closely united with God's Will are the lightnings of which Job speaks,—"Canst thou send lightnings, and will they go, and will they return, and say to thee, Here we are?" (*Job* XXXVIII. 35.) Lightning and thunderbolts being fire of the utmost subtlety, rise upwards by their own nature; but because God sends them downwards to the earth, forgetful of their own properties, they rush below with incredible swiftness, cleaving a way through iron, rocks, and whatever resists their course. And you may call those the lightnings of Christ who trample under foot their own will that they may obey the Divine Will. They would soar on high indeed, if they followed their own aspirations, but because God wills otherwise, they let themselves down even to the lowest depths, not unwillingly, but with the utmost readiness; they break through difficulties and impediments of every kind; they are not wearied with such constant motion, but when their mission is accomplished they return like lightnings, and stand before their Lord, and say,—"Lo! here we are! What shall we now do? We are ready even to die. Command

what Thou wilt." As, moreover, the lightnings leap (a thing to be observed), not from the water, or from the earth, but from a dense and well-closed cloud; so the will which is ready, and easily led to obedience in everything, issues forth from prayer and meditation, which soar on high like clouds, while the senses of the body are safe closed up on all sides. For if any one attentively considers with what wonderful obedience so many millions of angels in heaven serve the Deity, and how the Son of God Himself embraced the Will of His Father in the manger, coarse swaddling-clothes and straw, in journeyings, in agony, and on the Cross, he will not be able to restrain himself, but like lightning he will promise the most ready obedience, and will closely unite his own will to the Divine. And then at last he will with sincerity say the Lord's Prayer, and particularly the clause,—"Thy Will be done on Earth, as it is in Heaven."

4. That most famous passage of S. Augustine's is well worthy of attention, where, when examining the command given to the first Pair not to touch the Apple, he assumes the character of Adam and asks,— " 'If the tree is good, why may I not touch it? But if it is bad, what place has it in Paradise?' And to him God replies,—'It is in Paradise because it is good; but I forbid you to touch it because I desire that you should be an obedient and not a rebellious servant.' 'And why is this?' 'Because you are the servant, and I am the Lord.'" And here you have a thousand reasons contained in this one:—Because God is our

Lord, and has set before us His Will to be obeyed by us, and not to be questioned, and we are servants; it is therefore most fitting that we should walk in the way in which the Will of God leads us.

The apostate angel most craftily and wickedly asked in Paradise,—"Why hath God commanded?" (*Gen.* III. 1.) He ought to have asked,—Why do you not eat of the fruit of this tree? For to this question there would have been an immediate answer,—Because God has commanded us not to eat of it. But the most subtle serpent anticipated the reply, and framed his question,—"*Why* hath God commanded?" As often, then, as it is ascertained that God wills anything we must not after this inquire,—"*Why is this?*" There is a reason, the most urgent of all reasons,—GOD SO WILLS. When Abraham was bidden to slay his son, what excuses might he not have devised and urged! but he was silent and obeyed. This one reason was enough for him,—GOD SO WILLS.

5. Parents occasionally ask, in order to test the disposition of their children, whether they would not like, as the day is so fine, to go into the garden, or take a trip into the country? Supposing (they say) we put aside books for to-day, and look at some pictures instead. If the children answer,—"Just as our master and parents please," they exhibit a proof of excellent training, and sound discretion. But if they do not disguise their eager desire for walks and play, and before their parents have given their consent, fly out into the sunshine, they show a disposition of an inferior order;

and then the father very properly says,—"Stop, my boy; put away your playthings, you must go to school to-day." And then follow dejected looks, tears, and mutterings; no attention is paid to books, but the thoughts wander idly; oftentimes, too, there are fits of crying, and complaints against the tyranny of parents. Look at these silly children, so little inclined to yield to the wishes of their parents! And such very often are we ourselves! Most entirely given up to all sorts of fleeting pleasures, and instantly complaining when God, our Supreme Father, either disturbs our play, or calls us away to work. If we are wise we shall try to imitate children who are well brought up, and shall say nothing else than,—"Just as it pleases the Lord, our Father, are we ready and prepared to go, or not to go; to do, or not to do; to labour, or to suffer, according as our Father wills."

And here John Tauler appositely remarks,—"If God were to give you a choice, and say, 'Do you desire that I should exempt you from all the ills of body and mind, and restore you to paradise?' You ought to make no other reply than this,—'Thou art able, O Lord, both to take away sufferings and to leave them, according as Thou willest; but that will be most pleasing to me which is most agreeable to Thy Will.'" In this way of a truth we attain a fuller measure of grace than if we grasp at the greatest gifts, when following our own will. God is, certainly, no light exactor of virtues, but, like strict parents, He is wont to train His children in a severer way; and so when you see men who are good and pleasing to God, labouring, and toiling, and ascending by a steep road, while the evil are taking their ease, and are filled to overflowing with pleasure, reflect that the former are pleased with the moderation of sons, the latter with the licence of servants; that the one are restrained by a severe discipline, while the audacity of the other is encouraged. God does not allow one who is dear to Him to remain in the midst of pleasures; He puts him to the trial, and makes him endure hardship, and thus prepares him for Himself. We grow wiser in adversity; prosperity takes away right judgment.

And so, let us offer ourselves as empty baskets to God, either to be filled according to the Divine Will, or to be left empty. S. Jerome, rebuking Julian, says,—"You fancy that you are standing on the very pinnacle of virtues if you offer a portion from the whole. The Lord desires yourself as a living victim; give to God yourself, not yours."

CHAPTER V

WHAT ARE THE MARKS AND SIGNS OF A HUMAN WILL CONFORMED TO THE DIVINE

THE Romans thought nothing of a soldier who had not firm-set ribs, and arms muscular enough to carry any weight. And besides this it was needful that he should have polished and glittering weapons, and the most complete confidence in his general. And so, let no one vaunt himself as a soldier of Christ, let no one think that he is devoted to the Divine Will, unless he can detect in himself certain indications that his own will hangs entirely on the Divine Will in all things. And that every one may be able to put himself to the proof in this matter, let him look for the following marks or signs :—

1. *The First Sign.* To desire to do all things at the bidding of the Divine Will, and, therefore, to set about nothing without first imploring the Divine Aid. He who truly follows the Will of God takes no business in hand without first asking God to be his Helper. But if anything seems to be of more than usual importance, or of more than common difficulty in execution, he so much the more frequently implores aid from God. And let this be a fixed rule for those who have

to deal with weighty matters, and are entrusted with government, never to undertake anything hastily, without first asking counsel of God. No man living can easily estimate how much damage the whole world suffers from this cause: how many households are badly managed; how many kingdoms and provinces are improperly governed; how many unjust wars are undertaken; how many injuries are inflicted by one on another, through the neglect of this law. This is the most prolific source of evils; because masters of families, governors, rulers, and kings oftentimes are self-willed and arbitrary, and do not act according to reason, but by impulse; and do not consult the Mouth of the Lord, but follow impetuosity as their guide, and lean to their own understanding, and trust to their own shoulders, being very Atlases in their own eyes: and hence often arises a chaotic and disgraceful confusion of business to the injury of very many.

The princes of Israel sinned grievously, because they made a treaty with the Gabaonites, "and consulted not the Mouth of the Lord." (*Josue* ix. 14.) And we are none the more inclined to take warning on account of their error, but often plan great undertakings, "and consult not the Mouth of the Lord." We seek for the priesthood, we contract matrimony, we mix ourselves up in worldly business, and yet we "consult not the Mouth of the Lord." But far otherwise those noble generals, the Machabees, who never engaged in any battle without first having "consulted the Mouth of the Lord" more than once. For not only before the battle did they exhort their soldiers to prayer, and joined with them in their devotions, but they also continued this combined prayer even while they were fighting. And so Judas Machabeus, looking upon the hostile array before him, "stretching out his hands to heaven, called upon the Lord that worketh wonders, Who giveth victory to them that are worthy, not according to the power of their arms, but according as it seemeth good to Him." (2 *Mach.* xv. 21.) Nor did Machabeus only before the battle "consult the Mouth of the Lord" with the utmost earnestness in prayer, but by his example he inflamed his soldiers also to do the same, and so he and "they that were with him encountered the enemy, calling upon God by prayers." (Ver. 26.) And not merely at the beginning of the battle, but also in the very heat of the conflict they constantly called upon God, and so, fighting indeed with their hands, but praying to God with their hearts, they slew no less than thirty-five thousand, "being greatly cheered with the presence of God." (Ver. 27.) That is to say, they solemnly "consulted the Mouth of the Lord."

It is the advice of Cassian that before every action these versicles of the Church should be used,—"O God, make speed to save me. O Lord, make haste to help me." It was the practice of S. Pambo, whenever his advice was asked, to require time for commending so great a thing to God, nor could he endure to give any reply until he had first "consulted the Mouth of the Lord." And this practice was of so great use to him, that, when he was now near death, he affirmed that he did not remember that anything had ever been said by him of which he was sorry. Of a truth God immediately answers those who seek counsel of Him. "Thy ear hath heard the preparation of their heart." (*Ps.* IX. 17.) That man does not trust in God, nor does he carefully search out the Divine Will, who does not derive the beginning of all his actions from God. We must consult the Mouth of the Lord in all things without exception.

2. *The Second Sign.* It is a mark of true devotion towards the Divine Will, not merely not to shrink from sorrows and calamities when they are present, but willingly to seek them when they are absent, and for this reason, because God is far nearer by His Grace to those who are afflicted in various ways, than to those who enjoy uninterrupted prosperity. With great delight the Psalmist, Jesse's son, sings,—"Thou hast turned all his couch in his sickness." (*Ps.* XL. 4.) And this, according to S. Ambrose and S. Chrysostom, means that God soothes a sick person, or one who is otherwise afflicted, with such consolations, as if He prepared for him the softest bed. As ladies of rank sometimes wait on the sick from a sweet feeling of pity, so Christ our Lord exercises a special guardianship over such as are afflicted either with disease or any other calamity, if they only show themselves worthy of this heavenly protection. The Roman philosopher (SENECA, *de Provid.* 4. 5) moralizes very devoutly on this subject:—"Cease, I pray you," he says,

"to dread those things which the Immortal God applies to your souls to urge them onwards. Calamity gives occasion to virtue. One may truly call those people wretched who are indolent through excess of prosperity, and whom a sluggish tranquillity holds fast as it were on an unruffled sea. And so those whom He loves God tries, and causes them to endure hardships, and corrects them, and disciplines them; but those whom he appears to deal gently with, and to spare, he is reserving for evils to come. For you are mistaken if you think that any one is excepted. His own share of troubles will befall him who has been prosperous for a long time. Whoever seems to be in a low estate has his happiness deferred. But why does God afflict all good men either with ill-health or other troubles? Why, too, it may be asked, in a camp are the most perilous posts assigned to the bravest? A general sends his picked soldiers to attack the enemy in an ambush by night, or to examine the line of march, or to dislodge a garrison from some particular position. Not one of those who go forth says,—'The general deserves no thanks from me!' but,—'He has made a good choice.' And in the same way let those who are bidden to suffer things which to the fearful and slothful are subjects for tears, say,—'We seem to God to be thought worthy to have the trial made in us as to how much human nature is capable of enduring.'"

And how agreeable is this to that which Wisdom proclaims,—"For God hath tried them, and found

them worthy of Himself." (*Wisdom* III. 5.) Therefore, fly from pleasures, fly from that enervating happiness whereby men become effeminate, unless something interposes which may admonish them of the
human lot, like those who are stupefied with perpetual
drunkenness. God, therefore, follows the same plan
with good men, as a master does with his scholars,
who exacts a larger share of work from those from
whom he feels more sure of getting it.

Do you think that their own children were objects
of hatred to the Spartans because they tried their disposition by lashes inflicted in public, while their parents
themselves encouraged them to bear the strokes of the
whip bravely, and asked them, when they were lacerated and half dead, whether they should go on adding
gash to gash? And what wonder is it if God severely
tries noble souls? There is no such thing as an easy
and gentle proof of virtue. Does Fortune lash and
tear us? Let us endure it; it is not cruelty, it is a
conflict, in which the oftener we engage the stronger
we shall be. It is by endurance that the soul arrives
at despising the power of evils. Fire tries gold, and
misery tries brave men. Why are you astonished that
good men are shaken in order that they may be
strengthened? A tree is not firm and strong unless
the wind constantly blows against it; for by the very
disturbing force of the blast it is strengthened, and
fastens its roots more surely to the earth. Frail are
those trees which have grown in a sunny valley.

Behold, then, the most certain evidence of a human

will which is transfused, as it were, into the Divine, if it does not refuse to follow it even through rough and difficult places. Whosoever, therefore, has welcomed to himself the Divine Will with a hearty embrace will exclaim in the midst of troubles, with more earnestness even than Demetrius,—"This one thing, O my God, I can complain of concerning Thee, that Thou hast not earlier made known to me Thy Will; for I should have arrived before this at that point to which I have now attained when called by Thee. Dost Thou will to take away from me wealth or reputation? I was ready long ago to offer them. Dost Thou will to deprive me of my children? I have already put them aside for Thee. Dost Thou will to take any part of my body? Take it. It is no great offer which I make, for in a short time I shall relinquish the whole of it. Dost Thou will to take my spirit? And why not? I do not object that Thou shouldest receive what Thou hast given. Thou wilt take from a willing person whatever Thou shalt demand. I am driven to nothing, I suffer nothing against my will; nor do I *serve* Thee, O my God, but I *agree* with Thee." This is the true union of two wills.

3. *The Third Sign.* The greatest possible distrust of self. This is pre-eminently a Christian virtue, and one which was scarcely known at all to the heathen of old time. He who distrusts himself ascribes even his most prosperous successes not to his own strength or diligence, but entirely to the Divine Power and Goodness; but his errors, and whatever arises from

them, he imputes to himself, and he observes most faithfully the precept of S. Augustine,—"Let God be all Thy presumption, so as to acknowledge that without Him you can do nothing at all, but all things in Him." Nevertheless the man who is entirely distrustful of self, and hopes not for success through his own powers, does not neglect to do what he can, relying with all the surer trust in God in proportion as he has none in himself. He knows that he can do nothing, and yet that he can do all things, but only with God. He works, indeed, with all his might, but he looks to the Divine Will for all the fruit of his labour, accepting with composure all those things which are only ills to one who bears them ill. But how different with those who trust in themselves, their own strength, their own skill, their own prudence, and their own schemes! How eloquent they are in extolling their own performances; with what unsparing tongue do they speak their own praises; and in the meantime how carelessly do they behave in many things through excessive self-confidence! But he who rests entirely on the Divine Will is like a pair of scales, he descends the lower on one side in proportion as he ascends higher on the other. A general who has undertaken the defence of a fortified camp examines weak and ill-defended points before the enemy advances, he provides for the commissariat, he arranges his artillery, he prepares against every kind of attack, for he knows that he cannot trust the enemy. And in the same way the Christian says,—"I will not trust disease and death; I will fortify myself beforehand with sacraments; I will furnish myself with prayer and fasting as weapons; I trust neither myself nor death." But he who is presumptuous, and confident in his own strength, thinks that he is well enough prepared to meet all the attacks of his enemies; or at least hopes that it will be easy enough to prepare when occasion arises. He trusts himself and Death! And well does Solomon say concerning each of these,—"A wise man feareth, and declineth from evil; the fool leapeth over and is confident." (*Prov.* xiv. 16.)

4. *The Fourth Sign.* Most complete trust in God, whence it comes that when any one is injured or offended he does not immediately plan vengeance, but says to himself,—"God has seen and heard this, and He will avenge in His Own time." And by means of this one thing he rises superior to all his enemies, because he feels certain that even if they were to move hell itself against him, they could not harm him more than God permitted. But you may say,—"There are some who neglect no opportunity of doing harm to others. If they cannot inflict actual injuries they at least try to hinder their neighbours' profit." It is so, I admit; but he who trusts in God so acts as that no amount of diligence should be wanting on his part; but everything else he commits to Divine Providence. And fruitlessly do the wicked attempt to strive against it,—"There is no wisdom, there is no prudence, there is no counsel against the Lord." (*Prov.* xxi. 30.) How dishonestly did Laban deal with Jacob his son-in-

law! He changed his wages ten times that he might diminish his possessions; but it was to no purpose, since all things turned out to Jacob's advantage, for God suffered him not to hurt him. (*Gen.* XXXI. 7.)

Sennacherib threatened direst vengeance against Jerusalem; but neither he himself, nor his army, could escape the avenging Hand of God. An angel slew the army, and his sons slew him:—"And the Lord saved Ezechias and the inhabitants of Jerusalem out of the hand of Sennacherib, king of the Assyrians, and out of the hand of all, and gave them treasures on every side." (*2 Par.* XXXII. 22.) And so, my Christian friend, trust in God, and leave all vengeance to Him, for He is the Lord of vengeance. And let even the heathen teach you this. Tissaphernes, the Persian general, concluded a peace with Agesilaus; but it was only in pretence and not in reality, for he afterwards came with a vast army and summoned the Greeks to withdraw from Asia. But to the threats of the ambassadors Agesilaus dauntlessly replied,— "Tell your general that I heartily thank him for having broken the treaty, and so made both gods and men his enemies. My forces will swell through the perfidy of my foe!" Words almost worthy of a Christian! It is as if he had said,—that we should be saved "from our enemies, and from the hand of all that hate us." (*Luke* I. 71.) He who trusts in God has all his enemies as vassals, because he has God on his side.

But whatever a man who trusts in God desires, he

first of all seeks it from God. And here he lays down this rule for himself,—It either is good for me that the thing which I seek should be granted, or it is not good, but which of the two it is God knows best. If it is good for me, God will either grant it immediately, or at some more fitting time, in order that in the mean-time my patience may be exercised; if, however, God refuses me what I have asked, I am perfectly certain that my request was not for my good. In this way alone, and never in any other, does he who has yielded himself absolutely to the Divine Will present his peti-tions to God. They, on the other hand, who are ig-norant of this mystery of the Divine Will, either do not implore God's aid, or do so sluggishly and care-lessly, and before they do this weary out the patience of all their friends, and court the favour of as many as they can; and if they cannot effect their object in any other way, they even try to procure this favour by bribes, and they buy interest and honours, just as they would in the market.

S. John, who may be called the eye of the Lord, saw Christ carrying in His Right Hand seven stars. (*Apoc.* I. 16.) And what are these stars in His Hand? John himself, when unfolding this mystery, says,—"The seven stars are the angels of the seven Churches" (*Apoc.* I. 20), or the seven bishops of Asia. Behold, then, bishops and their mitres are in the Hand of Christ! But if a mitre anywhere wants an owner, there are numbers who offer their head for it; but they do not first hasten straight to the Hand of Christ.

They run indeed but oftentimes they reach the hands of kings and princes before they run to Christ. And the same thing happens in the pursuit of other offices and honours; human interest is sought, but the Divine favour only by a few, or after that of man. It is a transparent error; we ought to do the reverse: the Divine Favour and Will should be sought before all things. Sceptres and crowns are in the Hand of God; He apportions offices, dignities, places of trust, and magistracies; from Him, in the first instance, must all these be sought:—"As the divisions of waters, so the heart of the king is in the hand of the Lord: whithersoever he will he shall turn it." (*Prov.* XXI. I.) As a gardener who has a little stream of water at his command in his garden does not always guide it to the nearest or best tree, but oftentimes to one of feebler growth, or in whatever direction he pleases; so the heart of the king, like a stream, contains offices and preferment of every kind: but God, like a gardener, guides the water from this stream towards those whom He Himself has chosen, without, however, forcing man's free-will. And therefore they act with consummate folly who throw away so many prayers and bribes into the ears and hands of others, while God is saluted only in a cold and distant way. Oh! the madness of men! More purely are waters sought from the Fount itself.

5. *The Fifth Sign.* To be able to endure all things in noble silence. Consider, I pray you, the most patient JESUS, so nobly keeping silence amidst numberless

reproaches and torments. The Jewish priests stood
and constantly accused Him, but JESUS held His peace.
They laid various crimes to His charge, but JESUS
held His peace. They grew vehement against Him
with loud cries, and demanded that He should be
crucified, but JESUS held his peace. While He was
hanging on the Cross they ceased not to revile Him
with most bitter reproaches, but JESUS held his peace.
And so, too, the mother of our Lord was perfectly
silent amidst the greatest difficulties. S. Joseph perceived that she was with child, and therefore determined to put her away; and here the mother acted as
her Son did, so that it may be truly said of her—but
Mary held her peace, and committed all this to the
Divine Will and Providence. She heard that the Man
Who was so inexpressibly dear to her, her own Flesh
and Blood, was assailed with innumerable calumnies;
but Mary held her peace. She saw her son, Who was
perfect in innocence, fainting beneath the weight of
the Cross, she heard him groaning on it, she saw Him
dying in most bitter agony; but Mary held her peace.
This Son, and this mother, very many have imitated
successfully, for even when accused of the most grievous crimes they held their peace. David, that meek-
est of kings, understood the wondrous power of this
silence when he said,—"I was dumb and was humbled,
and kept silence from good things: and my sorrow
was renewed." (*Ps.* xxxviii. 3.) And again,—"I
was dumb, and opened not my mouth; because Thou
hast done it." (Ver. 10.) He brings forward no

other reason for his silence than this,—*"because Thou hast done it."* Therefore I hold my peace because I perceive that it is Thy Will. Thy Will, O my God, has pointed out this silence to me!

It sometimes happens that a master of excitable disposition goes into the servant's room, and disarranges the furniture, and throws everything into confusion, and then goes away lest he should be caught in the act. When the servant comes home and finds all the furniture in disorder he grows very angry; but when he hears that it has been done by his master, he holds his tongue and restrains his rage. And so David says of himself,—"I held my tongue, and spake nothing." And why? *"Because Thou hast done it."* And in the same way he who has yielded himself unreservedly to the Divine Will is conscious indeed of adversity, but comforts himself with the thought of Divine Providence; and knowing that he will do no good by idle complaints, he says,—"I have lifted up my eyes to the mountains, from whence help shall come to me. My help is from the Lord, Who made heaven and earth." (*Ps.* cxx. 1, 2.)

When King Assuerus and Aman sat down to their feast all the Jews were weeping. (*Esth.* III. 15.) But how quickly did this bloody tragedy change, and the evil which he had devised for others recoil upon its author! If a monthly want of light did not obscure the moon, which changes as it waxes and wanes, Philosophers would not know that it borrows its light from the sun; and thus we, too, from the daily want of things, learn that every blessing comes from God. Is any one sick? For the first time in his life he now knows how to value health, which he never would have prized so highly if he had not lost it. This is human nature, that nothing pleases so much as that which is lost. Does any one suffer from calumny? He now understands what a serious thing it is to injure the reputation of another, which he may often have done, and yet have thought it a trifling matter. Has any one been reduced to want? He now begins to recollect how he formerly bore himself towards those who were in need. And so he holds his peace, and, pondering on this, commits himself to the Divine Will.

But perhaps it is with difficulty that you hold your peace. Speak then; but only with your heart, and to God. Let the tongue be silent, and let the mind pray. Meditate upon the silence of Christ before the High Priest, upon the silence of Mary before those wicked citizens, upon the silence of David before his enemies. A person of greater dignity and influence than yourself reproaches you—hold your peace! An equal reproaches you—hold your peace! An inferior reproaches you —and even then hold your peace? This may be harder than the rest, but it is more noble. Leave him alone, and draw near to God. Pray for your enemy, as David did, according to that saying of his—"Instead of making me a return of love, they detracted me; but I gave myself to prayer." (*Ps.* cviii. 3.) He was accustomed to conciliate his adversary by *silence,* and

God by *prayer*. Therefore hold your peace, and commend yourself most absolutely to the Divine Will, constantly keeping before your mind the saying—*"Because Thou hast done it."*

6. *The Sixth Sign.* To attempt for the honour of God things which are difficult, and which are supposed to be scarcely possible. And how courageous was S. Paul in this! "I know," he says, "both how to be brought low, and I know how to abound (everywhere and in all things I am instructed), both to be full and to be hungry, both to abound and to suffer need. *I can do all things* in Him Who strengtheneth me." (*Phil.* IV. 12, 13.) And with an equally great and exalted mind, David says,—"Through God I shall go over a wall." (*Ps.* XVII. 29.) So that let Pericles come to life again, and build his walls to the Piræus, forty cubits high, and so broad that two chariots yoked together would have room enough to pass, and yet I, says David, will leap over them. Let the Carthaginians re-appear, and raise their triple wall, famous in every age, and I will leap over it. Let the architects of Babel come back, and build a tower whose top shall reach to heaven (*Gen.* XI. 4), and with the help of my God, I will leap over it; for by Him shall I be delivered from temptation. But David, promising still greater and more difficult things, says,—"In Thee I will run girded; in my God I will leap over the wall." (*2 Kings* XXII. 30.) It was too little for him to run and toil, but he desires to run even when clad in mail, and armed from head to foot. It was too little

for him to pass over a wall, however wide or high, but now he desires to pass over a barrier, even if it reaches as high as heaven. There can scarcely be a higher and wider wall put in the way as an obstacle than *his own will* is to each individual. But this wall he must cross and leap over. Let each one reflect thus:—"God desires that I should be patient, and chaste, and that I should quickly forgive my enemies; He wills that I should think and speak well of others. And why do I not will the same? Truly my will stands like a wall in the way of my doing this. But that wall need not terrify me. I shall pass over it; I shall leap over it, I can do all things through Him Who strengtheneth me."

He who meditates upon the acts of the saints will very often give utterance to those words of the royal Psalmist,—"God is glorified in the assembly of the saints." (*Ps.* LXXXVIII. 8.) "The Lord will give strength to His people." (*Ps.* XXVIII. 10.) Yea, He has given strength to His saints! And not to speak of ancient times, how great things did Francis Xavier, the apostle of Japan, dare to do for God! What wonders did he work! What walls did he not pass over! What fortresses did he not scale! You might say that he flew, if he could not approach his object in any other way. A thirsty man is sometimes wont to complain that a whole village seems to be on fire inside him, so fearfully does thirst oppress him; but the world itself might have been thought to be burning in the breast of Xavier, so ardently did he thirst for the salvation of all men. And what a fire did Xavier carry about in his soul, when with separate leaps, as it were, he passed from Italy to Portugal, from Portugal to India, from India to Japan, and from thence penetrated even to the most extreme borders of China, traversing country after country, and crossing sea after sea! Do you place in his way perils of land and sea? But such things, he says, the man does not fear who trusts in God. Or darkness of forests? A flame shines brightly enough in his breast. Or the raging ocean? Many waters cannot quench love. Or the secret attacks of robbers and pirates? But he is not safe, even at home, whom the Divine Will protects not. And so, trusting in God, he leapt over every wall, and in this way added to Christ, as Bozius affirms, three hundred thousand heathen. No one is ignorant, I suppose, that when meditating better things he is usually kept back by a thousand hindrances; but he must break through them by force, and must struggle upwards, even though Satan, with all his furies and appliances, stand in the way. Christ encouraging us to this says,—"If you have faith as a grain of mustard-seed, you shall say to this mountain, Remove from hence hither; and it shall remove; and *nothing shall be impossible to you.*" (*Matt.* XVII. 19.) Whosoever then has yielded himself absolutely to the Divine Will is confident that he can do all things.

7. In order that what I have said, as well concerning the knowledge of the Divine Will, as concerning

the conformity of the human will to it, may be perfectly clear to an understanding however uncultivated, I will now proceed to condense what precedes under this short summary.

Whatever is done in the world (sin excepted), by whomsoever or howsoever it is done, must be said to be done by the Divine Will. All things that are done, God wills to be done; but whatever God does not will most surely is not done. "How could anything endure, if Thou wouldst not?" exclaims Wisdom. (Chap. xi. 25.) Sin alone God *wills not,* but *permits.* He might, indeed, prevent sin; but, for reasons known to Himself, He does not prevent it.

Scotus, that theologian of marvellously subtle intellect, says that all things which are done or exist, which have been done or have existed, which shall be done or shall exist, are known to God by the Decree of His Will. And observe, good reader, that the freedom of man's actions is not hindered because God has foreknown and willed them from eternity; for He willed them on this account, because He foreknew that they would be done.

But let us proceed. God not only wills that whatever is done in the world should be done (sin excepted), but in reality He ever brings to pass that which is good, or rather, which is best. S. Basil the Great sets this forth very clearly when he says,—"This one thing we ought to take for granted, that none of those things which happen to us is evil, or such that we can desire anything better than it." And here S. Augustine is worthy of all attention:—"It is brought about," he says, "by the justice of the True and Supreme God, not only that all things exist, but also exist in such a way that they cannot at all be better." And what can be clearer? But hear his reason:— "Whatever," he says, "has befallen you, which really is for your advantage, know that God has caused it, as being the Creator of all good; for you cannot desire anything good in the case of a creature which has escaped the Maker of that creature."

8. As to the way in which God *wills* all things that are done, but *permits* sin, I propose to bring forward the following illustration:—Pope Julius II. ordered that Michelangelo, the most celebrated of painters, should paint the Last Judgment. The painter commenced the work, but, on account of his hostile feeling towards the Princes of the Church, he placed even Bishops and purple-robed Fathers in the flames of hell. The Pope very often visited the painter, and saw through the daring of the man, which was concealed under the rules of art; and, although he strongly disapproved of it, yet for certain reasons he pretended not to see it, thinking to himself—Let him only finish his work, and he will soon find out in prison the errors of his pencil, when he dines on nothing but bread and water. The Pope certainly wished that the Tribunal of the Supreme Judge should be painted for the benefit of those who looked upon it, and not for the injury or contempt of any one; but this injury he knowingly and willingly allowed in order to attain a

certain object. And in the same way God wills that we should paint for eternity, and produce immortal works; but we, with hand and affection which wander from His design, place sometimes one person and sometimes another in hell; that is to say, we are harmful in a variety of ways to those whom we esteem our enemies; and many other faults, too, we are guilty of while performing our task. Nevertheless, a picture is elaborated of things which are most entirely different in their nature; for there is a marvellous connection, dependence, and arrangement in details, so that particular objects, which, taken by themselves, seem to be unsightly, or at all events less beautiful than others, when brought into connection with certain other objects are far more beautiful than they were before. Moreover, God, Who is so boundless in patience, waits till the whole of this picture is finished; and for reasons of perfect Justice He shuts His eyes to our manifold errors, just as if He did not see them. But at the Last Day it will at length be made manifest what each one has painted worthy of eternity, and what faults he has committed in his painting. As, therefore, the Pope, or any King, desires that a certain fixed subject should be painted, and yet does not interfere with the judgment of the painter, but allows even faults to pass unnoticed, for reasons known to himself, so God wills that all things which are done should be done, but permits sin; and yet permits it knowingly and willingly, since He might prevent it. And in this way King David employed Joab as a

General. He by no means approved of his crimes, but for a long time he dissembled knowledge of them.

Nor can any one object here, why is man compelled to prevent sin when he can, and God is not compelled, though He always can? For over and above that God is the Lord and Ruler of all things, intent on the common good, but we servants and slaves, this consideration must also be added, that God produces from sin, the foulest of all things, some good which man cannot. S. Augustine (*Ench.* 10. 11), admiring this work of the Supreme Artificer, exclaims,—"From all collectively arises the wondrous beauty of the whole, in which even that which is called evil, being well arranged and put in its proper place, commends things which are good in a more remarkable way, making them the more pleasing and more deserving of praise from being contrasted with what is evil."

9. But you may object in the first place,—"Granted that all things which God wills are good, or even the very best that could happen, yet certainly they are not so *to me.*" But what are you saying, rashest of mortals? "God hath equally care of all." (*Wisd.* vi. 8.) And so in the perfection of His Providence He cares for you, and me, and each individual, as He does for all; and He wills not merely that which is *good,* but ever that which is *best,* both for you, and for me, and for each, and for all; and that which He wills He performs most efficaciously. S. Gregory (*Moral.* xvi. 5) most beautifully says,—"God bestows His care on *all* in such a way as to be present with *each.* He is

present *with each* in such a way as not to be absent at the same time *from any*. He rules what is highest, so as not to desert what is lowest. He is present with what is lowest in such a way as not to withdraw Himself from what is highest." "God hath equally care of all." Respecting His children, or those who are best beloved by Him, the case is certain and clear; but not even in respect of those who will be damned is it otherwise. God is their Father, their Preserver, their Defender, even to the latest moment of their life; and He will at last be their Judge, their Punisher, and the Avenger of such wilful rebellion against Himself.

But you may object, secondly,—"And how can so many incongruities follow the Providence and Care of God, if they are so great? And, to use a gentle term, how comes it that the most absurd of all absurd things are done? While I should shrink from saying that God sleeps, can I safely venture to affirm that He is aware of every trifling matter?" I reply, that God has an eye for all things, yes, even the most minute; and this S. John Damascene most aptly shows, replying to your dulness,—"God occasionally allows something which is absurd and preposterous to be done, in order that by means of the action which has the appearance of absurdity something great and wonderful may be effected; just as by the Cross He procured the salvation of men." And will you deny the truth of this? Therefore God does not indeed *will* sin, but *permits* it efficaciously; or wills to permit it, and from thence produces the most beneficial results, and those

which most redound to His Own glory. S. Augustine
(*In Ps.* VII.) lays this down clearly when he says,—
"Wherefore this ordinance also is to be ascribed to
Divine Providence, not because it makes sinners, but
because it orders them when they have sinned."
Wherefore, although for a man, regarded by himself,
it would be better not to have sinned, yet, if the whole
order of nature and grace is regarded, it is much better that sin was permitted by God. The testimony of
the Church is well known,—Happy is the fault which
has merited to have such and so great a Redeemer!
This much then must be both known and believed
concerning the Divine Will. And would that the human race would cease to be blind, if only in this one
thing, and would be ready to embrace the Divine Will
with as great promptitude as they can easily recognize
it!

BOOK III

CONCERNING THE BENEFITS ARISING FROM THE CONFORMITY OF THE HUMAN WILL TO THE DIVINE

"I walked at large: because I have sought after Thy Commandments" *Psalm* CXVIII. 45.

THE HELIOTROPIUM

CHAPTER I

HOW GREAT TRANQUILLITY OF MIND CONFORMITY OF THE HUMAN WILL TO THE DIVINE PRODUCES

I HAVE pointed out how we may recognize the Divine Will, and in what way we can unite our own to it. And now I must proceed to show what advantage follows if the human will is ever most closely united to the Divine.

1. So bountiful is God in riches and gifts, that not only has He decreed to bless us with never-ending felicity, but as though anticipating the day of Eternity, and in order to make us more ready and eager, He sends from His Own table a cup of the Heavenly Feast, and bids us taste a drop, at least, of eternal happiness. And so not even in the foul hospital of this mortal flesh is there wanting a foretaste, as it were, of that great and eternal banquet. Even in this lower world there is a certain kind of rest: even here there are consolations sent from Heaven. Nor is there need of any great outlay to attain them: the only

thing required is a will conformed to the Divine.

S. Peter had scarcely tasted a drop of Heavenly happiness on Mount Tabor when straightway he exclaims,—"It is good for us to be here." He might have been thought already to be inebriated with this nectar, for "he knew not what he said." (*Mark* IX. 4, 5.) It is too soon, O Peter, to expect this Heavenly Food and Drink: in a better place they will be given to you, but not yet.

S. John, in the Apocalypse, says:—"There was silence in Heaven, as it were for half an hour." (*Apoc.* VIII. I.) And here that kind of repose is signified, according to the interpretation of S. Gregory, which they attain in this world who desire to fulfil the Divine Will as it is done in Heaven; and on this account live, as it were, in the very entrance-hall of Heaven. David, panting for this, says,—"Who will give me wings like a dove: and I will fly, and be at rest." (*Ps.* LIV. 7.) And whither will he fly? To the most sweet contemplation of the Divine Will, which, when any one has reached, he at last begins to breathe freely, and to rest calmly. For nothing does he seek with such ardent prayers as this one thing,—"Thy Will be done on Earth, as it is in Heaven." Among the things which procure the greatest peace and tranquillity of mind this certainly is reckoned first, viz. to strive and aspire in all our desires towards constant obedience to the Divine Will. And so that excellent writer, Thomas à Kempis (*Imit. Christ.* III. 23), gives this precept,—"Desire always and pray that the will of

God may be entirely fulfilled in thee. Behold, such an one entereth within the borders of peace and rest." Whosoever, therefore, desires with that holy King to fly away and be at rest, may at once be borne on high with these wings and achieve wonderful things.

2. A writer of undoubted credit makes mention of a certain Religious whose clothes, if they were merely touched, restored many to health, so that he began to be held in veneration by the sick, and in admiration by his brethren; but all the while no single virtue seemed to shine conspicuously in him, for he spent his life in a Monastery, like the rest, and did not afflict himself with any extraordinary austerities. About this one thing alone he was accustomed to show the utmost solicitude, never to will anything but that which God willed. And so when he very often cured people without the aid of drugs, and was asked by the Superior what was the reason of it, he used to reply that he himself was surprised, and was filled with shame, because he scarcely equalled others in fasting and prayer, much less surpassed them. "It is as you say," replied the Superior, "we know that you are a man of cheerful disposition, and that in other things you are not better than the rest of us." At the same time he began to make minute inquiries, and to ask many questions, and to try to unlock the secret chamber of his soul. And then the Religious said,—" I have good reason to think that this favour is shown to me by God, because I have so conformed myself to the Divine Will that I should never wish to make a single movement in opposition to

that Will. And not only do I not fear that things will
ever be in such perplexity as that I should willingly lose
my confidence or complain, but no amount of prosperity
will, as I think, so far beguile me as that I should on
that account allow myself to be filled with immoderate
joy. For I accept all things, without distinction, from
the Hand of God; nor do I desire that what happens
should be done according to my own will: but I desire
that all things should be done as they are done. And
so nothing affects me with pleasure or pain, nothing
disturbs me, nor does anything make me happy, except
this single thing—the one and only Will of God.
Therefore, in all my prayers, this one thing I ask, that
the Divine Will may always be most perfectly fulfilled
in me, and in all created things." The Superior was
exceedingly astonished at this reply, and said,—" Tell
me, I pray, what sort of feeling you lately experienced,
and whether you did not take it to heart as much as the
rest of us, when a miscreant set fire to our House, and
when the stalls, and the barn, and so much corn, and
so many cattle, were burnt—an almost irreparable
loss?" To which the Monk replied,—"I would wish
you to know, reverend Father, that I felt no grief on
that account: for it is my fixed habit to thank God
for such things; since I am perfectly certain that whatever happens is done through the Permission of Divine
Providence, and that it is entirely for our advantage.
Therefore I feel no anxiety as to whether we have little
or much for sustaining life. I trust in God, Who can
as well support any one of us on a crust of bread as

with a whole loaf. And so I live happily and cheerfully." Upon this the Superior tried to raise various objections, and to press the Monk with all kinds of questions, in order that he might thus disclose, in an agreeable way, the hidden feelings of his soul. After many such attempts the Monk replied:—"Through the daily oblation of myself to the Divine Will I have come to such a state of feeling, that if I knew beforehand that I was to be cast down to Hell by an immutable Decree of God, I would yet not so much as desire to resist it, if it were only permitted me at the same time to know that it thus seemed good to God, and that He so willed. Nay more, if it were in my power to rescind that Divine Decree by saying the Lord's Prayer once only, I would not dare to do it, but would rather offer up these two prayers to God—That He would continue to fulfil in me His most Just and Holy Will; and that He would grant me this one grace,—that for all Eternity I might be restrained from thinking anything contrary to the Divine Will." The Superior was horrified at these words, and almost turned to stone. A silence ensued on both sides. At length he said,— "Go, good Father, go, and remain as firm as you can in your purpose. You have found a Heaven this side of Heaven; and on this account you can exemplify to us a grace granted but to a very few. It is a marvellous state of freedom to be capable of being disturbed by no one, and of being injured by no one! He who absolutely conforms himself to the Divine Will dwells in a fortress of perfect repose."

3. And so the Superior dismissed the Monk, being buried all the while in profound astonishment, and thus began to reason with himself :—"Now I see clearly how it is that this man, whom people were wont to esteem an object of ridicule, has this gift of healing. This wonderful union with the Divine Will carries him up to such an amazing height. And how could God condemn a man like this to eternal flames? It is utterly repugnant to Infinite Goodness. And in truth I am constrained to acknowledge that it is neither a long nor a difficult journey to this height of most enduring tranquillity. For there is no need here of extraordinary austerity of life, nor is the struggle to be maintained with long fastings and watchings. That one noble determination TO WILL accomplishes all this." But this resolution TO WILL must be renewed every day, and there must be a firm resolve not to allow anything which is contrary to the Divine Will. "And so," says S. Chrysostom (*Serm. de Zach.*), "to will makes to be able, just as not to will makes not to be able. Great is the force of the will which makes us able to do that which we will, and not to be able to do that which we will not."

But if in the morning a man commends himself to God in this way,—"O my Lord, and my God, I offer myself to Thee to fulfil all Thy Good-pleasure; this day I will knowingly and purposely do nothing contrary to Thy Will,"—and yet this same man, on the very same day, either yields to forbidden acts of profligacy, or rashly puts himself in the way of other occasions to sin, then he must be thought to be making a mock of God, and to hold out in one hand bread, but in the other a scorpion: and so to promise that he will be perfectly obedient to the Divine Will, and yet all the while be meditating designs against the money, or reputation and good-name of others, willingly to admit envy into his soul, not to restrain himself from anger, but deliberately to court it—this is to trifle with God, and to spur on vices when they move too slowly, and to open the door to them when they have scarcely yet asked to be admitted. And what sort of mark of love is this? It is just like,—"I love you, but take this blow from me." Or,—"I cannot endure to be separated from you, and yet, when opportunity serves, on a narrow mountain path, I will hurl down with my hand into the abyss beneath the very same person whom just before I flattered with my words." But we are wont to excuse our conduct with words of such utter indolence as,—"I could not help it." But S. Chrysostom (*Serm. de Zach.*) says in reply:—"No one will be able to be excused, as if he willed, but was not able; since it is plain that he was not able, because he was not willing; so that the unwilling may be condemned by the example of the willing, and the willing be rewarded, because he performed what he willed."

4. That conversation, then, between the two Religious is not hard to be understood, and we are constrained to confess that the way to such a height of tranquillity is not barred against anyone, and that the

door to this paradise is not shut against anyone; he who is capable of this one thing,—*to will that which God wills,*—has entered it already. None are repelled, of whatever rank, or sex, or age. But there are two points specially in the conversation which has been related, full of such wonderful instruction, that to have fairly mastered them is already to have gained the palm of victory.

First, to be most thoroughly convinced that whatever happens is done by Divine Providence, which disposes all things to its own end and happiness, as it has from all eternity pleased the most secret Judgment of God.

Secondly, to do what is in one's power to ascribe all things to Divine Providence with the fullest confidence, to live contented with one's own condition, not to inquire about another person's state, and not to envy another his happier lot. These are the qualities which lead us into a fortress of invincible tranquillity; this is the panoply of all virtues. But they never put this armour on who love the fleeting things of this life, as if they were their own, and were perpetual; or who wish to be looked up to on their account, and who do not trust enough in Divine Providence. Such as these collapse at the touch of the lightest injuries; they lie and mourn when false and fleeting pleasures desert their minds, which are vain and childish, and ignorant of all solid pleasure. But the man who does not allow himself to be inflated by prosperity, nor depressed by adversity, but trusts most fully in Divine Providence, retains a soul of well-tried firmness, which is invincible against either condition, and is defended with the panoply of all virtues. In a single word—*he wills that which God wills.*

CHAPTER II

WHETHER OR NO IT CAN BE THAT ONE SHOULD NEVER
BE SAD, AND WHETHER THIS STATE IS TO BE
BROUGHT ABOUT IN THE SAME WAY IN WHICH WE
CONFORM OUR OWN WILL TO THE DIVINE

SOLOMON, a very ocean and prodigy of human
wisdom, fearlessly declared,—"Whatsoever shall
befall the just man, it shall not make him sad." (*Prov.*
XII. 21.) That wisest of kings is speaking of casual
things which befall a person of upright mind contrary
to his will, just as if he said,—"Voluntary evils, such as
sins and injuries, make a man anxious, however good
he may be, and afflict him with grief; but those freaks
of fortune, such as loss of wealth or honour, failure of
health, and death of those who are dear, do not so
much afflict and torment an upright man, as to prevent
him from very often reckoning such things to be benefits, and not consider them evils, but believe them to
be for the exercise of his patience, and give God
thanks for them, as is right. For to an upright mind
every calamity is an occasion of virtue."

And that a just man may receive external evils of
any kind with steadfast and cheerful mind S. Paul
gives the most abundant testimony :—"I am filled with

comfort, I exceedingly abound with joy in all our tribulation." (*2 Cor.* VII. 4.) Not merely in hunger or thirst, not only in bonds or stripes, but in all troubles and difficulties,—*"In* ALL *our tribulation."* Nor am I affected with merely a passing joy, he would say, but —"I am *filled* with comfort, I *exceedingly* abound with joy!" even when I am beaten with rods, when I am stoned, when I suffer shipwreck. S. Martin, Bishop of Tours, was never seen, during a period of many years, by Severus Sulpicius either to be angry or sorrowful, but always calm and self-possessed. And thus in truth "whatsoever shall befall the just man, it shall not make him sad." S. Chrysostom (*In 2 Cor. Hom.* I) entirely confirms this when he says,—"There is nothing miserable, save the offending against God; but this apart, neither afflictions, nor conspiracies, nor any other thing has power to grieve the right-minded soul; but like as a little spark, if you cast it into a mighty deep you presently put it out, so does even a total and excessive sorrow, if it light on a good conscience, easily die away and disappear." And the same Doctor of the Golden-mouth, in order to bring the matter more clearly before our eyes, compares the mind to the sky, and says,—"The sky is higher than showers and storms. It is obscured, indeed, with clouds, and is thought to suffer, but it suffers nothing at all. And in the same way we too, even though we are thought to suffer, suffer nothing; that is to say, we are thought to be obscured with sadness, as if with clouds, but we are not made sad." S. Ambrose (*De Off.* III.

5) also says,—"Granted, that in such things, that is to say, in labours, there is some degree of bitterness. Yet what grief does not virtue hide? For I should not deny that the sea is deep, because its shore is shallow; nor that the sky is bright, because it is sometimes covered with clouds; nor that the earth is fruitful, because in some places there is only barren gravel; nor that crops are abundant, because they occasionally have wild oats intermingled with them. And in the same way believe that the harvest of a good conscience is sometimes interrupted by a bitter grief; but yet if any adversity or sorrow befall the sheaves of a blessed life, it is hidden, like the wild oats; or like the bitterness of the darnel is overcome by the sweetness of the good corn." Therefore "whatsoever shall befall the just man, it shall not make him sad." He will *feel* sadness, but will not *yield* to it. The sky will be covered with clouds, but will not be disturbed in its serenity. Darnel will mingle with the wheat, but will not harm it. To be *insensible* to one's own evils is not the part of any man; to be *unable to bear them* is not the part of a good man.

1. But it is not only Christian wisdom that receives this, for even to the ancients such vigour of soul was not unknown. Truly enough did the Bard of Venusium sing (Hor. *Carm.* III. *Ode* 3):—"A man who is just and firm of purpose neither the frenzy of citizens inciting him to wrong, nor the look of a threatening tyrant, shakes from his steadfast resolution. If the crumbling world totters to its fall, the ruins will beat

against a fearless man." Yes, let all things be thrown
into utter confusion, let the sky itself fall, and beneath
this crumbling mass the heart which trusts in God will
not fear. And most abundant are the promises which
may fortify such a heart beforehand. "Touch ye not
My anointed" (*Ps.* civ. 15), exclaims God, those, that
is to say, whom I have anointed with the oil of My
Grace. And truly is it said,—"The souls of the just
are in the Hand of God, the torment of death shall not
touch them." (*Wisd.* iii. 1.) And again,—"He that
toucheth you toucheth the apple of My eye." (*Zach.*
ii. 8.) And S. John bears record (1 *Ep.* v. 18),—"We
know that whosoever is born of God sinneth not (that
is to say, not violating charity by deadly sin); but the
generation of God preserveth him, and the wicked one
toucheth him not," with such power, that is to say, as
to be able to overcome him.

Sennacherib, King of Assyria, besieged all the cities
of Juda, but he was not able to take Jerusalem; nay,
he did not even lay siege to it, or see it. Isaias distinctly declares:—"Thus saith the Lord concerning the
king of the Assyrians, He shall not come into this city,
nor shoot an arrow into it, nor come before it with
shield, nor cast a trench about it." (*Isaias* xxxvii. 33.)
And so the just man, whose law is the Will of
God, is perfectly impregnable:—"Whatsoever shall befall the just man, it shall not make him sad." Even
though pain racks all his limbs, although poverty
pinches him, although a thousand troubles press upon
him, yet with erect and lofty soul he binds himself

closely to God, and even then conforms himself entirely to the Divine Will. And why should he not be able to do this? He has the arms of love free—arms which can never be bound by any fetters, if he *wills* that they should not be bound, arms which will cleave to the Divine Will with an eternal embrace, if he only desires it.

It is related of a man of great learning and piety, that, when he was in the utmost difficulties, he was accustomed to say,—"Hail, thou most bitter sorrow! Hail, thou that art full of grace and blessing!" And what is this but with Socrates the philosopher to drink the hemlock even with a smile? Or let me rather say, what is it but with the Apostle Andrew to embrace the cross, saluting it even at a distance? In this way, in truth, we salute the hedge (as the saying is) on account of the garden; and for the sake of the fruit we love the tree also.

2. But you may object that this is the way we talk in the schools, but that we live differently at home. Hunger, you say, disgrace, loss of goods, and painful diseases please no one, since they assail him so fiercely; and the man must be made of iron whose cheerfulness such battering-rams as these do not break down.

But if you will allow me to say so, you seem to be akin to the friends of Job, to whose faces he said,— "You are all troublesome comforters; my eye poureth out tears to God." (*Job* XVI. 2. 21.) It pours out tears; I deny it not; and this is not pleasure: but it pours them out to God; and this is solid joy. "God will

not cast away the simple nor reach out His hand to
the evildoer: until thy mouth be filled with laugh-
ter, and thy lips with rejoicing." (*Job* VIII. 20, 21.)
"Have pity on me, have pity on me, at least you my
friends, because the Hand of the Lord hath touched
me." (*Job* XIX. 21.) To be smitten by this Hand is
more blessed than to be caressed by any other. This
Hand of the Lord works a thorough cure, even by the
touch alone. When it smites it brings not disease, but
health, not death, but life. This was Job's reply to his
friends, and this is what I say to you. Why do we not,
then, award to God at least the same amount of praise
which we bestow on a surgeon, when he has skilfully
opened a tumour with the knife, and we say,—"Well
done, my good sir, from this wound which you have
made I look for health." We praise a physician also
when, with most beneficial effect, he mixes a viper with
his antidote to snake's poison. And why do we find
fault with God if He mingles with His medicines human mischief and injuries? Let us be assured that He
has a reason for what He does; even though there is
no evidence of it to us. But meanwhile, we who are
so full of complaints, murmur secretly against God,—
"O Lord, how sharply does thy Hand strike me! Thy
Arms are too strong to beat me!" But do not charge
God, my Christian friend, that He is too strong to
chastise you. It is you who are too delicate to endure
punishment. Only if it pleases you, must the wind be
bitter; if any one approaches you to let out some putrid
matter, you immediately think that you are going to

be killed. "The just is as an everlasting foundation. The just shall never be moved." (*Prov.* x. 25, 30.) He stands at length in that place whence nothing can drive him away, and where nothing can alarm him:— "Whatsoever shall befall the just man, it shall not make him sad."

3. Let the soul, then, carry itself high over all difficulties to God; resting on the Divine Will in such a way as that things which casually happen neither elevate nor crush it, and so that its true pleasure may be the contempt of pleasure. And the soul which is thus unfettered, which is fearless and firm, which is independent of ignoble fear, blind lust, or foul desires, to which God and the Divine Will is its one good, and its one evil declension from God and the Divine Will, such a soul as this, I say, shall not be made sad. When it is thus firmly fixed there must of necessity follow, whether it wills or not, perpetual cheerfulness, and a joy which itself is deep, and which springs from the deep. Other kinds of joy are either base or insecure, and altogether independent of man. And those with which the multitude are beguiled have but a slight and superficial pleasure. Whatever joy is of foreign growth wants solid foundation. But far otherwise is it with the joy of a just man, for that springs from himself, and is trustworthy and sure, and is continually increasing, and remains even to the end, observe, —remains even to the end. And this is evident even to reason itself, for virtue alone bestows joy, which is PERPETUAL and unshaken; since even if any difficulty

arises it only comes in its way like clouds, which are borne rapidly along beneath, and never entirely hide the daylight. It may be said with truth that the soul which is firmly fixed on the Divine Will resembles the condition of the Universe beyond the moon—"Broken in its perpetual calm by no cloud" (LUCAN), since that higher and serener part of creation is neither swept by clouds, nor driven to tempest, nor lashed into whirlwinds, but is free from every disturbing element. And in the same way the soul which is constantly fixed on the Divine Will is tranquil, and from being placed in a calm retreat, is equable and composed; nothing that happens will sadden it. Not, however, that the just man will be perpetually in the excitement of Society, or the distractions of the world; his joy is calm and secret, and is joined with gravity, and even with severity: for it consists in nothing but internal repose, and peace, and concord of soul, and greatness of mind combined with meekness. But such qualities as these are wanting to the wicked and to fools; for with them their very lusts rage and fight together; and in their souls there always are whole legions and encampments, as it were, of foul and bitter thoughts.

4. Thus, then, although the just man *feels* afflictions (for no amount of virtue deprives a man of the sense of feeling), yet he does not *dread* them, but looks down from a lofty height upon his sorrows, being altogether unconquered by them. The Roman philosopher (SENECA, *de Prov.* 2) says most truthfully,—"No evil can happen to a good man;"—just as if he were an-

swering an objector;—*adversity,* I grant you, may befall him, but *evil* never. Here, therefore, you are mistaken. For just as so many rivers which flow into the sea do not alter the taste of its water, nor indeed make any sensible change in it, so the violent assault of adversity does not affect the mind of a brave man. He remains firmly fixed in his position, and, happen what will, he colours it according to his taste; for he is beyond the control of all external things: nay, more than this, he is not even conscious of their power, but masters them, and raises himself up so as quietly and calmly to meet the difficulties which advance in his path. All adverse things he regards as discipline. And such a man in truth was Job; such was King David. "For though I should walk in the midst of the shadow of death," he says, "I will fear no evil, for Thou art with me." (*Ps.* XXII. 4.) "If God be for us, who is against us?" (*Rom.* VIII. 31.) "If God is for me," Paulinus used to say, "then even a spider's web will be to me like a triple wall; but if He is against me, then this same web, so slender as it is, will be able to restrain me better than any wall." Of a truth,—"The just cried, and the Lord heard them, and delivered them out of all their troubles." (*Ps.* XXXIII. 18.) David proclaimed to the world:—"I sought the Lord, and He heard me: and He delivered me from all my troubles." (*Ps.* XXXIII. 5.) Therefore,—"Blessed be God, Who comforteth us in all our tribulation, that we also may be able to comfort them who are in all distress, by the exhortation wherewith we also are exhorted by God."

(2 *Cor.* I. 3, 4.) Whatever, in fine, happens, it will not make the just sad. For as no one could touch the apple of Christ's eye, but he by whom Christ willed that it should be touched, so it is a most certain truth, that not so much as a hair can be taken away from the just man unless God so wills it. But if he knows what is pleasing to God, he immediately exclaims,—" 'Thy will be done on Earth, as it is in Heaven!' Whatever befalls me according to the Divine Will will not make me sad." And therefore Isaias the prophet sends out messengers, as it were, to all men of upright mind, and bids them say to them,—"Say to the just man that it is well." (*Isaias* III. 10.) But tell me, I pray you, O prophet, suppose that this man's beloved wife has died; nevertheless, he replies, say to him, *"it is well."* But suppose his house is burnt down; still say, *"it is well."* But he has lost his office and all his interest: *"it is well."* Or he has experienced a great falling away of honour: *"it is well."* He has already witnessed the death of all his children: still say to him, *"it is well."* Or he has lost an immense sum of money: *"it is well,"* —for he himself would have been lost if his money had not been lost before him.

Jacob slept in the open air; the earth was his couch, and a stone his pillow. It was a rugged sleep, I ween. But he saw angels ascending and descending, and the Lord Himself standing above the ladder. (*Gen.* XXVIII. 10-13.) And so to many people all things seem stony enough; but they know that angels, who never slumber, are watching around them, and they behold

God the constant spectator of their afflictions, so that nothing which happens to them makes them sad:—"The just are bold as a lion." (*Prov.* XXVIII. 1.)

Alphonsus, the celebrated King of Naples and Aragon, when he was quite an old man, used to read Livy and Cæsar every day, and translated the Epistles of Seneca into the Spanish tongue, and (lest you should think, good reader, that he was versed in profane writers alone) also read the whole Bible, Old and New Testament, together with commentaries on it, fourteen times, and this not in a hurried way either, but line by line. This king, I say, so justly famed for his piety and learning, has left the following Divine memorial to posterity, among many other sayings. Once upon a time he was asked whom he should call happy in this world, and he replied,—"I judge that man to be perfectly happy in this life who commits himself with entire devotion and affection to the Lord his God, and approves and receives whatever befalls him in no other way than as what is done by God." And may we not say that this is an oracle, and that it is a voice which comes to us from Heaven? An angel could not have spoken more truly or devoutly.

5. Heraclides of Alexandria (*Paradisus,* 1.) relates that he went to see S. Dorotheus, who, for sixty years, had lived a life of the greatest sanctity in a cave. Having been sent by him to a fountain to draw some water, he saw an aspic swimming in the pool, and instantly returned with the pitcher empty. Dorotheus smiled, and after looking at him for some time, said, as he

gently shook his head,—"If God were to allow the devil to throw aspics into every well, would you, then, abstain altogether from drink?" Presently he came out of his cave and went to the fountain, where he drew some water, and having made the sign of the Cross over it, he said, while drinking the health of Heraclides,—"Where the Cross is, there the devices of Satan are powerless." The just is bold as a lion, and will be free from terror. "Whatsoever shall befall the just man, it shall not make him sad."

But in order that what is here related in words may be exemplified in act, S. Chrysostom (*Hom.* v. *ad. Pop.*) furnishes us with two pieces of advice. First of all,—"When pains of different kinds are experienced in the body, it generally happens that one is less acutely felt than the other. For example, if a person has a finger which has been injured and is festering, and at the same time is suffering violent pain in his stomach or head, he says nothing about his finger, but complains of the pain he feels in his stomach or head. And in the same way," says S. Chrysostom, "if loss of money or of honour and reputation, or any other calamity, encourages you to grieve, then excite in yourself contrition for your sins, and begin to mourn over them. Meditate upon the unspeakable insults and pains undergone by Christ when scourged at the pillar, dragged along through the streets, and fastened on the Cross, and then recognize the punishment due to your sins. This sorrow will prevent the other from being felt, or will certainly mitigate it if it is felt." And so Christ says,—"Fear ye not them that kill the body, but are not able to kill the soul: but rather fear Him That can destroy both body and soul into hell." (*Matt.* x. 28.) Our Lord desires that fear should be vanquished by fear, and that the one should be consumed by the other, so that "whatsoever shall befall the just man, it shall not make him sad."

Secondly, a plaster must be applied to a part which is injured and not to a sound limb, nor to a part for which it is not adapted. Eye-salve is good for the eyes, but not for the arms. A pill is meant to be swallowed, and not to be used as a bandage for the foot. A cataplasm is to be applied to a sore, and not to the sound flesh near it. And precisely in the same way sorrow does not cure loss of money, or honour, or disease, or any ill of this kind. Wear yourself out, if you choose, with grief, do nothing but weep, and you will not be one whit the better; you will not bring back your money, or honour, or health by weeping, but you will increase your loss and pain. And the reason is this. Sorrow is the proper remedy for sin. By this antidote is that plague to be cured. Apply this cataplasm to that sore. Grieve that you have sinned, not that you have lost your money. And with great wisdom does S. Chrysostom (*Hom.* v. *ad. Pop.*) admonish us of this when he says,—"Has any one lost his money? He is overpowered with grief, but has not thereby repaired his loss. Has another lost his child? He has mourned, but has not brought the dead to life again. Has another been scourged? He has grieved, but has not

done away with the disgrace. Has another been attacked with a most painful disease? He has lamented,
and yet has not removed the disease, but has only made
it the harder to cure. Do you perceive that sorrow
profits none of these? But has any one sinned? He
has grieved, and has blotted out his sin, and has dis-
charged his debt." Most plainly does S. Paul say,—
"You were made sorrowful according to God, that you
might suffer damage by us in nothing. For the sorrow that is according to God worketh penance steadfast
unto salvation; but the sorrow of the world worketh
death." (2 *Cor.* VII. 9, 10.) Sorrow, therefore, is
both a medicine and a poison, according to the way in
which you use it. Ten thousand times, then, do I repeat,—"Whatsoever shall befall the just man, it shall
not make him sad."

CHAPTER III

I AFFIRM that next after the Heavenly Lamb, Which is wont to be daily offered, the offering of one's own will is the sacrifice most acceptable to God. S. Jerome, writing to Lucinius (*Ep.* 28 *ad. Lucin.* and *Ep.* 103 *ad Paulin.*), draws the following admirable distinction:—"To offer gold," he says, "is the act of beginners, not of the perfect. Crates, the Theban, did this, and so did Antisthenes. To offer oneself to God is peculiarly the act of Christians." He has given *all* to God who has offered *himself*. And God, desiring this one thing, says:—"My son, give Me thy heart." (*Prov.* XXIII. 26.) When you have given this you will be accounted to have given everything.

1. But in order that this offering of one's heart or will may be acceptable to God, it is necessary that he who makes the offering should be in a state of grace. S. Basil remarks upon that verse of the Psalms,— "Bring to the Lord, O ye children of God, bring to the Lord the offspring of rams" (*Ps.* XXVIII. 1.)—"Be a child of God before you offer those things which are pleasing to God."

You ought at least to mourn that you have fallen from grace, and endeavour to return. A contrite and a humble heart God will not despise. S. Augustine (*De Quantit. Animae,* 20) says most strikingly:—"I could wish that I might do nothing else than restore myself to Him to Whom I chiefly owe myself, and that I should thus become to God that which the poet (HORACE, *Sat.* II. 7) speaks of, a friend and servant of my Lord." And exhorting all others to the same, he says,—"Believe in God firmly, and trust your entire self to Him as much as you can. Refrain from wishing to be, as it were, your own, and under your own power; but profess yourself to be the servant of that most merciful and beneficent Lord. For so He will not fail to raise you up to Himself, and will permit nothing to befall you but for your profit, even though you know it not." And again, further confirming this, he says,— "We can offer nothing more acceptable to Him than that we should say with Isaias, 'Lord, possess us.'" (*Isaias* XXVI. 13. Septuagint.) Some there are who offer wax or oil for trimming lamps in churches. These votive offerings cost much money; but they are not on that account the best, or perfect. Another vows abstinence from wine, or determines to give larger alms; it is a costly vow, but yet not the best of all. In this case what could poor men do? God does not ask your oil or wax; but that which He redeemed—your soul; offer this to Him. And if you ask me how I am to offer to Him my soul which He already has in His Own power, I reply, by holy manners, by pure thoughts,

by fruitful works. In this way Anna offered her Samuel; thus the most blessed Virgin offered JESUS; thus
John the Baptist was offered while yet an infant: and
in the same way S. Gregory Nazianzen, S. Dominic, S.
Bonaventure, S. Bernardine, and S. Bernard, having
been offered to God by their parents, grew up to be
men of most saintly lives. But if it profits so much to
be offered by *others,* how greatly will it profit to be
offered by *oneself?* And this King David most fully
carried out when he said:—"I will freely sacrifice to
Thee." (*Ps.* LIII. 6.)

It is wonderfully gratifying to each one of us when
any one unreservedly devotes himself to us. Once
upon a time, when many people were making offerings
of various kinds to Socrates, according to their means,
Æschines, who was a listener, but a poor man, said,—
"I can find nothing worthy of you which I can give,
and it is only in this way that I am conscious of my
poverty; and so I give you the only thing which I have
—*myself.* And this gift, such as it is, I pray you to
take in good part, and remember that when others gave
much to you, they kept back more for themselves." And
by this gift of his Æschines outdid the spirited gener-
osity of Alcibiades, which was equal to his wealth, as
also the munificence of all the rich young men. Do
you perceive, then, how his soul found means to be
liberal, even in the midst of poverty itself? We must
not inquire of *what value* things may be, but with what
sort of *intention* they are given, and with what readiness of will. That man gives much to God, yea, he

gives everything, who daily transfuses himself and his will into the Divine Will. And this must be done not merely once or twice every day, but very often; yea, a hundred or a thousand times, and specially so when any one feels that he is wavering, or is being assaulted by temptation, or perceives that he fails of success in any-thing, or that things turn out according to his wishes, then he must cry out,—"O my Lord, and my God, I offer myself to Thee to fulfil all Thy Good-pleasure. Thy Will be done!" And this produces patience in ad-versity, and sobriety and moderation in prosperity. This restrains the afflicted, even when all things turn out most gloomily, from giving way to impious speeches and impatience. This increases merit; this in a wonderful way makes God favourable to man; this is a shield against every calamity.

2. S. Bernard (*Serm. de Quadrupl. Deb.*), wishing to persuade all people to this, says,—"I have but two small things, or, rather, two very small things, body and soul. Or I might more truly say, I have but one small thing, my will; and shall I not surrender it to the Will of Him Who, though He is so great, presents me, insignificant as I am, with such great blessings, and Who purchased me wholly with His whole Self? Otherwise, if I retain it, with what sort of face, with what eyes, with what mind, with what conscience, can I appeal to the bowels of the mercy of our God?" S. Chrysostom, speaking of the blessed Paul daily offering himself to God, says,—"Abel offered a sacrifice, and on that account is praised; but if we examine Paul's

victim it will be found to be as superior to Abel's as heaven is higher than the earth. For he did not offer sheep or oxen, but day by day he sacrificed *himself*. Nor, indeed, was he satisfied with such sacrifices as this, but because he had already devoted himself to God, he studied to offer the whole world also." And so that man of fire, being inflamed with such zeal through the oblation of himself, avoided no labour, and shrank from no danger, being perfectly ready to endure all things for God.

In the reign of Diocletian, a priest named Epictetus, and Astion, who lived a most religious life in the East, were seized by Latronianus and thrown into prison. Whereupon Epictetus said,—"If the judge shall examine us to-morrow, my excellent Astion, and inquire about our name, our parents, and country, let us make this single reply, 'We are Christians; and this is our name, our kindred, and our country.' But if God wills that we should be torn to pieces by tortures, let us say nothing in the midst of them but this, 'Lord JESUS, Thy Will ever be done in us!'" The next day they were summoned from the prison to a judgment-seat which had been prepared in the middle of the market-place; and Latronianus sitting on the tribunal, while all the people were standing round, began to inquire of what family, tribe, and country they were. To which Epictetus replied,—"We are Christians; and the children of Christian parents." "That is not my question," said Latronianus; "tell me your names; this is not the first time I have known of the perfidy of your sect."

To which again the holy martyrs replied,—"We are Christians; we worship Christ JESUS, and detest idols." When he heard this the judge was furious, and ordered them to be stripped of their clothes and to be cruelly beaten; but with eyes raised towards heaven, they still exclaimed amidst the bloody stripes,—"Lord JESUS, Thy Will be done in us." Whereupon Latronianus bitterly mocked them, and inquired,—"Where is that Defender of yours, Whose aid you are imploring? Let Him come and deliver you from my hands." And then the holy martyrs cried out afresh,—"We are Christians; may the Will of our God be done in us!" The judge was excited almost to madness at these words, and ordered the martyrs to be carried to the "Horse,"* and to be savagely torn with its iron hoofs. But not even thus could any other words be wrung from them than,—"We are Christians, thou tyrant Latronianus; may the Will of our God be done in us!" The judge, thinking it derogatory to his dignity that he should be outdone in this way, ordered lighted faggots to be applied as they hung above them. And still nothing else was heard than before,—"We are Christians; may the Will of God be done in us!" When they had been released from all these tortures they were led back to prison. After being a spectator of this tragic sight, Vigilantius, who was an assessor of the judge, from having heard the expression so often repeated,—"We are Christians; may the will of God be done in us,"— felt persuaded that it was an incantation of wonderful

* An instrument of torture.

power, which could entirely take away the pain of grief, and even in the midst of tortures themselves prevent their being felt. He commenced, therefore, repeating these same words, as a most potent charm against every kind of injury, and he said nothing when standing, sitting, walking, at home, abroad, retiring to rest, or rising from his bed, but these same words,—"We are Christians; may the Will of God be done in us!" And in this way he spent three days, while God showed mercy upon him as on a child of good disposition. At length, on the fourth day, impelled by some secret power, he rushed out into the street, and began to cry out before all the people,—"I am a Christian, thou tyrant Latronianus; may the Will of my God be done in me!" Being admitted into the prison of the martyrs, he was baptized with all his family; and, in order to show his gratitude to his teachers, he buried them after they were beheaded. The next day Latronianus ordered the priest Epictetus and Astion to be brought before him; and determining now to act with craft, he inquired,—"Are you ready to sacrifice to the gods? or do you still persist in your madness?" To whom Epictetus replied,—"You are wasting your labour, Latronianus, for we do not worship these monsters of hell; you will wrest our lives from us more easily than this determination. We have already said, and for thousands and thousands of times will continue to say,— 'We are Christians; may the Will of God be done in us!'" Upon this Latronianus began to roar like a lion, and cried out to the ministers of death around him,—

"Bring quickly vinegar and salt; let these wretches feel that they have wounds; and be not sparing over them, but rub their lacerated limbs with vinegar and salt." But the martyrs altered not a single word of what they had said before. The confession of each was alike unflinching in its steadfastness,—"We are Christians; may the Will of God be done in us!" But as they still survived these tortures, they were thrown into prison again, and were brought out afresh after thirty days, and were wounded in the face with large stones, and most cruelly beaten with ashen sticks. But even then they both broke forth with the same exclamation,—"O Lord our God, Thy Will be done in us!" At length sentence was passed upon them that they should be put to death outside the city. As they were being led along they encouraged one another with these words,—"Praise the Name of the Lord, because in all things the Will of our God is done in us!" When they had reached the place of execution they cried out, with a loud voice,—"Blessed art Thou, O Lord, Thou God of our fathers, and worthy art Thou to be praised and highly exalted, because not the will of man, but Thy Will, is in all things done in us!"

The time had now come when their heads were to be struck off with an axe, and then a noble rivalry arose between these most glorious athletes as to which should first receive the stroke; one deferring to the other for honour's sake. Whereupon Epictetus, who was sixty years old and grey-headed, using the authority which belonged to his age, said that he desired that Astion should be despatched first. Nor did Astion long resist, for he said,—"O my father and venerable priest of God, the Will of God and thy will be done!" Having said this, and commended his soul to his Maker, he offered his head to be struck off. And then Epictetus throwing himself forward on the body of Astion, and embracing it tightly, presented his own head also to be cut off; and thus both of them finished their life by a most holy end.

3. Behold, then, two mirrors of brightest polish, in which perfect devotion of human will to the Divine is reflected in a wonderful way. And so let every one prepare himself, that, whatever hardships he may experience, he may still repeat without ceasing these self-same words,—"I am a Christian; may the Will of God be done in me! These things seem to me of a truth to be exceedingly hard, and most grievous to bear, but the Will of God be done! I was not, I confess, expecting an event so sad, but the Will of God be done! This man has behaved most unjustly towards me, but may the Will of God be done in me!"

Jehu, who was a most valiant general, wrote a letter and sent it to Samaria to the rulers of the city; but they delayed not to choose ambassadors and send them to Jehu, to say on their behalf,—"We are thy servants, whatsoever thou shalt command us we will do." (4 *Kings* x. 5.) And how often does Almighty God send a letter to us, and admonish us in various ways, and set before us His Own Will to be followed? And what message should each one of us deliver to be carried back but this,—"We are Thy servants, whatsoever thou shalt command us we will do."

Elias, the Thesbite, contended with the priests of Baal as to which were the worshippers of the True God; at length they came to an agreement that the side should prevail whose sacrifice was consumed by fire from heaven. And when these pretended priests had cried aloud for a long time, and yet not the smallest indication of any spark of fire from Baal appeared, Elias ordered every part of his sacrifice to be thoroughly steeped in water, and immediately fire fell from heaven and burnt up the whole of it. And how much labour and weariness, I pray you, is there on all sides among so many Christians! how much clamour and excitement! They are hot and cold by turns; they run and struggle; they spare no pains, and yet, for the most part, *the fire is wanting,* that is to say, *true devotion to the Divine Will!* Rarely and coldly do we pray,—"Thy Will be done, O Lord!" And so it happens that we very often both cry aloud and sacrifice, but to no purpose, since we have no care for that most noble of all sacrifices,—*the oblation of our own will.*

Once upon a time two persons asked S. Macarius to teach them how to pray. He replied,—"There is no need here of a great flow of words. The hands must very often be spread out towards God, and you must cry,—'O Lord my God, as Thou willest, and as it seems good to Thee, so be it done,' since He knows what is for our good." An excellent way of praying!

Pachomius also used constantly to pray that the Will of God might be fulfilled in all things.

Alphonsus Salmeron relates that there was once a man who, instead of a prayer, repeated the whole alphabet letter by letter, especially when harassed by some perplexing difficulty; and added to it this clause:—"Do Thou, O Lord, join the letters together, and bestow that which is most pleasing to Thee and best for me!"

This agreement, then, of the human will with the Divine is, of all things which anyone can offer to God, the greatest and most acceptable sacrifice and holocaust. For in all other cases a man offers *his goods* merely, but in this, *himself*. In other cases he offers himself only in part; but in this case he gives his entire self in such a manner as that the Divine Will should dispose of him and his in any way, and at any time, that it sees fit, no reservation or exception being made for himself even in the smallest particular. And, therefore, as much as the part differs from the whole, so does this sacrifice differ from all others.

CHAPTER IV

THAT ALL HUMAN PERFECTION CONSISTS IN THE CONFORMITY OF MAN'S WILL TO THE DIVINE

ALL human actions derive their value from *the end* for which they are done; hence they are either good or bad according to their end. But, as an end and aim of our actions, we shall find nothing better or more sublime than the Divine Will, that is to say, than God himself; and, therefore, there are no actions better or more sublime than those which are nearest to this end. And hence that saying of S. Basil the Great, that the whole sum of sanctity in a Christian man consists in his referring the causes of all things, great and small alike, to God alone, and most readily submitting himself in everything to the Divine Will. This is that virtue of *resignation,* so often and so greatly commended by the Holy Fathers and masters of the saintly life; it is the commencement of all tranquillity, as being that which places a man in the Hand of God, by far the safest of all resting-places, in such a way that he no longer desires to be his own, but God's, and not to live to himself, but to God, and to do everything for God's sake, being contented alike with adversity and prosperity. And this virtue God so greatly loves and delights in, that, when rewarding King David with a title of the highest honour, He called him—"A man according to My Own Heart, who shall do all My Wills." (*Acts* XIII. 22.) For that King kept his own heart so entirely fixed on the Divine Heart, that he stood ready and prepared to perform every indication of God's Will. And in this same way one may daily merit much if he refers to the Divine Will all those actions which in themselves are neither matter of blame or praise, such as eating, drinking, walking, and sleeping; and does not eat or drink merely because he is hungry or thirsty, but because it pleases God that it should be so. An ox or a cow would say,—"I eat because I am hungry; I drink because I am thirsty; I lie down because I wish to go to sleep." But far otherwise should a Christian man speak, who is able to desire, eat, drink, stand, sit, and sleep, not because it is pleasant to him, but because it is approved by God.

1. The Heliotrope, as I have said (Book II. chap. ii. 3), a flower most devoted to the sun, is accustomed ever to look towards it when it sets, and at all hours to turn round with it, even on a cloudy day. And let the will of man emulate the natural inclination of this flower, and constantly regard the Divine Will as its Sun, even on cloudy days, and in troublous times. And in this in good truth all sanctity of life consists, as a Theologian most admirably says,—"The sum of a Christian life, and the compendium of all virtues is, to conform oneself in all things to the Will of God, so

as to will the same, and not to will the same. As
often, then, as God commands anything, let each say
readily for himself, 'Yea, Lord, this will I do.' And
as often as He forbids anything, 'Yea, Lord, this will
I not do.'" The sum of humility, according to S.
Bernard, appears to consist in our will being brought
into subjection to the Divine Will, as it is right it
should be. All things, indeed, are subject to God as
their Creator, for all things serve Him; but from man,
who is endowed with reason, He exacts a subjection
which is voluntary.

2. The Acts of the Saints abound with stories showing the marvellous power of the human will when
joined to the Divine.

Those miracles of old time are well known—the rod
of Moses, the mantle of Elias, the staff of Eliseus, the
apron of Paul,* the shadow of Peter. Of a truth such
men as these obtain from God the power of ruling
over created things, in return for which they give to
Him the best thing which they have—their will. By
this law of transfer man deals with God as if he were
to say,—"My whole will I deliver to Thee, O Lord;"
while God says,—"And I deliver to thee my sovereignty, that thou shouldest be lord over beasts, that
thou shouldest rule over the sea; in a word, that thou
shouldest be a kind of God in the earth." For the
most benign Creator wills not to be outdone in liberality. When anyone gives to Him that which he
holds dearest, He does not deny him the most excel-

* Acts xix. 12.

lent gift which He has, that is, to rule over all things. And as, in the olden time, King Alexander said of His beloved Hephæstion,*—"You are not mistaken, for he, too, is Alexander," in like manner it may be said of the man who is entirely devoted to the Divine Will,—"He, too, is God," through a most intimate union of his own will with the Divine.

It is related that there was once upon a time a husbandman whose land usually produced more abundant crops than that of his neighbours. On being asked how this was, he replied that there was nothing wonderful about it, for that he had a most perfect agreement with the sky, and there was never any kind of weather but just what he wished. His neighbours laughed at him, and said that this was impossible. "Not so," he said, "for the favour of heaven always answers to my wishes; since I never wish for any other changes of weather than those which God wills. Inasmuch, then, as the Divine Will is my will also, God wills that more abundant crops should spring up for me than for you, who very often are at variance with Heaven, and the Divine Will." Truly,—"The creature serving Thee the Creator abateth its strength for the benefit of them that trust in Thee." (*Wisdom* XVI. 24.)

3. The children of Israel presented a petition to Pharao, by the hand of Moses, in these words:— "The God of the Hebrews hath called us, to go three days' journey into the wilderness and to sacrifice to

* Because of his close resemblance to the King.

the Lord our God." (*Exod.* v. 3.) And many say that the path to heaven is a "three days' journey." On the first day's journey the road is called *Purgative,* on the second *Illuminative,* on the third *Unitive.* And by this road, indeed, we approach closest to God, when the human will is most firmly bound to the Divine. Our Lord proclaims (*Luke* xviii. 19):—"None is good but God alone." And hence arises that saying of the holy Fathers and Theologians:—"As the Divine Intelligence is the rule of entire TRUTH, and cannot be deceived, so the Divine Will is the rule of entire GOOD, nor can it be distorted. And as it cannot be that anything should be conformed to the Divine Intelligence and not be TRUE, so nothing can be conformed to the Divine Will which is not GOOD." S. Chrysostom admirably says,—"That which is in accordance with the Divine Will, *although it seems to be wrong,* is nevertheless pleasing and acceptable to God. And, on the other hand, that which is contrary to the Divine Will, and other than what He wills to be done, although it is thought to be acceptable to God, is nevertheless the worst and most pernicious of all things."

The Book of Kings furnishes an example of this. A prophet, who had been sent by Divine command to rebuke Achab, because, contrary to the Will of God, he had spared the King of Syria, whom he had taken prisoner in battle, in order that he might not be recognized by his face when delivering the message, went to a neighbour "in the word of the Lord," and said,—

"Strike me." (3 *Kings* xx. 35.) But he refused to do so, for he was afraid to smite a prophet. But quickly he heard the fearful sentence,—"Behold, thou shalt depart from me, and a lion shall slay thee." (Verse 36.) And it happened as he said. "Then he found another man, and said to him: Strike me. And he struck him, and wounded him." (Verse 37.) And this he not only did without punishment; but also earned commendation for what he had done. "And what could happen more contrary to all expectation?" asks S. Chrysostom. "He who smote the prophet escaped without harm, while he who spared him suffered punishment. Of such moment is it to follow the rule of the Divine Will, or to despise it." When the Divine Will points out anything to anyone it is impiety even so much as to ask,—"Why is this?" It must stand us in place of all reasons that *God so wills.* Therefore it is the safest height of Christian perfection to yield oneself as entirely as possible to the Divine Will, and to cease to be one's own that we may become God's.

CHAPTER V

THAT CONFORMITY OF THE HUMAN WILL TO THE
DIVINE IS THE SUPREME GOOD IN LIFE

THE brother of the Prodigal was indignant that
he who had squandered his patrimony should be
welcomed home with so sumptuous a feast; and so,
looking upon this as an act of injustice to himself, he
refused to enter his father's house. But the father,
who was very full of pity, in order to appease his son,
went out, and began to entreat him not to spoil the joy
of the day by dissension.   "And he answering said to
his father, Behold, for so many years do I serve thee,
and I have never transgressed thy commandments; and
yet thou hast never given me a kid to make merry with
my friends: but as soon as this thy son is come, who
hath devoured his substance with harlots, thou hast
killed for him the fatted calf." (*Luke* xv. 29, 30.)
But that excellent father, in order to quiet his rage,
"said to him, Son, thou art always with me, and all
I have is thine." (Verse 31.) Do you not know that
you are as much master in the house as myself, that
we have but one purse, and that all my goods are
yours? And being soothed at last by these words he
was content to go in.

And in the same way God, Who is most benignant, preserves a man devoted to His Will, and inflames him thus:—"Thou art ever with Me; thou art in My Intelligence, in my Memory, and in My Will. I ever regard thee; I embrace thee with singular favour; all I have is thine; My Heaven, My Angels; yea, My Only-Begotten Son is thine; and more than this, I Myself am thine, and will remain thine; I will be thy Reward exceeding great through all eternity." (*Gen.* xv. 1.)

Nor is this enough for that most loving Father, but in order that the man who is devoted to the Divine Will may know how much he prevails with God, He further bestows upon many the power of doing such things as can be done by Divine Strength alone. "The works that I do," says Christ, "he also shall do, and *greater* than these shall he do." (*John* xiv. 12.) This is the Sovereignty of God, of which I have already spoken (see preceding Chap.); this is His most loving promise; this is to be regarded by Him with perpetual favour. God holds a divided empire, as it were, with man, since all things which are God's are also man's, yea, even God Himself. S. Paul affirms most confidently,—"All things are yours; whether it be Paul, or Apollo, or Cephas, or the world, or life, or death, or things present, or things to come: for all are yours; and you are Christ's; and Christ is God's." (1 *Cor.* iii. 22, 23.) Yours they are, not as yet indeed in possession, but for your use, and for this end, since all things were made that they might

[178]

minister to your salvation. The world and all created things are yours, for they all serve the body and soul. Life is yours, so that you may devote it to the sole Will of God. Death is yours, that by it, as through a door, you may pass into Paradise. Present things are yours, prosperous and adverse alike, for you use them to advance in virtue. Future things, too, are yours, since you will enjoy them at your pleasure. All things work together for your good. (*Rom.* VIII. 28.) The Lord has granted you your heart's desire. (*Ps.* xx. 3.)

I. The son of Themistocles used to boast that the entire Athenian republic was governed by him, since all the citizens willed what he willed. And while people were wondering at this vaunting speech of the young man, he added,—"That which I will my mother wills also (for she loved her son most tenderly), and that which my mother wills my father, Themistocles, also wills; and it is well known that whatever pleases my father at once pleases all Athens. And in this way," he said, "the Athenian republic is quietly brought under my government." And in the same way, but with a better right, a man whose will is perfect may say,—"That which I will the whole host of heaven wills also; for that which I will God wills (since I never will anything but that which He wills), and that which God wills, all the orders of the blessed and all the degrees of the angels will also." To such a man as this the Father repeats these most soothing words, —"*All I have is thine.*" But the wicked are rebels still; and yet the time will come when they also will be made subject to the just:—"The just shall have dominion over them in the morning." (*Ps.* XLVIII. 15.) As long as the night of this life lasts monstrous acts of wickedness are perpetrated, and are not discovered; the Divine Will is resisted, and God keeps silence; but "in the morning," in the last day when all shall rise again, then "the just shall have dominion over them." All the power of the wicked shall consume away like a worn-out garment; and then will it be said afresh,—"*All I have is thine.*" Most truly does S. Paul say,—"He that is joined to the Lord is one spirit" (1 *Cor.* VI. 17), through this consent of the will, from which man derives tranquillity of conscience, and sanctity of life, so as ever to flourish and bloom.

Brocardus relates a wonderful story about certain places in the Holy Land, solemnly asserting that nothing is told by him but what he saw with his own eyes:—"Before one of the gates of Jerusalem," he says, "there is the spot, distant about a spear-cast from the city, where our Lord addressed the multitude, and at this same place is pointed out a stone on which that woman stood who cried out, in the midst of our Lord's address, 'Blessed is the womb that bore Thee, and the paps that gave Thee suck.' (*Luke* XI. 27.) The hill is never covered with sand, although in the neigh-bourhood it flies about like snow driven with the wind, and settles on everything else. And besides this, both in summer and winter, this grassy spot, by some won-

derful property, preserves its verdure perfect." Now
there is great resemblance between this ever-verdant
hill, as I may so say, and the man who receives the
Divine Will into his inmost heart, so as to exclaim,—
"I desire that Thou, O my Lord, shouldest address
me here; to Thee will I listen." So perfect a mind as
this is never buried beneath the sandy waves of troubles, nor can anything ever come so much amiss to
a man of a disposition like this, as to prevent his
saying,—"Thou dealest gently with me, O Lord, and
sparest me too much; I have merited severer treatment; I feel these afflictions indeed, however light they
may be: but not *what I feel,* but *what Thou willest,* I
regard; and because Thou permittest these things, I
have no desire so much as to open my mouth against
them. Whatever I see pleases Thee pleases me. I
am perfectly satisfied with all Thy Decrees. I am
fully prepared to obey every indication of Thy Will.
Bid, command, ordain, change, as Thou willest. Too
foolish should I be, and wicked, if I were to require to
restrain Thee, or place a limit to Thine Ordinances!"
Such a man as this a perfect army of misfortunes will
never be able to vanquish; nor will the loss of anything tear him away from God. Here at least he is
invincible; he flourishes both in summer and winter,
in adversity as well as in prosperity.

2. When Jehu the general met Jonadab, he addressed him kindly and said,—"Is thy heart right as
my heart is with thy heart? And Jonadab said: It
is. If it be, said he, give me thy hand. He gave him

his hand. And he lifted him up to him into the chariot." (4 *Kings* x. 15.) And that which Jehu did,
Christ the King of all the world did also. He came
to Samaria, which, by its very name, signifies this
world bristling with thorns; and for this purpose He
came, that He might destroy all the family of wicked
Achab and the false priests of Baal, that is to say,
that He might root out pride, lust, idolatry, and every
kind of sin. And here Christ found Jonadab, a man
of good will, to whom He put the question,—"Is thy
heart right, as My Heart is with thy heart? If it be,
give Me thy hand, and mount into My Chariot, and
come with Me." To such an one God stretches out
the right Hand of His Grace, and raises him up into
the lofty Chariot of His Will; and in this he is borne
along. For,—"Come with Me," He says, "and I will
lead you by the way of the Cross; this is the very
path to life, even that life which is eternal. Fear not;
sit by My side, I will not suffer you to fall; by this
narrow path will I conduct you to Heaven. Come
with Me, that you may ever be with Me, and by My
side." This is that safest of all places in the world
which Job so exceedingly longed for when he said,—
"Deliver me, O Lord, and set me beside Thee, and let
any man's hand fight against me." (*Job* XVII. 3.) I
shall endure, he means, and come out safe from a thousand blows, being perfectly secure in Thy keeping.
When a man has once reached this Chariot of the Divine Will, it is easy for him to insinuate himself into
the closest intimacy with Christ, yea, and to become

a kinsman of Christ, and to be united to Him by the closest ties of relationship; for our Lord Himself declares,—"Whosoever shall do the Will of My Father That is in Heaven, he is My brother, and sister, and mother." (*Matt.* xii. 50.) And here Euthymius very rightly exclaims,—"O admirable virtue which exalts those who attain to it to such a height of honour as to make them the very kinsmen of Christ!" Of a truth the union of the human will with the Divine is the supreme good in life.

A saintly man used to say,—"Whatever you wish to be, that you are!" For so great is the power belonging to our will, when united to the Divine, that whatever we seriously and with our whole intention desire to be, we may be. No one ardently wishes to be lowly, patient, modest, or liberal, who may not be that which he desires to be,—"Whatever you desire to be, that you are." The same holy man further adds:—"If it is not in your power to do, or offer, great things, yet have at least *a great will,* and stretch this to infinity. Are you poor? You can still be of that mind, that, if riches were yours, you would bestow them liberally on the needy. Is your strength small? Still you may so offer yourself, that, if you had a thousand souls and a thousand heads, you would not refuse to lay down the thousand souls, and heads, and lives for Christ. Are you afflicted? And do you think yourself wretched? Unite your will to the Divine, and you will be perfectly happy. That man is truly wretched who knows not how to rule himself,

[183]

and for possession of whom vices contend, as cities do for the birth-place of Homer; who, by a most disgraceful alternation, is one while the slave of ambition, at another, of avarice, at another, of anger or envy, at another, of drunkenness or lust. Scarcely ever is he his own, and much less God's, because he is never able to rule himself. The poet sings of Hercules,—"When he had made all things his slaves, he himself fell a slave to desire and anger." And we may say nearly the same of such a man as I am describing. Although he possesses all things, yet he wants himself; he is not his own, but is the slave of money or passion, and many other vices. "The patient man is better than the valiant: and he that ruleth his spirit, than he that taketh cities." (*Prov.* XVI. 32.) If you desire to bring all things into subjection to yourself, submit yourself to the Divine Will. You will rule many, if the Divine Will rules you.

3. In all ages of the world God has ever had certain from among men whom he has chosen to Himself to be His friends, whom He might admit to intimacy, to whom He might unfold many of His secret designs, and to whom He might manifest Himself by daily favours. And of these some are, as it were, of the first order of nearness to Him, others of the second, and others of the third. That is to say, some are more closely united to God than others. Men of this kind we call "Saints."

Now the very first step to saintliness of life is to surrender oneself absolutely to the Divine Will in all things. That man attains to the greatest sanctity of life who descends deepest into the Divine Will. And so blessed Paul, desiring this one thing in his converts, says,—"We cease not to pray for you, and to beg that you may be filled with the knowledge of His Will." (*Col.* i. 9.) It is not enough for him that the Divine Will should be recognized by his children in the Faith, but he desires that they should be *"filled"* with this knowledge. He desires that they should descend as deeply as possible into the Divine Will. For Paul knew that when he had obtained this from them they would advance very rapidly, and without difficulty, in the pursuit of all kinds of virtue.

How fitting, moreover, is it that that which from eternity has been pleasing to God should be pleasing also to man. When Harpagus had dined off the flesh of his own son, and King Astyages (who had prepared that banquet) ordered the remaining limbs, such as the head, and arms, and feet, to be brought forward, and inquired,—"How did you like it?" He replied,— *"Whatever the King does I like."* Ah! miserable wretch! is it so great a matter to you to throw off the man that you may please a beast? And should not we Christians the rather say this one thing under all circumstances,—*"Whatever God does pleases me?"*

The gross flattery of the Romans used formerly to subscribe to the petitions which were presented to the Emperor,—"The most devoted servant of your Deity and Majesty." Christians, too, present petitions when they pray. And therefore let every one always add, both to his prayers and works,—"To Thy Deity and Will, O my God, I am most devoted." To devote one's whole will to the Divine Will, and closely to bind it there, is the supreme good in life, and is in reality heaven out of heaven, as I shall now proceed to show.

CHAPTER VI

THAT CONFORMITY OF THE HUMAN WILL TO THE DIVINE IS HEAVEN OUT OF HEAVEN, AND TRUE HAPPINESS OF LIFE

"**B**LESSED art thou, and it shall be well with thee" (*Ps.* cxxvii. 2), whoever thou art, that hast perfectly attained to this conformity of thine own will with the Divine, and hast eagerly embraced everything as from the Hand of God. This will be thy happiness in this lower world; thou wilt experience a perpetual joy, and a gladness known only to a few; for this happiness they enjoy who are united to God in the closest friendship. "Blessed art thou, and it shall be well with thee," for sure is that saying of S. Paul,—"The kingdom of God is not meat and drink; but justice and peace, and joy in the Holy Ghost. For he that in this serveth Christ pleaseth God, and is approved of men." (*Rom.* xiv. 17, 18.) For as in Heaven there is no change, and no yesterday or to-day (if I may so speak), but a continual and equable inflowing of eternal pleasure, which is itself unvarying, and yet not wholly enjoyed at one and the same time, "for a thousand years in Thy sight are as yesterday, which is past" (*Ps.* lxxxix. 4); so, in like manner, those also

who have attained to this union of their own will with
the Divine are now well-nigh unchangeable, and whatever sorrowful vicissitude befalls them they restrain by
the empire of reason. All their meat, and drink, and
delight, is the Good-pleasure of God; and so restless-
ness and anxiety depart, or else from these there would
daily spring first one kind of trouble and then another
without number. Their will is so sweetly lulled into
repose by the Will of God, that, since they see that
all things proceed from Him, and that His most Holy
Will is fulfilled in all things, even their very troubles
and sorrows bring with them a portion of joy, for in
these troubles and sorrows they discover the Divine
Will, and more surely so than in the greatest prosperity. And so if haply there is anything which assails their deep tranquillity, there is certainly nothing
which can overthrow it. "They that trust in the Lord
shall be as Mount Sion: he shall not be moved for
ever." (*Ps.* cxxiv. i.)

i. And this was the ground of that unruffled peace
with which the ancient Fathers were sustained, and, as
it were, beatified. They were not exempt indeed from
an accumulation of various troubles. Diseases very
often harassed their bodies, and anxieties assailed
their minds; for in proportion as each one became
more saintly, the sorer was he for the most part afflicted. Whence, then, did they derive such unvarying serenity of mind? Whence such great firmness
and cheerfulness of exterior? How was it that they
kept such a perpetual paschal feast, sabbath, as it were,

after sabbath? From no other cause, in truth, than from the most perfect oblation of self to the Divine Will. It was with vain and edgeless attack that calamity of every kind rushed upon him whom the Divine Will had thus forearmed:—"Whatsoever shall befall the just man, it shall not make him sad." (*Prov.* XII. 21.) These saintly men, therefore, were both happy and blessed, for in all things they recognized and worshipped the Will of God, and so on this alone they reposed, and by it were gladdened and sustained. It chanced that two persons were conversing upon this subject, when one of them said,—"If it really is the case that all things which happen proceed from the Divine Will, and in such a way that not even a single sparrow falls to the ground, as Christ testifies, without God having foreknown it from all eternity, and willed it, we shall be happy, and shall be incapable of ever being unhappy, if we receive this." "Yes, perfectly happy shall we be," said the other, "and shall even now almost dwell in Heaven; but few are able to receive this in all its fulness; not because it is hard of reception, but because they do not apply their minds." This also may doubtless be a reason, viz., because this truth is so seldom and so obscurely laid down in sermons. Oftentimes learned subjects, and those which are pleasing to the ear, are discoursed of; but such topics are comparatively useless, and to be acquainted with them is scarcely any help at all towards heaven. This must be taught and enforced, this must be constantly inculcated, viz., the way in which each person

[189]

may best devote himself, and all that belongs to him, to the Divine Will, and may become possessed of a heaven this side of Heaven.

S. Catherine of Siena, a virgin remarkable for her sanctity, was wont to say that men of upright minds were as like as possible to our Saviour, for as He never lost His tranquillity of soul, even in His utmost agony, so neither did they lose it, since it consists in the conformity of their own will to the Divine. Nor does it hinder this tranquil happiness that their sufferings are great, for such things oftentimes increase it. Job was none the less united to God when suffering the bitterest afflictions than he was when surrounded with pleasure; nay, I would even go so far as to affirm that Job when in want, and covered with sores on a dunghill, was far more closely united to God than he was when living in splendour. The calmness of a mind united to the Divine Will cannot be obscured by any clouds of sorrow. The leaves of the Heliotrope never fade, according to Pliny; and so concerning such a man, you may say,—"His leaf shall not fall off: and all whatsoever he shall do shall prosper." (*Ps.* i. 3.)

2. Once upon a time one of the Persians, boasting to the Greeks about the multitude of his own people, said,—"To-morrow we shall hide the sun with our arrows." To whom the Greek playfully replied,— "I am glad to hear it, for we shall fight the better in the shade." And so the man who is truly devoted to the Divine Will exclaims,—"Let the whole power of hell assail me, let enemies advance, and let them

hide the sun with their darts, yet shall not my heart fail me, for I shall fight all the better under this shade." "Nevertheless, as it shall be the will of God in heaven so be it done." (1 *Mach.* III. 60.)

Cassian (*Coll.* XII. 13) relates that a man of Alexandria, who was of a great age, was surrounded by idolaters, like a lamb by wolves. They all united in pinching, and pushing, and driving him hither and thither; heaping on him a thousand curses and a thousand injuries, and treating him like a ball which is tossed from hand to hand. At length one of them asked him in mockery what miracles his Christ, Whom he vaunted so much, had shown? Whereupon the old man calmly replied,—"He wrought this miracle, that I should endure the injuries which you heap upon me, without losing my tranquillity of mind, and should be ready to endure even greater injuries for love of Him, if you were to proceed to inflict them." And this is in truth a great miracle, and one which even now is daily performed by those who surrender themselves entirely to the Divine Will. Such as these know how to stand fearless in the midst of whirlwinds and tempests, and erect among ruins; and to look down upon all human things as beneath their feet. The old miracles are revived; the bush which Moses saw and which burnt with fire, but was not consumed; the three Hebrew Children who fell down bound in the flames at Babylon, and yet remained uninjured and untouched. And so, no doubt, many sorrowful things befall good men; and here it is not that they

lack the sense of feeling, but impatience. Every kind
of adversity they view as a trial of themselves, and
refer it all to the Divine Will. And so they do not
dread hardships and difficulties, nor do they murmur
at all about God and the Divine Permissions. Whatever happens they believe it to be for their good, and
turn it to a good account, and refer everything to the
Divine Will and Providence.

They say that Mount Olympus in Macedonia is of
such a wonderful height that neither wind, nor rain,
nor snow, ever reach its summit. "Olympus rises
above the clouds." (LUCAN, *Pharsal.* 2.) There the
sky is clear and bright, beyond all the fierce conflicts
of tempests. But this spot allows no birds or other
living creatures to rest upon it, for the exceeding
rarity of the atmosphere prevents respiration. The
knowledge of this fact was arrived at as follows:
There were certain people who attempted the ascent
every year, and who used to carry with them wet
sponges fastened to their nostrils, which made the air
denser, and thus promoted respiration; and when they
had ascended the peak of the mountain they wrote
certain letters on the dust, and after the lapse of a
year they found that they had not been disturbed, but
were just as if they had been recently written; and
this was a convincing proof that neither rain nor wind
ever visited that spot. And such is the condition of
the man who has reached this most exalted height of
union with the Divine Will. He is a Mountain, an
Olympus, higher than the clouds, above storms, out of

the reach of wild beasts, unapproachable by winds.
Here the clouds of sorrow are hurried along beneath
him. Here is profound and most delicious repose in
the sole Will of God. "In peace," says S. Augustine,
"is perfection, where there is nothing which opposes;
and therefore the sons of God are men of peace, since
there is nothing in them which strives against God.
And this is the peace which is given on earth to men
of good-will: this is the life of a complete and perfectly wise man." Admirably has Dorotheus (*Serm.
de Obed.*) said, that the man who in all things endeavours to follow the Divine Will is borne along in
a chariot, together with all the crosses which otherwise would have been borne by him; while others,
who do not understand this short and easy way of
travelling, follow behind on foot, and either drag along
heavy crosses in a gloomy way, or carry them with
pain and difficulty.

3. That this perfect union with the Divine Will is
the supreme happiness out of heaven Philo (*De Sacerd.
Muner.*) testifies, when he says,—"While the question
is about offering gifts to God, regard is had to the
benefit of those who offer. For as long as they are
accustomed to cut off a part of their daily food for
God, they never fall into forgetfulness of Him: and
nothing in this world can happen more fortunately for
a man than this." And to this sentiment a Theologian and preacher of our own day subscribes. "I
have sometimes thought," he says, "whether any art
could be devised by which a man might be perfectly

happy out of the heavenly condition of the Blessed;
and I am persuaded that there is this one way—*if he
surrenders himself entirely* to his Creator and His most
Holy Will, keeping back no part of himself."

And great assistance in making this truth known
does the god Cynocephalus render; who is a beast in
the formation of its hands and feet, but like a man in
the rest of the body. It is the peculiarity of this
creature that it is governed by the moon through some
secret influence. For when the moon grows old the
eyes of the Cynocephalus fail so much that when it
has come to its last quarter, and has disappeared, the
eyes of the beast stare wide open, without any power
of sight, and in a similar way all the functions of its
body fail. But when the moon is young, and re-ad-
justs its golden orb, the eyes of the animal expand, and
its whole body regains its strength, so that, being re-
created, as it were, and restored to its former condition, it raises itself up on its hinder-feet, and with a
wonderful prostration of body, and with hands raised
up in veneration to the ring of the moon, it worships
that heavenly body with suppliant gesture. And by
this worship the animal protests and proclaims that it
ascribes all its happiness to the moon, since it owes
all that it possesses to the liberality of that heavenly
body. And so it happens, that, when the moon reaches
the full, a ring shines round the head of the Cynocephalus like a crown. A very wonderful union between a planet and a brute, that the animal knows how
to return thanks to its nourisher with such great signs

of submission, and with such an humble form of worship, and to offer itself as a slave! And what are we doing, Christian friends, if we are either less wise, or inferior to an animal void of reason? God is most perfect Light; yet, as far as we are concerned, that Light either waxes or wanes according as we prepare ourselves to receive it. When it fades within us our eyes become dim; we pine away, and fall to the ground, and faint, and perish: but when it increases we are illuminated, and grow, and are strong and healthy. Let us, therefore, submit ourselves as perfectly as possible to this Lord, and to His most Holy Will, being ready to obey its every indication. This procures for us a crown, and not only that of eternal glory, but an illustrious one even in this fleeting life. We are transformed into God, when our will is transformed into the Divine.

And how I wish, Christian friends, how I wish, that day and night you would do nothing else, and care for nothing else, than that your will should in all things be the Will of God, than that the Divine Will should transfuse itself into yours! It is the worthiest of tasks for you to strain every nerve that you may only will or not will that which God wills or wills not. Believe me, it is good for us thus to cleave to God; it is good for us thus to be joined to the Divine Will, and to place our trust in the Lord God. This is true blessedness. This is HEAVEN OUT OF HEAVEN.

BOOK IV

CONCERNING THE HINDRANCES TO CONFORMITY OF THE HUMAN WILL WITH THE DIVINE

"I called and you refused." *Prov.* I. 24.

THE HELIOTROPIUM

Book IV

CHAPTER I

THE CHIEF HINDRANCES TO CONFORMITY OF THE HUMAN WILL WITH THE DIVINE

WHEN the keys of a house or a city are entrusted to anyone, there is at the same time committed to him the power of entering that house or city at his pleasure; but sometimes Christ is long seeking for the keys to the inmost chambers of the heart before He obtains them, and gains free access thither. So little nobility of feeling do we show to that most bountiful of all guests!

Ludovicus Blosius tells a story of S. Gertrude the virgin, which is well worthy of being known. Our Lord appeared to her, and said,—"In this hand I carry health, in the other disease; choose, my daughter, which you like best." And what could Gertrude do? Should she choose health, it would seem like presumption. Should she prefer disease to health, it would be put down to excessive modesty. It certainly is the custom among men that, when a friend offers a choice of this kind to a friend, he should choose the worse of the two, in order to show his modesty, and on this principle Gertrude ought to have chosen disease, in order to escape the torments of the other world. And she would not have made a foolish choice, after the example of S. Catherine of Siena, who preferred a chaplet of thorns far before a crown of gold. But Gertrude, with greater wisdom, and to her greater profit, chose neither, but folding her hands in the form of a cross upon her breast, and throwing herself upon her knees, exclaimed,—"O my Lord, this only I desire of Thee in all my prayers, that Thou wouldest not regard my will, but Thine Own: and so I am ready to receive either; neither do I choose. To Thee, O Lord, it belongs to decide whether Thou wouldest leave with me this or that." To whom Christ replied,—"Whosoever desires to be often visited by Me, let him offer to Me *the key of his will,* and never ask it back from Me." And Gertrude, being thus instructed, composed a little prayer, which she arranged according to the following form,—*"Not my will, but Thine be done, O my most loving* JESUS!" And this she continued to repeat, according to her rule, three hundred and sixty-five times a day. And this little prayer seems preferable to a thousand other prayers. He will have done well indeed who has frequently repeated it day and night, and with all the more earnestness when adversity presses upon him with the greatest vehemence. No one can be so engrossed with business, or laden with cares, but that ten, twenty, thirty or even a hundred times every hour, he may repeat this short form,—*"Not my will, but Thine be done, O my most loving* JESUS!"

But it seems perchance to some one to be no light matter always to obtain from himself this *to will.* At times the will resists, and refuses to be driven to perform things which are so meanly thought of, and so hard to bear. It is necessary, therefore, that he who desires that his own will should be as closely united as possible to the Divine should offer himself as being ready and prepared to do those things especially from which his corrupt nature shrinks. The rebellious will must be forced, therefore, to do that, above all other things, which it hates the most.

1. And first of all, let the man who is devoted to the Divine Will offer himself to *the loss of all things,* and say,—"O my Lord, I offer myself to Thee, being just as ready for poverty as I am for riches (it is hard indeed, but salutary), nor do I refuse to bear even that poverty of soul which deprives me of consolations, and leaves me barren of every feeling of sweetness. If it thus seem good to Thee, O my God, let my heart become like the most barren ground. Thou, O Lord, hast pledged me, not in costly and fragrant wine, but in wormwood, and in wine mingled with myrrh. To Thy favour, then, will I respond even from this bitter cup. I know, O Lord, that Thy cellar abounds in choicest wine, and the most generous hippocrass; but, in order to try Thy servants, Thou art wont to pledge them in this dead and acid

drink. Therefore I will drain, O good JESUS, the cup Thou shalt present to me, however bitter it may be."

Once upon a time God made a clear manifestation of Himself to one of His chosen friends, and soothed his soul with consolations of various kinds. It was as though he were perpetually standing on Mount Thabor, before the radiant presence of Christ. "And why is this?" he used to say to himself. "Do we not live in a place of sorrow and mourning, and does the time demand such sweet consolations?" And so he prayed against this great comfort of soul. God granted his prayer, and for the space of five years exercised him with many cares and difficulties. At last He sent an Angel to replace the man's mourning by consolation; but he, with perfect composure, and steadfastness of purpose, said,—"I seek for no other consolation but this alone, that I may know that it pleases God that I should be afflicted with sorrow. The Divine Will is to me the greatest alleviation of all griefs. Only let me please God, and I care not whether I am healthy or sick."

S. Chrysostom (*In Matt. Hom.* VIII. 4) justly extols the virtue of S. Joseph, the betrothed husband of the Blessed Virgin, in this particular:—"When he had heard these things," he says, "he was not offended, neither did he say,—'The thing is hard to understand. Didst thou not say just now that He should save His people? And now He saves not even Himself; but we must fly, and go far from home, and be

THE HUMAN WILL WITH THE DIVINE

a long time away. The facts are contrary to the
promise.' Nay, none of these things doth he say
(for the man was faithful), neither is he curious about
the time of his return; and this though the Angel had
put it indefinitely thus,—'Be thou there until I tell
thee.' But nevertheless, not even at this did he shudder, but submits and obeys, undergoing all the trials
with joy." Joseph was perfectly prepared for com-
mencing his flight, for leaving his country, and for
enduring want of every kind. The Divine Will soothes
all miseries.

When an offering of oneself to *poverty* has been
made, we must then proceed further.

2. To the first oblation, then, of self, let there succeed a second, *to be lightly esteemed.* And this S.
Paul enjoins, when he says,—"In all things let us
exhibit ourselves as the ministers of God, in much
patience, in tribulation, in necessities, in distresses, in
stripes, in prisons, in seditions, in labours, in watchings, in fastings; by honour and dishonour, by evil
report and good report; as deceivers, and yet true; as
unknown, and yet known; as dying, and behold we
live; as chastised, and not killed; as sorrowful, yet
always rejoicing; as needy, yet enriching many; as
having nothing, and possessing all things." (2 *Cor.*
VI. 4-10.) Let the man who is devoted to the Divine
Will say,—"Lord, I offer myself to Thee for any ignominy and contempt; and that especially for which
I have afforded no cause. For Thy sake I do not
shrink from being neglected, despised, cast down, and

even trodden under foot." This pill is hard and large, but yet it must be swallowed, since it comes from Christ's Dispensary. Christ Himself not only exposed Himself to every kind of injury, but He endured them also as the most abject of men. He was "made a curse for us: for it is written, Cursed is every one that hangeth on a tree." (*Gal.* III. 13.) How many of the Saints were thought in the old time to be the wickedest of men; and they knew how they were esteemed, but endured it, however much they may have felt the pain. It is one thing to be *esteemed* wicked, another *to be* so; and this last we all of us learn in our cradles without a master, while few only know the former; and those only know it perfectly who receive all contempt from the Hand of God, and from the Divine Will, just as they would receive great honours.

It seems to me that the Mother of our Lord, the Blessed Virgin Mary, was united to the Divine Will with all her heart, when Joseph her betrothed husband, being alarmed at her being great with child, was thinking about putting her away. And was not the Virgin silent? Had she not committed to the Divine Will whatever opinion might be formed about her? And by this illustrious example many of the Saints were moved; for although they were accused of the most heinous crimes, yet they held their peace, and bore the ignominy, and committed themselves entirely, with all their ignominy, to God.

S. Emmeramnus, Bishop of Ratisbon, was not only

accused of a most abominable crime, but was also tormented with the utmost cruelty; for, at the command of Lambert, who was the son of the prince, he was fastened to a ladder, and having been thus prepared for torture, his fingers and toes were cut off, then his ears, nose, arms, and feet; at last his tongue was pulled out, and not long after his soul followed. And could this holy Bishop, and so many other innocent people, endure with calmness the extremity of ignominy? How comes it then that we, who are guilty of a thousand offences, bear with such impatience contempt so trifling, and an act of injury which is of the smallest possible magnitude? If the Will of God, from which all these things spring, is really dear to us, we shall not easily be disturbed by any contempt however grievous; yea, rather each one will be the greatest possible despiser of himself.

After our Lord had risen from the dead, He said to Magdalen, who was about to embrace His feet with the deepest reverence,—"Do not touch Me; for I am not yet ascended to My Father." (*John* xx. 17.) Just as if He had said,—"You will often see Me, Magdalen, and you will not be denied that privilege of touching and kissing Me, which was granted to many of the women of Jerusalem, who ventured to do it as well as you." Christ, indeed, now that His sufferings were all over, and He had endured death, might justly have forbidden that He should be touched; but because He had not as yet ascended to Heaven, the home of immortality, He not only permitted Himself to be touched by His beloved Disciples, but by women also. And yet we, vile and contemptible men of earth that we are, who not merely have never ascended to the habitations of the Blessed, but have not as yet descended either into the grave,—we, I say, who are still mortal, and exposed to all sorts of miseries, nevertheless cry out so often,—"Do not touch me! Do not touch me!" In our frenzy we often allow our tongue to run on in a thousand foolish ways. But what monstrous ignorance of the Divine Will possesses us, my Christian friends, and makes us so sensitive as not to be able to endure to be addressed with even a single phrase less honourable than we think our due? He who understands the mystery of the Divine Will, voluntarily offers himself to contempt of every kind, and exclaims,—"O my Lord, I am most worthy to be despised, and cast out by all; and therefore, when I see that I am suffering that which long ago I have merited, I will not take it amiss! I know, O Lord, that no one will ever despise me who has not first of all received the power to do so from Thee. I will not, therefore, complain; but will make myself viler than I am, and will be lowly in my own eyes."

3. When the soul is now prepared for Poverty and Contempt, there follows a third Oblation of self—*to every kind of sickness*. Hanging-lamps of silver and other metals are made with such skill, and are supplied with so clever a fastening at the joints, that wherever and however they are carried they are never upset, but always remain lighted, and always look upwards to-

wards the sky; and whoever is truly devoted to the
Divine Will is like a lamp of this kind; for, however
roughly and improperly he is handled, he still looks
towards God and the Divine Will, always standing
upright before his Maker, to Whom he frequently
offers himself thus:—"If Thou willest, O Lord, that
my body should be worn out and feeble, or if Thou
willest that I should be a living corpse, deprived of
all strength, wasting away with disease, afflicted with
pains, or confined for years to my bed, behold, I am
ready and prepared! If it so please Thee, even the
most weary sickness will be more pleasing to me than
health, however lasting; and it will be equally my
pleasure either to be well, according to Thy Will, or
to fall into sickness, and to give thanks for it." That
which the great master of virtue, John Avila, taught,
in the following words, is very well worthy to be
noted:—"It avails more," he used to say, "to thank
God *once* in time of tribulation, than six thousand
times in prosperity." For most people know how to
thank God when it goes well with them, but few indeed in adversity!

Ludovicus Blosius relates that a virgin, remarkable
for her saintliness of life, on being asked by what
acts of discipline she had arrived at such perfection,
replied,—"Never have I been so much overwhelmed
by grief as to be prevented from asking to endure
greater sorrows for love of God, thinking myself unworthy of gifts so singular."

Such force, then, must be applied to the will, as

that it should learn to be indifferent about good and bad health, and to be prepared for either. But we must proceed.

4. Fourthly, let the will of man voluntarily offer itself *to death* of every kind, and let it not look for a quick passage or a protracted life otherwise than as it pleases God. Let, then, one who loves the Divine Will exclaim,—"I desire neither to live long, nor to die soon, but in either case to obey Thee, O good JESU. Nor do I prescribe by what kind of death I would desire to die. By whatever kind Thou shalt will to call me to Thyself, by that I am ready to go. But only, O my Lord, would I desire to pray against sudden death; yet not even here do I wish to strive against Thy Will. If Thou willest that I should depart by a sudden stroke, so be it done, as Thou willest. By Thy grace I will ever strive to live in Thy grace. I know that, 'the just man, if he be prevented with death, shall be in rest.' (*Wisd.* IV. 7.) And so I neither shrink from early death, nor desire it to come late; neither do I shudder at a miserable death, or one which my eyes loathe to look upon. We are constrained to believe that many fall asleep in death most placidly, and yet are hurried away to hell, while many depart by a horrible and painful death, and are received into heaven. This judgment is too deep to be capable of being disclosed to human eyesight. And therefore will I cheerfully welcome both an easy and a painful passage, as it shall seem fit to God. For whether we live or die we are the Lord's. 'None of

us liveth to himself, and no man dieth to himself.' "
(*Rom.* xiv. 7.)

S. Martin, Bishop of Tours, when about to yield
up his soul, said,—"If I am still necessary to Thy
people, O Lord, I refuse not labour. Thy Will be
done!" And so the Church, extolling his virtue, says
—"O wonderful man! who wast not overcome by toil,
and who couldest not be conquered by death, who
neither fearedst to die, nor refusedst to live!"

To LIVE and TO DIE, then, must both be embraced
and received according to the ordinance of the Divine
Will. Does God will that we should live? Let us
live, whether it be in happiness or misery; only let us
be aspiring towards happiness. Does He will that we
should die? Let us meet death with a soul which is
thoroughly prepared for it; and, as an old writer admonishes us, let us at least not advance sluggishly
towards death, since it is that which summons us to
immortal life.

But how few are there, alas! who die without a
murmur! Who does not depart this life struggling
against death, and full of sorrow? But this is not to
commit oneself entirely to the Divine Will; nor to be
content with the time allotted to us. It is our duty
to keep in readiness the things which are allowed to
us for an uncertain period, and, when called upon,
to yield them up without complaint. It is the part of
an unprincipled debtor to reproach one to whom he
owes money. The days will always be few if you
count them. Reflect that the chief good does not

consist in time. As far as you can, turn it to good account. It does not help your happiness at all that the day of death is postponed, since life is not made *happier,* but only *longer* by the delay. How much better it is not to count the years of others, but to value one's own in a kindly spirit, and reckon them as gain. You ought not to complain about that which is taken away, but to return thanks for that which is given. Since, therefore, it pleases the Divine Will that I should now die, now will I die, and now will I die with cheerfulness.

5. Fifthly, let the man who is devoted to the Divine Will yield himself to God as being perfectly ready to *endure all things* which can happen either in time or in eternity, and this without the smallest exception or reserve. The eaglet, if it is worthy of its race, is said to gaze upon the sun with steadfast eye; and the human will, if it is perfect, burns in such a way for the Divine, that it voluntarily offers itself to *endure all things*, nor does it make any exception. And who in this can be nobler than Paul, who followed the Divine Will through naked swords, glittering spears, showers of stones, and stormy seas, through whirlwinds, and the fiercest tempests, through places pathless and remote; nothing could close the way so as to hinder him from following the Divine Will? No, not the fear of prisons, not the scourging with rods thrice repeated, not the cloud of stones, not the dread of shipwreck, not the whole host of perils, not the daily need of dying! So inflamed was S. Paul with the Spirit of

God, that, if you had bidden him go into the fire, he would have gone. "For I wished myself," he says, "to be an anathema from Christ for my brethren." (*Rom.* IX. 3.) "What sayest thou, O Paul," inquires S. Chrysostom, "hast thou not already said, 'Who shall separate us from the love of Christ?'" Even so, Chrysostom; but because Paul loved Christ alone he desired to be plucked away from Christ and His sweet companionship, but only on this condition, that more people should be brought to love Him; and so Paul, under the dominion of blind love, as it were, desired to be separated, not indeed from the love of Christ, but from blessedness and glory with Christ. Behold, how steadfastly this eagle fixed his eyes on the sun of the Divine Will! Of such importance, moreover, is this so energetic a conformity to the Divine Will, that, in comparison with it, it is of little matter if even a thousand worlds should smile. With most of the holy martyrs there was but little difficulty in pledging tyrants in their own life-blood as a thing of the most insignificant value. In the midst of their tortures they abounded with Divine consolations, and so they easily despised their sufferings, and even death itself. S. Lawrence reclined on the red-hot gridiron like a weary traveller on a bench. S. Andrew saluted the cross as if it were a royal couch. S. Stephen welcomed the shower of stones like drops of dew. The man, then, who daily faints beneath the weight of so many troubles, and feels that he is slowly dying, and who nevertheless yields himself up to the power of the Divine Will, and offers himself as perfectly ready to endure all things, achieves a great matter indeed, provided, as I have said, that IN ALL THINGS he is equally ready to follow the Will of God. And so it ought to be; for all the faculties both of body and soul, and those things which we call the gifts of fortune, we receive from God; and how, then, can we make *any exception* in restoring them? That commonest of sayings in the schools, "No rule is without an exception," is utterly inapplicable here, for the rule of the Divine Will is without any exception. S. Bernard sets before us an illustrious example of this when he bids us listen to the man whom God found after His Own Heart:—"My God," he says, "my heart is ready, my heart is ready; ready for adversity, ready for prosperity, ready for abasement, ready for exaltation, ready for all that Thou shalt command. Dost Thou will to make me a shepherd? Dost Thou will to set me up as the king of Thy people? My God, my heart is ready, my heart is ready. But if He shall say to me: 'Thou pleasest me not:' I am ready, let Him do that which is good before Him." (2 *Kings* xv. 26.) An abasement of soul and surrender of his own will worthy of such a devout prince! For observe, if God says, Thou pleasest me not; I will that you should not be king; I will that you should not live,—"I am ready!" says David; "let Him do that which is good before Him." If God's command had been, I will that you shall again be an exile and fugitive, and in place of a wicked father-in-law shall have a most abandoned son, who shall seek his father's crown and life; still David says,—"I am ready!" But if God were to command, I will that you should again live in caves and dens of wild beasts, that you should again become a mendicant, and every day be in peril of your life; yet still David says,—"I am ready!" But if God were to say, I will that you, instead of receiving your revenues, should, in the time of your calamity, be defamed with reproaches, even by your subjects, and should have stones cast at you, and should be cursed with dreadful imprecations; not even this do I refuse, says David,—"Let Him do that which is good before Him." What heroic valour in that most holy prince, by which alone he would have been acceptable to God, more especially when he said this weeping, and covered with sackcloth! So great a thing did the man after God's Own Heart esteem it to *please God* that he would most gladly have purchased this grace at the expense of his liberty, children, riches, kingdom, nay, and his very life itself!

Only let David be able to obey the Divine Will, and with the greatest alacrity could he say, in reference to all such things as these,—*"My heart is ready, O God, my heart is ready."*

CHAPTER II

I

ONCE upon a time some of the dregs of society,
and a large gang of thieves, night-prowlers, and
burglars, presented a petition to the judges, praying
them to do away with gibbets, so that some regard
might be shown to the eyes and noses of passers-by.
The judges replied that, if they desired the practice of
hanging to be done away with, they must themselves
first of all put a stop to the habit of stealing, and that
they, for their part, would not hesitate to remove
crosses and gibbets if their petitioners would first put
an end to felonies. Upon this, one of the thieves
more daring than the rest replied,—"Venerable sirs,
we are not the originators of felonies. That, therefore, which we did not introduce we cannot do away
with." To which the judges answered,—"Neither did
we invent gibbets, good sirs, and therefore we will
not abolish them."

The first parents of the human race were detected
in an act of wrong. This is the origin of all acts
of wickedness; hence arises the contagion of sin, and

hence, too, the punishment of hell. And we who are distant descendants of this race of thieves complain that hell is ordained for us, and therefore we often present petitions to God, and ask,—"Only, O Lord, cast us not down into the outer darkness! If Thou, O Lord, wouldest destroy the flames of hell, Thou wouldest immediately deliver us from fear." But God replies most justly,—"You, on your part, remove your guilt, and I, on My part, will extinguish the fire of hell. Let your sins come to an end, and the fierceness of these flames shall be mitigated." But we continue,—"Nay, but, O Lord, we are not the originators of wickedness, and why do we suffer for the fault of others, and for that which is born with us! This is original sin." But again God answers,—"Neither am I the cause of hell, but pride and disobedience are. Nor was it the original design of hell to torment men, but devils, for hell-fire is 'prepared for the devil and his angels.' (*Matt.* xxv. 41.) You cannot, therefore, complain that you are involved in the evils of others."

S. Bernard, illustrious among the faithful servants of God, long ago proclaimed, in words as few as they are clear, in what way the fire of hell may very easily be extinguished. These are his words (*Serm.* 3, *de Resur. Dom.*):—"*Let there be an end of your own will, and there will be no such thing as hell.*" And he assigns the following forcible reason:—"For what does God hate or punish but one's own will? Against what will hell-fire rage, but against one's own will? Even now, when we suffer from cold or hunger, or any such

thing, what is injured but our own will? But, if **we**
voluntarily endure these things, there is then a com-
munity of will established (that is to say, between
God Who sends such things, and man who endures
them). Moreover, with what fury one's own will
fights against the Lord of all Might let those who are
the slaves of their own will hear and tremble. For, in
the first place, when it becomes its own master, it
withdraws and separates itself from the Government
of Him Whom, as its Author, it is bound by right to
serve. But will it be content with this act of injustice?
By no means. It adds another still, and, as far as lies
in its power, seizes and plucks away by force everything which belongs to God. For what limit does
human cupidity propose to itself? Would not the
man who gains a trifling sum by lending his money at
interest, try in the same way to gain the whole world,
if it were not utterly impossible, and if his capacity
only equalled his inclination? I affirm, with confidence, that the entire world would not be enough to
satisfy a man who is guided by his own will; but how
I wish that he would be contented even with that, and
would not (horrible to speak of!) vent his rage against
the very Author of all things! Thus he becomes like
some cruel animal, the fiercest of wild beasts, the most
ravenous of she-wolves, the most savage of lionesses.
This is the most loathsome leprosy of soul, on account
of which he ought to wash himself in the Jordan, and
follow the example of Him Who came not to do His
Own Will. Whence also, during His Passion, He ex-

claimed,—"Not my will, but Thine, be done." *"Let one's own will come to an end, and there will be no hell!"* It is not, therefore, a childish and idle question,—"Can the flames of hell be extinguished, and in what way?" They certainly can. They are not vain prayers to ask God to destroy hell. He is ready to do it. He demands but this one thing as the reward for His labour,—*"Let man's own will come to an end, and there will be no hell!"* But who can so far stimulate all men as that each should surrender his own will, and cause it to rest entirely on the Divine? Do you, my friend, if you are in earnest, do you master your own will, and you have at once removed that place to which you would otherwise have been bound, and where you would have been tormented in hell, just as much as if hell itself were destroyed, and its flames were extinguished. *"Let one's own will come to an end, and there will be no hell."* "The eye," says one, "is the door and messenger of the heart. Close the eye, and there will be no desire of having. Let the will come to an end, and, lo! hell is closed!"

2. How many there are, alas! who endure manifold and great sufferings, but against their own will, and in a spirit of resistance; for they do not surrender their own will to the Divine. God wills that they should suffer, and most clearly declares this to be His Will, when He sends their sufferings upon them; and this with just as much certainty as if a voice were to come from Heaven and say,—"I will that you should suffer." But even thus they would not be

willing to suffer; and, if they could only have done so, would long since have thrown off the burden which they bear. Behold, then, man's own will entirely wanting in conformity to the Divine!

Parents know what a work of labour it is to educate those children in whom wilfulness is not early crushed. How many times must they cry out every day,—"Hold your tongue; be quiet; attend to this; leave that alone." Sometimes they are so restless, and make such a disturbance in the house, that even a mother of the greatest gentleness becomes angry; and, seizing a stick, or anything else that she finds in her anger, vents her rage first on one, then on another, and upon whichever child happens to be nearest. Sometimes she shows her rage in words only, and cries out,—"You are no children of mine! I do not own you; I see nothing that belongs to me in you: you do not take after the disposition either of your father or mother. Away with you, you good-for-nothings!" And God deals with us in the same way as parents treat their restless and wilful children. How often does he threaten a drunkard or a lustful man? How often does He set before the one, by means of silent accusations, his drunkenness, and before the other his wanton life? How often does he dissuade from such vices, and say,—"See how you are injuring your body and soul! You are exhausting your pocket and strength; you are forfeiting My grace and heaven. You know, indeed, that such things are forbidden by Me. You know that it is My Will that you should

utterly shrink from all such vileness as this; nor are
you ignorant how thoroughly I abominate and detest
a will which struggles thus against Mine." At last
the most gentle Father seizes a rod, and punishes the
wickedness of His child in such a way that he may
feel that he is being punished. But when this has
many times been done, and the child does not effectually amend, or abandon his vicious habits, then at
length the Father becomes angry, and says,—"Why
should I smite you any more? In vain have I smitten
My children, for they refused to receive correction."
"But the multiplied brood of the wicked shall not
thrive, and bastard slips shall not take deep root, nor
any fast foundation." (*Wisdom* IV. 3.) Depart, ye
wicked ones; I will let you go according to the desires of your heart, and let you walk in your own in-
ventions. (*Ps.* LXXX. 13.) And this is the most
grievous form of the Father's anger, and more to be
dreaded than any punishment.

And in the same way God deals with a proud and
arrogant man, and rebukes him thus:—"You please
neither Me, nor men; although, despising Me, you
very greatly desire to please them. You are laughed
at by the very persons who you hoped would approve
of your arrogance. You long ago knew My Will.
You know that I cannot endure anyone who is proud,
no, not even an Angel; and much less, therefore, a
man. Who knows not that I resist the proud in a
singular way? And yet you persevere in your haugh-
tiness!" And in the same way, God, by His secret

impulses, draws on to amendment the covetous man, the angry, the jealous, and the slanderer, and in various ways sets forth His Will for them to follow. God leads each by the way which is best adapted to him. It was said before the face of Saul, the king of Israel, —"When thou wast a little one in thy own eyes, wast thou not made the head of the tribes of Israel? And the Lord anointed thee to be king over Israel. Why then didst thou not hearken to the voice of the Lord: but hast turned to the prey, and hast done evil in the eyes of the Lord. Forasmuch therefore as thou hast rejected the word of the Lord, the Lord hath also rejected thee from being king." (1 *Kings* xv. 17, 19, 23.)

Whoever, therefore, you are who still resist the Divine Will, come, I pray, come, and I will take you not to the school of eagles, but to that of ravens, and receive, I pray you, a lesson from them.

3. Why, I would ask, did God will that Elias the Thesbite should receive his food from ravens, who became, as it were, the ministers to his wants? What is the meaning of this? The most thievish of birds carry dinner and supper to one who lives in the desert, with faithful and ready obedience. God, then, willed this, my good friend, in order to teach you how even dumb creatures, in spite of their natural propensities, obey His Will. What is more wonderful than that meat should be carried by a raven, who is exceedingly greedy of flesh, and most rapacious at the same time, although he might have devoured it a hundred times

over as he went if the Will of God had not ordered otherwise? But some one may object here,—It is easy enough for God to compel any animal to do His bidding. They do not, however, obey because they are willing, but because they are bound to do so. It is as you say, and even on this ground it would be right that you should be perfectly obedient to the Divine Will, because God does not drive you on with *compulsory* commands, but with *voluntary.* He wills that you should serve Him with a *free service,* and should, therefore, obtain the greater reward.

But let us turn aside, I pray, from the school of the ravens into the cave of the winds, where even their fury is subservient to command. Our Lord "commanded the winds and the sea, and there came a great calm. But the men wondered, saying, What manner of man is this, for the winds and the sea obey Him!" (*Matt.* VIII. 26, 27.) Did not the very rocks mourn over the sorrowful spectacle of our dying Lord, testifying their grief by rents, which had never been seen before? (*Matt.* XXVII. 51.) Man alone becomes petrified into a rock, and too often persists in that wilful course which he has commenced. "The heart is perverse above all things, and unsearchable, WHO CAN KNOW IT?" (*Jer.* XVII. 9.) Yea, WHO CAN KNOW IT? Once begin to examine this whirlpool, and you will discover there the most hidden thoughts, which strive against God with such secret murmurings as,—"Dost Thou will, O Lord, that I should love my enemies? That I should submit myself to all?

That I should renounce my pleasures? It is a hard command, and my will inclines me otherwise. What, then, shall I do? I will use a little dissimulation, and will not strive against my own will over-strongly; neither will I obey Thine over-much." O inscrutable and wicked heart of man!

A story is told of M. Aurelius Marius how that one day he was made emperor, held the reins of government for the next, and on the third was slain by a common soldier, who, as he plunged his sword into his breast, exclaimed,—"This is a sword which you yourself have made;" for Marius had risen from a blacksmith's forge to the imperial crown. And in the same way the man who resists the Divine Will very justly hears the taunt,—"This is the sword which you yourself have made. You stab yourself with your own weapon, that is to say, WITH YOUR OWN WILL." There is a reason underneath, says Cæsarius, why the will is so prone to sin; for the Devil has two agents more wicked even than himself,—the Flesh and the World,—and by these the will is urged on. The Flesh lusts, the Devil inflames lust, and the World interposes itself, so that when lusts are kindled they may not be extinguished. Many are the sins which spring from the Flesh. Manifold are the baits which the World presents. Numberless are the wiles which the Devil employs. And so that is fulfilled which was formerly shown to Jeremias the prophet,—"Seest thou not what they do in the cities of Juda, and in the streets of Jerusalem? The children gather wood, and the fathers kindle the fire, and the women knead the dough, to make cakes to the queen of heaven, and to offer libations to strange gods, and to provoke me to anger." (*Jer.* VII. 17, 18.) And for whom are these cakes kneaded? For the queen of heaven, or the moon; for the sun is the king of heaven; and the human will is very like the moon, for it delights in continual changes. In honour of this queen cakes are made. The Flesh, like a loving child, supplies faggots of wood, that is to say, lusts; and the Devil, the father of pride, stirs the fire. Vanity, its mother, presents a lump composed of various ingredients; she heaps in snares, beguiling words, soft invitations to sin and pleasures; and so a delicious cake is made, and a noble sacrifice is prepared,—not for God, but for one's own will.

4. S. Augustine, in his exposition of the hundredth Psalm, most beautifully sets before us this perverseness of the human will as follows:—"The heart of a man who wisheth not anything contrary to anything that God wisheth is called straight. Attend. Some one prayeth that something may not happen; he prayeth, and it is not hindered. Let him ask as much as he can; but something happeneth contrary to his own will; let him submit himself to the Will of God, let him not resist the Great Will. For our Lord Himself thus explaineth it, showing our weakness in Himself, when He was about to suffer, saying,—'My Soul is sorrowful even unto death.' But what were those words save the sound of our weakness? Many as yet

weak are saddened by coming death; but let them have a straight heart; let them avoid death as far as they can; but if they cannot, let them say what our Lord Himself said, not on His Own account, but on ours. For what said He?—'O My Father, if it be possible, let this cup pass from me.' Behold, thou hast the *human will* expressed; now see the *righteous heart*—'Nevertheless, not as I will, but as Thou, Father, wilt.' If, therefore, the righteous heart followeth God, the crooked heart resisteth God. Suppose something untoward happeneth to him, he crieth out,—'God, what have I done unto Thee? What sin have I committed?' He wisheth himself to appear just; God unjust. What is so crooked as this? It is not enough that thou art crooked thyself; thou must think thy rule crooked also. Reform thyself, and thou findest Him straight in departing from Whom thou hast made thyself crooked. He doeth justly, thou unjustly; and for this reason thou art perverse, since thou callest man just, and God unjust. What man dost thou call just? Thyself. For when thou sayest—'What have I done unto Thee?' thou thinkest thyself just. But let God answer thee,—'Thou speakest truth; thou hast done nothing to Me; thou hast done all things unto thyself; for if thou hadst done anything for Me, thou wouldest have done good; for whatever is done well is done unto Me, because it is done according to My commandment. But whatever of evil is done, is done unto thee, not Me; for the wicked man doth nothing except for his own sake, since it is not what

I command.'" And the same most holy bishop (*In Ps.* cxxiv. 2) speaks again of this perversity of will as follows,—"'Therefore God is good unto Israel.' But unto whom? 'Even unto such as are of a clean heart.' Who are of a clean heart? They who do not censure God; who direct their own will by the Will of God, and do not endeavour to bend the Will of God into conformity with their own will. It is a short commandment, that man make straight his heart. Dost thou wish to have thy heart straight? Do thou do what God willeth; do not wish God to do that which thou dost will. * * * They who are right in heart, and who follow the Will of God, not their own will, reflect upon this. But they who wish to follow God, allow Him to go before, and themselves to follow; not themselves to go before, and Him to follow. And in all things they find Him good, whether chastening, or consoling, or exercising, or crowning, or cleansing, or enlightening, as the Apostle saith,—'We know that to them that love God, all things work together unto good.'" (*Rom.* viii. 28.)

And worthy offspring of the eagle are such as these, who, with steadfast eye, gaze upon the sun, and who earnestly incline their own will to the Divine! But far different is it with those who often dispute with God. At one time the severity of the weather displeases them; at another, a storm of rain. Sometimes they complain that it is too cold; at other times, that it is too hot. One while God does not give them enough for their wants; at another time He permits this or that wicked man to be exalted; while at another He does not punish their enemies, as it seems to them that they deserve to be punished. Thus, they are perpetually making excuses, and are constantly full of complaints. God does nothing of which they entirely approve. This is that crooked heart; this is that will of one's own, about which S. Bernard must also be heard after S. Augustine.

5. "One's own will," says S. Bernard (*Serm. 71, in Cant.*), "is a great evil; for by this it comes to pass that your blessings are no blessings to you, because He Who feeds among the lilies will taste nothing at all which is polluted by contact with one's own will." And in another place (*Serm. 2, de Resur. Dom.*) :— "But all such evils of a similar and dissimilar kind spring from the single root of one's own will; for this has two blood-thirsty, insatiable daughters, who cry out, 'Give us more, give us more;' since never is the soul satiated with vanity, nor the body with pleasure, as it is written (*Eccles.* 1. 8)—'The eye is not filled with seeing, neither is the ear filled with hearing.' Fly this blood-thirsty one, and you have forsaken all, for she draws all things to herself! Throw her down, and how manifold a yoke have you cast away! Man's own will, subverting the heart, and closing the eyes of reason, is an unquiet evil, which, ever pressing on the spirit, devises things which should not be thought of." And again (*Serm. Quomodo Voluntas nostra, &c.*) :— "Whence come offences, whence arises confusion, but that we follow our own will, and rashly determine in

our heart what we wish; but in case our purpose happens to be frustrated or hindered, we are immediately ready to give way to impatience, and murmuring, and offence, not reflecting that all things work together for good to those who are called to be Saints according to God's purpose, and that that which seems to us to be chance is the Voice of God pointing out to us His Will." And once more (*De Dupl. Bapt.*):—"Let us beware of our own will, therefore, as we should of a most poisonous and mischievous viper, which is able by itself to destroy our souls."

John the Abbot, when he was very near death, was asked, as Cassian testifies (*Instit.* v. 28), by those who stood round his bed, to give them some short piece of advice as a parting bequest. Whereupon he said, with a sigh,—"I never did my own will, and never taught anyone to do what I had not first done myself." But there are few such men as this now-a-days; scarcely one out of a hundred thousand. But countless is the number of those who, when dying, might rather say,— "As far as I was able, I have lived for my own gratification. I have yielded myself entirely to my own will. I have taught much, and given many precepts which I myself have not performed." That most excellent old man, Pimenius, replied to one who asked him in what way devils fought against us,—"Devils do not fight much with us, because we do their wills; but our wills become devils to us, and harass us. And this is illustrated by the following apologue:—The trees on Mount Lebanon conversed together, and said,

'How large and high we are, and yet we are cut down by a small piece of iron; and, what is worse, the weapons with which the mischief is done to us are taken from ourselves; for, to enable the iron axe-head to wound us, it receives its handle from ourselves.' And such a tree is man. The instigation of the devil is the iron, and the human will is the handle."

And how much better preacher was Job on the dunghill than Adam in Paradise! "As it hath pleased the Lord, so is it done," said the former. "I heard Thy Voice, and hid myself," said the latter.

CHAPTER III

IN WHAT WAY MAN'S OWN WILL IS TO BE BROUGHT INTO SUBJECTION TO THE DIVINE IN ALL KINDS OF ADVERSITY

THE will neither of an Angel nor a man can be good, unless it is in union with the Divine Will; but the greater the harmony is, the better and more perfect it will be; and the less it is, so much the worse and more miserable. The sole Will of God is the measure and rule of all wills in heaven and earth; nor can any will ever be called right, unless it is directed according to this standard.

1. When the Psalmist so frequently praises *the right in heart,* S. Augustine very learnedly, and very appositely to our present subject, explains this rectitude of heart, and says (*In Ps.* xxxii. Exp. 2, 1),—"Ye see how many dispute against God, how many are displeased with His works. For when He would do contrary to the will of men, because He is the Lord, and knoweth what He doth, and regardeth not so much our will as our benefit; they who would have rather their own will to be fulfilled than God's, would bend God to their will, not make right their will unto God. 'Praise,' saith he, 'becometh the upright.' Who are

the upright? They who direct their heart according to the Will of God, and whom, if human frailty disturb them, Divine Justice consoleth. For, although in their mortal heart they may privately wish something which may suit their own immediate case or interest, or their present necessity, yet when they have understood and learned that God willeth otherwise, they prefer the Will of the Better to their own will, the Will of the Omnipotent to the will of the weak, the Will of God to the will of man; for, far as God differs from man, so far the Will of God from the will of man. To have a proper will, it is difficult that this should not happen to thee: but think straightway Who is above thee; think of Him above thee, thyself below Him; Him the Creator, thyself the creature; Him the Lord, thyself the servant; Him Omnipotent, thyself weak; correcting thyself, submitting to His Will, and saying,—'Nevertheless, not as I will, but as Thou wilt.'

"Wherein art thou severed from God who now willest that which God willeth? Then shalt thou be upright, and praise shall become thee, for praise becometh the upright; but if thou art crooked, thou praisest God when it is well with thee, blasphemest when it is ill. Which ill, indeed, if it be just, is not ill; but just it is, since it is done by Him Who can do nothing unjust. And so thou wilt be a foolish boy in the house of thy Father, loving thy Father if he fondle thee, and hating Him when He scourgeth thee; as if He were not, both when fondling and when scourging, preparing for thee the inheritance. But see how praise becometh the upright. Hear the voice of the upright praising from another Psalm (*Ps.* XXXIII. 2) :—'I will bless the Lord at all times, His praise shall be always in my mouth.' What is 'at all times?' That is always. And what is 'I will bless?' That is, 'His praise shall be in my mouth.' At all times and always, whether in prosperity, or in adversity; for if in prosperity, and not in adversity, how *at all times?* How always? And we have heard many such words from many. When any good fortune befalls them they exult, they rejoice, they sing to God, they praise God; nor are they to be disapproved, nay, we must rejoice in them; for many praise Him not even then. But they who have now begun to praise God, on account of their prosperity, must be taught to acknowledge their Father also when scourging them, and not to murmur against His Hand when He corrects them, lest, remaining ever perverse, they deserve to be disinherited; so that being now made upright (what is upright? so that nothing which God doth displease them), they may be able to praise God even in adversity, and to say, 'The Lord gave, and the Lord hath taken away; as it hath pleased the Lord so is it done; blessed be the Name of the Lord.' To such upright, praise is becoming, not to them that will first praise, and afterwards blame. Learn to give thanks unto God both in prosperity and in tribulation. Learn to have in thy *heart* what every man hath on his *tongue:—The Will of God be done.* The common speech of the people is mostly saving doctrine. Who saith not daily,—*What God willeth that let Him do?"*

2. This beautiful dissertation of S. Augustine in a wonderful way both explains and confirms the entire doctrine concerning the Divine Will, which, on this account, should have the greater claim on our attention, since the holiest and wisest of men have ever desired that it should be understood as thoroughly as possible by all, more particularly since the entire Christian life hinges on it. But I cannot yet leave Augustine, that clearest of writers, whose words are quite worthy of being quoted as they stand. This saintly Bishop of Hippo, then, points out in the following words (*In Ps.* xxxvi. 16) in what way, even in adversity, we must not depart a hair's breadth from the Divine Will:—"As I have said, those are OF A RIGHT HEART who follow in this life the Will of God. The Will of God is sometimes that thou shouldest be whole, sometimes that thou shouldest be sick. If when thou art whole God's Will be sweet, and when thou art sick God's Will be bitter; thou art not of a right heart. Wherefore? Because thou wilt not make right thy will according to God's Will, but wilt bend God's Will to thine. That is right, but thou art crooked; thy will must be made right to That, not That made crooked to thee; and thou wilt have a right heart. Is it well with thee in this world? God be blessed Who comforteth thee. Doth it go hardly with thee? God be blessed, because He chasteneth and proveth thee;

and so wilt thou be of a right heart, saying,—'I will bless the Lord at all times; His praise shall be always in my mouth.'"

And not only did S. Augustine, the Bishop of Hippo, teach this doctrine, but David also, the King of Israel, in a remarkable way, both by precept and example. For when he was flying from his rebellious son Absalom, and the priests had taken up the Ark of the Covenant as a defence in their flight, he ordered it to be carried back into the city, and said,—"If I shall find grace in the sight of the Lord, He will bring me again, and He will shew me it, and His tabernacle. But if He shall say to me: 'Thou pleasest me not:' I am ready, *let Him do that which is good before Him.*" (*2 Kings* xv. 25, 26.) See how that once powerful king was self-conscious and composed even in his miserable flight, and extremity of trouble, and with what earnest gaze he looked towards the Divine Will! "I shall return," he says, "if it pleases God; but if He thus say, thou pleasest Me not, *let Him do that which is good before Him.*"

If, Christian friends, we were as willing to embrace this doctrine with our understanding and reason, as we easily might, there would scarcely be any further difficulty in enduring misfortunes; nor would any evil of such huge proportions press upon us, but we might bear it calmly and readily. Our Lord, before His Passion, spoke words in the Garden of Gethsemani about the Will of His Father and His Own, which prove that there is nothing which more completely nerves the soul to endure calamities of any kind than the union of the human will with the Divine. How manifest was this in our Lord Himself! Before His prayer He was fearful, sad, and pale; He trembled at and shrank from the shadow of approaching death. But after His prayer, after so great reverence had been shown to His Father's Will, He exclaimed, as if His strength were renewed,—"Rise, let us go." (*Matt.* xxvi. 46.) Let us meet our enemies of our own accord and welcome them: let us make an end of this bloody tragedy! And here also S. Augustine (*In Ps.* xxxii. Exp. 2, 2) remarks with great beauty: —"Whereupon Christ having put on Man, and proposing a rule to us, teaching us to live, and granting us to live, showed also man's private will; whereby he figured both His Own and ours, because He is our Head, and we, as ye know, belong to Him as real members. 'Father,' saith He, 'if it be possible, *let this Chalice pass from Me.*' This was the human will, wishing something proper to itself, and, as it were, private. But because He willed man to be right in heart, that whatever in him was somewhat crooked, He might make straight to Him Who is ever Right, 'Nevertheless,' saith He, '*not as I will, but as Thou wilt.*' He showed, as it were, man's proper will; He showed thee, and corrected thee. Behold, saith He, Thyself in Me; for Thou also canst will something proper to Thyself, though God will otherwise."

3. S. Catherine of Siena says of herself,—"Christ has instructed me that I should prepare for myself a

THE HUMAN WILL WITH THE DIVINE

secret chamber within myself." And what kind of chamber is that? *The union of the human will with the Divine.* At the first entrance it seems to be but a narrow dwelling-place; but he who desires to accustom himself to it will find out at length that it is larger than heaven, and more secure even than the best fortified camp; for here no troubles can ever force an entrance. This is an asylum of perfect safety from every calamity. The spirits neither of the upper or lower world are able to harm him who in all things keeps his own will in harmony with the Divine. This is his single law—As GOD WILLS, SO LET HIM DO. Beautifully does S. Augustine say (*In Ps.* LXI. 11):— "There cometh my pain, there will come my rest also; there cometh my tribulation, there will come my cleansing also. For doth gold glitter in the furnace of the refiner? In a necklace it will glitter; in an ornament it will glitter. Let it suffer, however, the furnace, in order that being cleansed from dross it may come into light. This is the furnace, there is the chaff, there gold, there fire; into this bloweth the refiner: in the furnace burneth the chaff, and the gold is cleansed: the one into ashes is turned, of dross the other is cleansed. The furnace is the world, the chaff unjust men, the gold just men; the fire tribulation, the re-finer God. That, therefore, which the refiner willeth, I do. Wherever the Maker setteth me, I endure it. I am commanded to endure; He knoweth how to cleanse. Though there burn the chaff to set me on fire, and as if to consume me; that into ashes is burned;

I of dross am cleansed. Wherefore? Because to God shall my soul be made subject."

Lo! true subjection of the human will to the Divine is the origin of every blessing. Most rightly did that pious author (Luiz of Granada) say,—"There is no greater sacrifice, and none more pleasing to God, than in every tribulation to conform oneself to the Good pleasure of the Divine Will."

And here that illustrious patriarch Abraham is very greatly to be praised; for, in order to make it known to the whole world that he did everything according to the command of the Divine Will, God, as though sometimes changing His Will, exercised him first with one command, then with another, and these to all appearance contradictory, and manifestly severe. But Abraham ever showed himself perfectly obedient to every indication of the Divine Will; and this one thing he endeavoured to do with all his might, to yield his whole self, and all that belonged to him, as cheerfully as possible to the one and only Will of God.

The Jews observe that Abraham was severely tried ten times, as to whether he would constantly will that which God willed. Let me enumerate the different trials:—

(1.) He is commanded to leave his country and kindred, and go into a strange land.

(2.) On account of scarcity of corn he is again driven into Egypt as a wanderer.

(3.) In Egypt he runs the risk of his life with Pharao the king: his wife also imperils her chastity, and is parted from her husband.

(4.) On account of the constant quarrels of the servants, he separates from Lot, whom he loved most tenderly as a son.

(5.) In order to deliver Lot, when he had been taken prisoner in war, he arms his servants against the four kings.

(6.) He is constrained, at the earnest desire of Sara, to cast out from his house Agar, his faithful servant and concubine.

(7.) He is commanded to be circumcised when now an old man.

(8.) Abimelech, King of Gerara, takes his wife again.

(9.) A second time he is commanded to drive away from his house Agar, with her son Ismael.

(10.) He is told to slay, with his own hand, his only and most beloved son Isaac, who had been miraculously born, and who had been brought up in hope of fulfilling the promise of a posterity.

What an accumulation of calamities! besides many others, not less bitter, although not so well known. And yet Abraham remained Abraham; that is to say, like himself, and a most constant observer of the Divine Will. He thoroughly understood that the Divine Will was the greatest alleviation of all his miseries.

And here it is to be observed that Mount Moriah, on which it was appointed that Isaac should be of-

fered as a victim to God, has passed into a proverb,—
"Whereupon even to this day it is said: In the mountain the Lord will see." (*Gen.* XXII. 14.) And this
hill "the Lord will see" must be climbed by all who are
in affliction. Let all who are in trouble and adversity
assure themselves that God from all eternity foresaw
all those things which are happening to them, and
also decreed that they should be done at the very time
in which they are done; and that this same Divine
Providence will always be ready to help them and
theirs.

4. Let this example teach us, moreover, that deaths
and calamities of all kinds are sent from God. For
as God sends war upon that province, and pestilence
upon this, so He sends to one man gout, to another
disease in the kidneys, and to a third fever; but this
war and that pestilence, this gout or disease in the
kidneys, or fever, are sent by God and the Divine
Will. This is a sure and certain fact. But how is
this or that province to conduct itself in reference to
the war or pestilence? And how are men to behave
in reference to their diseases? Have they the right
not to will that which God wills? No, they have not.
But is there, then, no opportunity for defence? Only
if God allows it. What did Abraham do when about
to sacrifice Isaac on Mount Moriah? He looked round
and saw a ram caught in a thicket; and he was offered
up in place of Isaac. And, in the same way, let the
kingdom which is scourged with war, the province
infected with pestilence, or the man who is harassed

with gout, look round for a lawful remedy, and employ it to avert the war, to remove the pestilence, to alleviate the gout.

If God wills that the one should be averted, the next removed, and the other mitigated, He will secretly send a ram; that is to say, He will supply the means either of alleviation, or of restoring things to their former condition. But if there is no remedy, or if it is used without success, it is then perfectly clear that God wills that Isaac should be sacrificed, that the kingdom should be devastated by war, that the province should be wasted by the pestilence, and that the man should be tortured by the gout. And the way of reasoning is the same in reference to poverty, and contempt, and all other calamities and miseries. So that when God points out a way of relief, Isaac is set free; but if not, he must be slain. And therefore in all such things let the human will submit itself with perfect resignation to the Divine.

S. Remigius, Bishop of Reims, foresaw that there would be great scarcity of corn the next year; and accordingly he collected a large supply of grain for the support of the people. But some of the very persons for whose benefit the holy man had resolved to do this were men of drunken and reckless habits, who said over their cups,—"What is our old Jubilee about? (for he had already been a priest for more than fifty years). What does he intend to do? Is he going to build a new city? What do so many heaps of corn mean? He seems to wish to monopolize the market.

Come and let us lay a trap for the old man, and play off a trick upon him." It was easy enough to stimulate men whose evil feelings were roused, and who were already hurrying on too fast. And so these madmen rushed headlong from the house, and one of them exclaimed, while applying a lighted torch to the measures of corn,—"Let us see how fast hungry Vulcan will devour Ceres!" This act of wanton daring was soon told to Remigius the Bishop, and he at once mounted his horse, and hastened with all speed to the burning heaps of corn. But when he arrived the flames had already forced their way through the whole of the wheat, and could not be extinguished by any amount of labour. And what could the sorrowful Bishop now do? Should he kill himself with grief, and either give way to wild lamentations, or utter all kinds of curses against the doers of the mischief? He did this,—he dismounted from his horse, and, because it was winter, he approached as close as he could to the conflagration, as if to warm himself, remarking at the same time,—"A fire is always pleasant, particularly to an old man." Behold, then, the soul of a perfect man, entirely devoted to the Divine Will, and therefore enjoying supreme tranquillity in every condition of life! He would have wished indeed, as far as lay in his power, to check the fire which had broken out, but because there were no means or possibility of subduing the flames which still continued to spread, he committed what had happened entirely to the Divine Will, and with unruffled brow repeated those words of Job,—"The Lord gave, and the Lord hath taken away: blessed be the name of the Lord." (*Job* I. 21.)

And in the same way must we act under all other circumstances. When some evil is imminent or already present, and we are not able to check it by lawful means, let us say from the bottom of our soul,— "THE WILL OF GOD BE DONE!" Let Isaac be sacrificed, if the ram is not sent in his stead. Let my son be slain, if God so commands. Perish my house, perish my goods, perish everything, *if only the Will of God be done.*

5. One who plays upon the harp tightens or loosens the strings until they give the proper sound; and so it is necessary that the man who desires to yield himself entirely to the Will of God should exercise, and keep under, and bind his own will until it is reduced to obedience, and should teach it, moreover, how it conduces to all happiness, if it conforms itself in all things to the Divine Will, as blessed David exclaims,—"Shall not my soul be subject to God? for from Him is my salvation." (*Ps.* LXI. 2.) The literal translation of this verse from the Hebrew is,—"Yet shall my soul keep silence to God, for from Him is my salvation." And this exactly harmonizes with my meaning; for this was the intention of King David,—"Whatever befalls me, whether it be prosperous or adverse, I still resist not the Divine Will; I do not try to disturb the Ordinances of God. Even if things turn out never so unpropitiously, yet I do not murmur. I keep si-

lence before every Permission of God, being perfectly contented at all times with the Divine disposal of events. Afflictions of all kinds may be mitigated by being borne with calmness."

Whoever, then, imitates this wisest of kings (and it will be easy enough for any one to do so, if he only desires it) will endure all kinds of adversity and calamity with quiet and unruffled mind. Never will so much as a single word escape him, as if he complained of his troubles being too frequent and too grievous. The Divine Will will be to him an alleviation of all distresses. Nor can he ever be so completely overwhelmed with misery as not to be able to exclaim with that most devout writer (THOMAS À KEMPIS, l. III. 50) :—"Holy Father, thus hast Thou ordained, and thus hast Thou willed; and this is done as Thou hast commanded. Nothing is done on earth without Thy Counsel and Providence, and without cause. Behold, O beloved Father, I am in Thy Hands; I bend beneath the rod of Thy correction! Strike my back and my neck that I may bend my crookedness TO THY WILL; that I may walk according to all Thy commandments, and may above all things ever seek for the Will of Thy Good-pleasure."

And they who refuse this discipline will always be unhappy, "ever learning, and never attaining to the knowledge of the Truth." (2 *Tim.* III. 7.) But they who centre all their energies in knowing the Will of God, and following it, will endure adversity of all kinds not merely with patience, but with joyfulness and thanksgiving. Well has that illustrious preacher said (John Tauler) :—"Esteem every day to be lost in which you have not, for the love of God, *broken your own will*."

CHAPTER IV

A MOST REMARKABLE INSTANCE OF A MAN WHO REFUSED TO SUBMIT HIS OWN WILL TO THE DIVINE

THE Prophet Jonas was a striking example of a man who with great reluctance delayed to yield himself to the control of the Will of God, and was on that account afflicted for so long and in such various ways, until he submitted his entire will to the Divine.

1. Let us hear what command the Divine Will gave to Jonas. "Arise, and go to Ninive." (*Jonas* 1. 2.) This was the first part of the command. The second was—"And preach in it." (Ver. 2.) Jonas arose indeed, and left the place where he was, but he went not to Ninive. He "rose up to flee into Tharsis from the Face of the Lord." (Ver. 3.) And here was a two-fold act of disobedience—not merely not to preach in the city in which he was bidden, but not so much as to go to it. Quickly, however, did God follow him as an Avenger, and fought with wind and sea, and every inclemency of the sky, against the rebellious will of Jonas. "The Lord sent a great wind into the sea: and a great tempest was raised in the sea, and the ship was in danger to be broken." (Ver. 4.) But not even yet did the fugitive perceive that the tempest was closing

around him, for "Jonas went down into the inner part of the ship, and fell into a deep sleep." (Ver. 5.) Nothing however is worse, nothing is more perilous than false security; and so the angry sea grew rougher and rougher, and the clouds which gathered on all sides obscured the light of day. The sailors hurried trembling to their duties; they furled the sails before the tempest, and threw out into the sea whatever seemed to burden the ship. But when the storm still continued, they determined to have recourse to lots,— "And the lot fell upon Jonas." (Ver. 7.) When, therefore, they questioned him, he replied,—"I am a Hebrew, and I fear the Lord the God of heaven, who made both the sea and the dry land." (Ver. 9.) But is it so, Jonas? Do you really fear God? Then why do you not obey the Will of God? Many people speak in this way. "We fear God," they say, but all the while they neglect the Will of God. But this, my good friends, is not to fear God—to cry out against His Will. Nor would the sea be quieted by these words of Jonas, but raging more and more, it increased in fury, and caused huge mountains of waves to roll against the ship. And so Jonas is at last thrown out into the sea; but he first confessed his sin, saying,—"I know that for my sake this great tempest is upon you." (Ver. 12.) How honestly and truthfully have you spoken, Jonas! Your own will stirred up all this rage of the sky, this battle of the winds, this wondrous disturbance of the stormy sea; it is the sole cause of all this! You were commanded to go to Ninive, not to Tharsis. But

a master is waiting for you in the sea who will teach
you to will, and to will not, the same as God. "And
they took Jonas, and cast him into the sea, and the sea
ceased from raging. (Ver. 15.) Now the Lord prepared a great fish to swallow up Jonas." (Chap. II, 1.)
Such are the fruits of following one's own will! In
this way must we be taught to receive the easy yoke
of the Divine Will. And thus Jonas, who was now
shut up in the living body of a whale, and who went
down almost to the lowest depths, while balancing un-
certainly between the living and the dead, exclaimed,
—"When my soul was in distress within me, I remembered the Lord." (Chap. 11. 8.) Yes, at length
we come to ourselves, and begin TO WILL that which
for a long time we resolutely willed not. And now,
Jonas, are you willing to go to Ninive? I am willing
to go. Are you willing to preach to the Ninivites? I
will preach to them. Are you willing to perform the
vows which you made in the belly of this monster?
I will perform them. "And the Lord spoke to the
fish: and it vomited out Jonas upon the dry land."
(Chap. 11. 11.) The former commands of the Divine
Will are then repeated:—"Arise, go to Ninive, the
great city: and preach in it the preaching that I bid
thee. And Jonas arose, and went to Ninive, according to the word of the Lord." (Chap. 111, 2, 3.)
Jonas has now cast out his own will; he now altogether
wills that which God wills; he now hastens with all his
might to the place whither he was at first commanded
to go; he now lifts up his voice, and exhorts the people

to repentance; he now submits himself to, and obeys, the Divine commands. Would that he may continue to do this to the end, and not return to his own will.

2. Alas! for the fickleness and inconstancy of the human will! That which a moment ago was God's, now begins to be his own again! "And Jonas was exceedingly troubled, and was angry." (Chap. IV. I.) And here are the worst signs of man's own will again contending with the Divine. He who brings his own will into harmony with the Divine is never so far disturbed by troubles as to break forth into rage and vent his indignation against God. And what is it, I pray you, Jonas, which again drives your will, so lately in perfect harmony with the Divine Will, into such a state of disagreement with it? Hear the fresh cause of variance:—"Is not this what I said," he exclaimed, "when I was yet in my own country? therefore I went before to flee into Tharsis: for I know that Thou art a gracious and a merciful God, patient, and of much compassion, and easy to forgive evil." (Chap. IV. 2.) This, then, is the point of variance between the Will of God and that of Jonas. God willed to spare the Ninivites; Jonas willed that they should be punished; and he says that his soul had forewarned him that it was vain for him to utter threats, since the execution of vengeance would not follow upon them, for that God was easily appeased. It seemed, then, that nothing was left but to pray to God,—"And now, O Lord, I beseech Thee take my life from me: for it is better for me to die than to live." (Chap. IV. 3.) It may be

better for you, Jonas, but perhaps *not so pleasing to God.* But your own will does not take this into account; it thinks only of what is pleasing to itself; but whether this pleases God or not, it has little care. "Then Jonas went out of the city, and sat toward the east side of the city: and he made himself a booth there, and he sat under it in the shadow, till he might see what would befall the city." (Chap. IV. 5.) And not even yet is his will at rest. He leaves the city, that he might the more conveniently behold its destruction. But why does Jonas leave it? Why does he not continue to exhort the citizens to lasting penitence? What need is there of his making for himself a new habitation with a creeping plant? A thousand houses in the city would have received the welcome preacher of penitence. But this did not please his will, for which not only the largest cities, but the world itself, are sometimes too narrow. Jonas thought that immediately after he had left the city fire would be rained from heaven, and the city be utterly overthrown; for thus God had commanded the prophet to threaten,— "Yet forty days, and Ninive shall be destroyed." (Chap. III. 4.) And for this reason Jonas places himself in safety, and quietly waits to see whether God will give any effect to His threatenings; or whether he will so quickly blot out all the iniquity that had been committed, and spare that most abandoned city. For a long time he waited to see the expected sight from heaven; and when the sky continued calm, and no flames flashed from it, or stones burst forth from it;

when vengeance seemed entirely to sleep; when the pleasure also which he derived from his ivy began to fade; when the sun struck fiercely upon his head; and when the great heat caused him to faint, then at last, Jonas, bearing so great patience of God with utter impatience, and growing very angry, "desired for his soul that he might die, and said: It is better for me to die than to live." (Chap. IV. 8.) And when he was asked whether he thought this anger right, he presumptuously replied, "I am angry with reason even unto death." (Chap. IV. 9.) Consider, I pray you, the cause of such impotent rage. Jonas poured out so much bitterness, and well-nigh fainted for grief, "because it had not fallen out to him as he imagined." (1 *Mach.* VI. 8.)

O Jonas, what implicit faith does your will exhibit, but chiefly in itself and its own instincts! Why are you so troubled at the Divine pity and patience? Do you not know that it is God's property to pity and spare? Do you wish to invest Him with the impatience of man, so that when He is injured He should strike at once; and when provoked, should immediately send forth His thunderbolts? This savours of man's nature, and not of the Divine. Such is our disposition, that when scarcely touched we assail the person who touches us with blows and kicks; when hardly injured at all, we strike with the most passionate blows; for nothing, in truth, are we better prepared than for vengeance. We run, or rather we fly, when we are going to punish. But not such is God.

"The Lord is gracious and merciful, long-suffering, and of great goodness. The Lord is sweet to all: and His tender mercies are over all His works." (*Ps.* CXLIV. 9.) "Neither will God have a soul to perish, but recalleth, meaning that he that is cast off should not altogether perish." (2 *Kings* XIV. 14.) But why, O Jonas, do you grieve so much that your palace of ivy is destroyed by a worm? You neither taught the worm to gnaw, nor the ivy to grow. The Lord gave it to you, and the Lord has taken it away from you; why then do you show your wrath against Him? But if the destruction of that shading ivy is a matter of such grief to you, should not the overthrow of a city, which is as large as a kingdom, cause you sorrow? And therefore, my good Jonas, conform your own will entirely to the Divine Will. Has the ivy perished? You will that it should have perished. Is Ninive preserved? You also will that it should be preserved. Nor is there any further reason why you should grieve, except on account of your own will not having been brought into immediate subjection to the Divine.

3. Behold, Christians, what is the effect of being under the influence of one's own judgment and will, and into how great errors this one thing draws even the saintliest men! We can effect nothing so long as we have not entirely subdued our own will. While this rises up and opposes the Divine Will, no gifts, or vows, or prayers, or sacrifices are acceptable to God. Pleasing to God is fasting, pleasing are alms, pleasing is earnestness in prayer, *but only so far as each is in*

harmony with the Divine Will. One's own will, indeed, knows how to be liberal in offerings of money, to set apart times for fasting, to have recourse to prayer; but all these acts are utterly hateful to God if they are not conformed to the Divine Will. And so God, when forbidding fasts (wonderful indeed to relate) and sacrifices, and other things acceptable to Himself, says,—"Do not fast as you have done until this day." (*Isaias* LVIII. 4.) And what, then, was the fault of this fast of the Jews? It savoured too much of their own will. "Behold in the day of your fast your own will is found, and you exact of all your debtors." (Ver. 3.) I love the fast, but I hate man's own will, which spoils the fast. If any one sets before a man who dislikes onions a dish of the most costly food, but which tastes of garlic, it will neither please him, nor stimulate the jaded stomach. It will excite a nausea, and not a desire for food. And in the same way fasting is like food of delicate flavour, and is commended by the angel,—"Prayer is good with fasting." (*Tobias* XII. 8.) But if the onion and garlic of one's own will are mingled with it, then away with it, for this food from the heavenly table is turned to loathing. S. Chrysostom says,—"He who sins and fasts does not fast for the glory of God, nor humble himself, but spares his substance." Man's own will defiles and destroys everything.

And this constitutes the extreme misery of those who are cast down to hell, that they rage with such perversity of will, that throughout all eternity it will never be in harmony with the Divine Will. The damned will never will that which God wills, nor will they be *able* to will it. S. Augustine says with great force:—"Such will be their will, that they will ever have within themselves the punishment of their wick-edness, but will never be able to entertain a single feeling of goodness; for as those who shall reign with Christ will have no traces of evil will left in them, so those who shall be condemned to the punishment of eternal fire with the devil and his angels, as they have no period of rest remaining, will also be incapable of having a good will." And what could there be more full of terror than hell, even if there were in it only this single punishment,—to be for all eternity utterly alienated from the most holy Will of God, *and never to be able to be brought into harmony with it?* There-fore, O my God, so that I may forsake my own will, teach me to do Thy Will!

CHAPTER V

WHAT THINGS CHIEFLY STRENGTHEN THE PERVERSITY OF ONE'S OWN WILL

AMONGST those grievous sins with which our Lord upbraids the city of Jerusalem is this,—"Jerusalem, Jerusalem, thou that killest the prophets, and stonest them that are sent unto thee, how often would I have gathered together thy children as the hen doth gather her chickens under her wings, *and thou wouldest not.*" (*Matt.* XXIII. 37.) See the obstinacy of man's own will—the origin of all sins! I *willed,* says God, but you *willed not.*

The Abbot Pastor used to say (*Doroth.* Serm. 5.)—"Our own will is an iron wall, shutting us out, and separating us from God. 'And thou wouldest not.' Hence those tears!" And in the same way S. Augustine says (*Conf.* VIII. 5)—"I sighed, being bound, not with the iron of others, *but with my own iron will.* My 'TO WILL' was holding me like an enemy, and had forged a chain for me, and had bound me."

But the three following things wonderfully strengthen one's own will.

1. *Evil custom.* S. Augustine (*Conf.* VIII. 5, 11) explains this when he says,—"From a perverse will,

in sooth, lust is formed, and while obedience is yielded to lust, custom is formed; and when no resistance is offered to custom, necessity is formed; and by means of these links, woven one into the other (whence I called them a 'chain') a hard slavery held me fast bound. But the new will which had begun to arise in me, that I might worship Thee freely, O my God, and desire to enjoy Thee, was not as yet capable of overcoming that former will, which had become so strong by habit. And so my two wills, one the old, and the other the new, the former carnal, the latter spiritual, were at war between themselves, and by their discord caused distraction to my mind; and the worse will, which was habitual to me, had more power over me than the better, to which I was not accustomed."

And so, when faults turn into *habits,* no further room is left for remedy. For this is the characteristic of all sins, that, unless they are ejected as soon as possible, they are seldom, and only with difficulty, expelled when they have acquired strength. S. Gregory (*Mor.* IV. 25) says with truth,—"When a sin has become *habitual,* the soul resists it the more feebly, even if it desire to do so, because it is fastened to the mind by as many chains, as it is bound by the recurrence of evil habit." It is easy to restrain those who are of tender years, but hard those who have grown old in a habit. "Woe to the pot whose rust is in it, and its rust is not gone out of it!" (*Ezech.* XXIV. 6.) "Over hard, indeed, and undesirable does sinful habit make the way of virtue." (S. JEROME, *Ep.* 14 *ad celant.*)

Most truly also does S. Chrysostom say (*Hom.* VII. *in* I *Cor.*),—"There is nothing so firmly established among human things as the tyranny of an inveterate habit." And so S. Augustine (*Serm.* XIV. *de Verb Dom.*) admonishes us, and says,—"Let the sinner revive as soon as possible; let him not descend into the depth of the sepulchre; let him not lay above himself the weight of habit."

Once upon a time Plato severely rebuked a young man who was playing with dice; whereupon the youth said sharply to his rebuker,—"What trifling things you find fault with!" But Plato immediately replied, —"That is not trifling which has become a habit." When the Cretans wish to use the most withering form of cursing, against those whom they violently hate, they pray that they may take pleasure in evil custom; and so, by a kind of wish which does not sound intemperate, they find a most effectual way of gratifying their revenge. For fruitlessly to desire something, and continually to dwell on the thought of it, is a kind of pleasure which is but one step removed from destruction.

2. The second thing which exceedingly strengthens one's own will is *want of patience*. Such is our impetuosity, for the most part, that, when we do not obtain what we want at a particular time, we are at once driven to impatience, and sometimes even to madness. Yes, such we are; utterly impatient of delay! How often may one hear a man who is destitute of patience say,—"I wish to have it now; I want it instantly; I

cannot wait; I cannot endure to be put off; unless it
is done immediately, I shall be in despair." And so
Saul, the king of Israel, could not wait for Samuel,
even for the one or two short hours which remained;
and therefore his foolish act was charged upon him in
the presence of all the people. (1 *Kings* XIII. 13.)
And in the same way it very often happens with ourselves in our dealings with God, that, if we do not at
once obtain that which we wish to have, we fall from
our resolution, and give way to sorrow and lamentation. Our prayers are very often like that request of
the dancing girl:—"I will that forthwith thou give
me." (*Mark* VI. 25.) And thus we often so far ex-
haust all hope and patience as to rush headlong into
impatience and despair. "Be of good comfort, my
children, cry to the Lord, and He will deliver you out
of the hand of the princes your enemies." (*Baruch*
IV. 21.)

It is a mark of great virtue not to wish that your
desires should be granted at once. Unwearying patience is of the greatest power, for it can bring into
leaf and flower even that barrenest of trees, which has
been tended for three whole years. Hence the following counsel of the Son of Sirach:—"Endure: and
make not haste in the time of clouds. Join thyself to
God, and endure, that thy life may be increased in the
latter end. Take all that shall be brought upon thee:
and in thy sorrow endure, and in thy humiliation keep
patience. Behold the generations of men: and know
ye that no one hath hoped in the Lord, and hath been

confounded. For who hath continued in His commandment, and hath been forsaken? Woe to them that have lost patience. And what will they do, when the Lord shall begin to examine? They that fear the Lord, will prepare their hearts, and in His sight will sanctify their souls." (*Ecclus.* II. 2 and foll.) But man's own will ever strives in a contrary direction, and imperiously demands what it desires, in this way:— "Give me at once; let it be done forthwith; immediately grant it; let there be no delay; and let there be an end to all hesitation." And therefore we stand in constant need of the caution,—"Wait, till we see what end the thing will have." (*Ruth* III, 18.) "If it make any delay wait for it, for it shall surely come, and it shall not be slack." (*Hab.* II. 3.)

While our Lord was hanging on the cross His enemies urged Him in various ways that He might not will to see the end of His sufferings. "If Thou be the Son of God," they say, "come down from the cross." (*Matt.* XXVII. 40.) And well does S. Chrysostom reply,—"On this account He came not down from the Cross, because He was the Son of God. The patience of Christ was waiting till it might be permitted to Him to say,—'IT IS CONSUMMATED.' And that which we see done in the Head we must imitate in the members also. The Will of the Father must be obeyed, even to our latest breath."

And here Ludovicus Blosius speaks so beautifully that I would fain quote what he says in his own words: —"Happy, therefore, is the man," he exclaims, "who, when suffering under trouble and pain, does not seek for a way of escape, but endures them to the end, and to the very last extremity, not even wishing to come down from the Cross, unless God shall release him, and take him down. Happy indeed is he who so descends into the abyss of the Divine Good-pleasure, and so resigns himself to the terrible and secret Judgments of God, as to be ready to remain in pains and afflictions of this sort, not merely for a single week, or a single month, but to the Day of Judgment, or even for eternity; not refusing to undergo the torments of hell itself, if God so will. And this kind of resignation, in truth, far surpasses every other kind. In comparison with this it is nothing to give up even a thousand worlds."

3. The third thing whereby one's own will acquires undue strength is *perpetual fickleness*. It is not enough to go round with the Moon, and to assume first one appearance, and then another; but we change every day, and every hour. One thing pleases us in the morning, and another in the evening. To-day we will; to-morrow we will not. We are never the same, and are inconsistent with ourselves, so wisely do we wander in different paths. Every day we change our plans and wishes. Like clouds we are driven hither and thither by any wind that blows. And this is one of the most common characteristics of our own will that, when it refuses to be bound to that firmest of pillars—the Divine Will—it surrenders itself in vain and transitory things, with which it cannot help un-

dergoing many a change. And through this instability of our own will, which is of such magnitude, we desire indeed to resist our daily vexations; and yet by this very means we often create for ourselves vexation out of vexation, whilst we so anxiously strive to avoid it. Thus it is that we roll the stone of Sisyphus, and fill the pitcher of the Danaides, while we will and will not the same thing, oftentimes in the same hour. Our will, and that which depends upon it, all our saintliness of character, is not an impregnable tower built on the summit of a mountain, or planted on a lofty rock, but a house of mud, which gives way and collapses before every attack. Granted that you are upright, that you begin this or that business well, that you manage this or that affair admirably—and I would not deny it— but how long, and how constantly will you do this? Alas! how easily do we change at the whispering of every wind, and are often cast down in a disgraceful way! We are, in truth, manifold in form, and are at times utterly unlike ourselves; neither do we play the part of one man, but of many.

Free-will, therefore, makes us our own; an evil will makes us the Devil's, a good will God's. "For they," says S. Bernard (*De Grat. et Lib. Arbit.*), "who wish to be their own, that like gods they may know good and evil, become not merely their own, but the Devil's. It is our own will, in truth, which makes us the slaves of the Devil, and not his power. But our will will not be perfect until it is brought into entire subjection to its Creator. Assuredly it is better

for us not to exist at all than to remain our own."
S. Augustine says that the young of eagles go through
the following kind of ordeal:—they are suspended in
the talons of the male bird, and are then exposed to
the full rays of the sun. The one who looks sted-
fastly at the sun is acknowledged as a true offspring,
while the one who is unsteady in his gaze is allowed
to fall. And we vile men of earth are more truly
under the power of the will of God than the eaglets
are in the talons of their parent. We depend on God
more than a ray does on the sun, or heat on fire.
God has more power over us than the potter has over
the clay, and yet from this Sun of ours—the Divine
Will—we wilfully turn away. Are we bidden to forgive an enemy? We refuse to do so. Or, to restrain
our unbridled lust? We are just as unwilling. To
subdue our impotent rage? And this, too, we are unwilling to attempt. To abstain from this or that evil
habit? We are very slow, indeed, in wishing to do
it; or, in other words, we quietly refuse to do it.
O progeny, not of eagles, but of owls, who follow not
the Sun of the Divine Will, but the darkness of their
own will! But hence springs every kind of evil, and
every kind of punishment.

Ludovicus Blosius relates that our Lord once revealed himself to a certain holy Virgin, and said,—"I
desire that you should know that almost all the punishments by which men are afflicted in the world consist
in their own will; for if the will were duly ordered and
conformed to My Will, it would be free from punish-

ment. For although the man who is endowed with this holy and well-ordered will may feel toil and pain, yet, whatever he willingly suffers for love of Me, he endures without punishment as it were; for he bears it with entire readiness, considering and knowing that it is My Will and Permission that he should suffer. In every bodily suffering his mind is free, since his will is in all things conformed to, and united with Mine. And so, when his own will has been laid aside, the soul of that man is tranquil and rejoices in peace."

CHAPTER VI

THAT NOTHING BELONGING TO ONE'S OWN WILL IS TO BE RETAINED, AS WELL IN DIFFICULTIES OF ALL KINDS, AS IN DEATH ITSELF

IN things of trifling importance we yield our will without much difficulty to the Divine Will; but in those which are of greater moment, as, for example, loss of riches, honour, or life, then shifts and excuses occur to us; there are delays and impediments; there is great perversity of our refractory will; and here our own TO WILL, and NOT TO WILL, stand in opposition to God's TO WILL and NOT TO WILL.

But why do we wretched mortals strive in vain? The Divine Will stands, and will for ever stand, like an immovable rock. We shall not draw that to us, but that will draw us to itself. We should laugh if a man, who had fastened his boat to a rock, were to continue pulling at the rope, and fancying that the rock was approaching him, when all the while he himself was drawing nearer and nearer to the rock. And is not our folly greater? since, although bound to that rock of the Divine Will, we desire, by our dragging and struggling, that it should follow us, and not we follow it.

1. There are some who instruct both themselves and others in the Divine Law, and such as these consecrate their understanding indeed to God. But where is their *will*, that most precious of all gifts? This they keep for themselves, making an unequal partition with God. Admirably, in the old time, was one thus accustomed to pray for another:—"May God be gracious to you, and give you all a heart to worship Him, and to do His Will with a great heart, and a willing mind." (2 *Mach.* 2, 3.) They, indeed, worship God with a very narrow heart, and a thoroughly unwilling mind, who in any simple and easy matter yield their own will; but when there is to be a risk of goods, or some point of honour, or when their life is hinging on the act, they, in such a case, retain the right over their own will with the utmost tenacity, and remain their own. Ah! you are not volunteers such as those of old, who of their own will enrolled themselves for service, promising to fight for their masters; and for this reason they were invested with the rights of citizenship, and were rewarded with their liberty. But if those who are so contumacious and refractory against the Divine Will would willingly yield themselves, and voluntarily submit their own will to that Supreme Will, of a certainty they would obtain a right to Heaven, and would be free to all eternity. Amongst those volunteers, David, the king of Israel, is conspicuous. "In me," he says, "O God, are vows to Thee, which I will pay, praises to Thee." (*Ps.* LV. 12.)

There is nothing under Heaven so free as the will of man. All other things obey the Creator with marvellous subjection. Man alone possesses such liberty, that he wills whatever pleases him, even though it be repugnant to Heaven, to hell, and to God. There is nothing so much in our own power as the will: it is competent for man, as often as he pleases, to say NO, and to refuse, even when God Himself assents. And this is the prolific source of all sins, when God says,— "I will that this shall be done," and man dares to speak against it, and say,—"I will not do this;" or when God says,—"I will not that this should be done," and man says,—"I will to do it;" and as often as God says,—"This is my Will," and man, nevertheless, replies,—"But it is not mine." And on this account God complains most grievously. "Of old time," He says, "thou hast broken My yoke, thou hast burst my bands, and thou saidst: I will not serve." (*Jer.* II. 20.) This is the very root of all sins. Let there not be this impious "I WILL," and there will be no sin. That, in truth, is the most excellent medicine which cures the disease in such a way as to pluck out also the root of the disorder. Now the proper remedy of sin is Penitence, which then only is true when it represses this rebellious struggle, and thoroughly subjects the human will to the Divine. But the first act of the will is TO LOVE, as it is of the ears to hear, and of the eyes to see. He who loves anything in earnest yields his heart and will to it with pleasure; nor does any labour, or pain, or danger separate him from it; and

so the will, which truly yields itself to God, esteems all
things as nothing in comparison with God, and cheerfully embraces as well what is bitter as what is pleasant and sweet, according as it knows it to be pleasing
to the supreme Will. And this was King David's state
of mind when he said,—"In me, O God, are vows to
Thee." "I know not how to thank Thee, O my Lord,
because I feel in myself this happiness and readiness
towards Thy Will. May the promises made to Thee
by me be kept in my inmost heart, lest they come to
nothing." Let the will of a Christian man, then, be
such a cellar, that from it may easily be taken whatever
pleases the taste of his Lord. Let it be a rich store-
room, which is furnished with every kind of food and
drink. If the master wishes for oil, or honey, or perfumes, or wine, whether it be Chian, Thasian, or Cre-
tan; oil, and honey, and perfumes are produced, and
wine which is not cheap and common, but such as he
has ordered to be brought. If the master desires a
partridge or a fatted capon, the partridge or capon is
at once produced. If he wishes for bread which is
snow-white, and of the first quality, the bread is ready;
if he asks for anything else, whatever he wishes for
flies to him at once. And such let our will be. Let it
be both an oil-store, a honey-chamber, and wine-cellar,
as well as a store-room of every kind of household
stuff, so that whatever pleases the palate of our Master
may be produced from thence; and let this be done in
such a way, indeed, that if God desires a soul ready
for poverty, disease, ignominy, or death, He may find

one so perfectly prepared for Himself as to say,—"In thee, O man, are My vows."

2. There was once a Bishop whose name was, "What God wills." And let this be both the name and the single study of all Christians—*what God wills*. It is the sign of an ill-disposed man only to say, "What God wills," when neither laborious or weighty commands are given. He excels all, who, when poverty oppresses, when disease harasses, when contempt assails, when death calls him, still pronounces with most willing mind—*what God wills!* If He wills that riches, or health, or reputation, or even life itself should be taken away—*what God wills!* So let it be done! Neither does he question why he must die now, or at this particular place, or with this particular kind of disease, but he is thoroughly prepared for everything; this one thing alone he constantly repeats—*what God wills!* Most forcibly has Seneca said (*Ep.* 30),— "What do you require in order to be good? To WILL to be so."

3. Of how great importance the conformity of our will to the Divine is in a mortal sickness, Ludovicus Blosius teaches very admirably in the following way: —"Let each person who is dying rest on the merits of our Saviour JESUS Christ, rather than on his own. Let him trust in His goodness, and in the prayers of the Blessed Virgin Mary, and the Saints, and Elect of God. Let him set before his eyes the most bitter Passion and Death of Christ, and remember that ineffable Love which constrained Him to suffer such hu-

miliation, and into those gaping Wounds, and into that fathomless deep of His unbounded Pity, let him cast himself, and hide himself, with all his sins and shortcomings. For the greater glory of God let him offer himself, as a living sacrifice, to the Lord, so as patiently to bear, according to His most acceptable Will, and from sincere love to Him, every bitter pain of weakness, and even death itself; yea, and whatever the Lord shall see fit to send upon him in time or eternity. If he shall be able really to do this—if, I say, from pure love he shall have offered himself with a ready mind, and with entire resignation of self, to endure every punishment, for the honour of the Divine Justice—that man shall neither enter hell, nor any place of torment, even if in his single person he shall have committed all the sins of the whole world." No exercise, then, can be more beneficial in the last condition than that one should resign himself afresh to the Divine Will; humbly, lovingly, and entirely trusting in the boundless Mercy and Goodness of God. For it is impossible but that he who departs this life with such true and perfect resignation, and with a holy trust in God, should at once attain to the heavenly kingdom. For as no punishment at all, nor any fire of torment can affect God, so neither can they touch the man who is thus united to God by conformity of will, and by love. In such a state of soul did that justified thief die upon the cross, who did not ask from the Lord salvation for his body, but dying willingly for his sins, and for the glory of God, resigned him-

self entirely to the Divine Will, and offered himself
wholly to Christ, that He should do to him whatever
He willed. For nothing but Mercy and Grace did he
seek when he said,—"Lord, remember me when Thou
shalt come into Thy Kingdom." (*Luke* XXIII. 42.)
But if at the near approach of death the infirmity of
our nature mourns or trembles, such mourning and
trembling must be cast down before God by means of
resignation, and sure trust in Him must be excited.
Let the Death of Christ assuage the pain of your
death. He has gone before you, and so, too, has a
countless host of His Elect. Let it not grieve you,
then, to follow. The body which you are about to lay
aside is but a vile garment. What matter if it turn to
corruption, and be hidden for a time in the earth?
Hereafter, this same body of yours will rise again, and
then it will be immortal, incorruptible, glorious, and
clothed with light. You should reflect also how resigned and ready for death were those elder saints,
Abraham, Isaac, Jacob, Moses, David, and others like
them, when the Door of the Kingdom of Heaven was
not as yet open. And so we read, at the end of
Deuteronomy, that the Lord said to Moses when he
had ascended the Mount:—"This is the land for which
I swore to Abraham, Isaac, and Jacob, saying: I will
give it to thy seed. Thou hast seen it with thy eyes,
and shalt not pass over to it. And Moses the servant
of the Lord died there, in the land of Moab, by the
commandment of the Lord." (*Deut.* XXXIV. 4, 5.)
See, with what a resigned mind Moses, the Friend of

the Most High, welcomed death, according to the Good-pleasure of God. He crossed not over indeed into that visible land, but he was received into the invisible and better Land, that is to say, into the secret abode of peace, and the Limbo in which the souls of the just used then to rest in great tranquillity. But *now* an entrance to the heavenly country is opened to us by Christ our Lord.

And therefore, my excellent Christian friend, when you feel death to be near, or even before you are conscious of its approach, unite your will as perfectly as possible to the Divine Will, and commit yourself entirely to it; and neither think nor speak anything but this one thing—*whenever it seems good to God.*

4. But that WHENEVER comes amiss to nearly all men. They know, indeed, that they must die, and they desire to die, *but not yet.* They wish to pay the debt they owe to nature, *but not yet.* They are anxious to be received into Paradise, *but not yet.* And in this way we wretched ones are so mad as to desire to cease to be wretched, *but not yet,* and to wish to be happy and blessed, *but not yet.* But why, miserable man, are you erecting for yourself so high a gallows, as to have many steps, by means of which you may know that you are proceeding the more leisurely to death? Why do you wish for so many years to be added to your life, in which to look forward to your death with the lingering torment of thought? Go you must, whether it be to-day, or to-morrow. But I know what deceives many. When death knocks at the door, they think

that an importunate creditor has arrived before the time. Fools! That is the time, WHENEVER it seems good to the Lord of death. Why do you try to avoid it? Why do you plead your unripe years? Why do you ask for delay? For a long time past you have been ripe for death. Delay, if granted, will make you none the more prepared or ready; for even after this you will wish to prolong the time, being perhaps all the less prepared, as the delay granted to you has been greater. A respite from death has made not a few all the worse. It is a bad preparation for death to be unwilling to die. He has gained half who wills it, whenever He wills it, Who can will nothing that is evil. Therefore, away with hesitation, and say to your soul, WHENEVER and HOWEVER it seems good to God, so let it be done!

5. Job, who was well versed in bearing troubles, pleased God more, as S. Chrysostom testifies, by a few words only, than by all his alms, bountiful as they were; for when he, who was so sorely afflicted on all sides, could say,—"As it hath pleased the Lord so is it done: blessed be the Name of the Lord" (*Job* i. 21)— he commended himself to the Divine Will more than when he made the most bounteous offerings; for, as we learn from S. Bonaventure (*De Grad. Virt.* 24):— "It is a sign of greater perfection to endure adversity with patience, than to devote ourselves zealously to good works; since God stands not in need of our works." (*Ps.* xv. 2.)

He, therefore, who sincerely seeks the Divine Will,

esteems it alike whether he be whole or sick, since the Will of God is our entire good. In sickness, then, we must only so far trust the physician and his medicines as that all the while our entire confidence be placed in the Providence and Will of God. And when King Asa did not do this, he was justly rebuked, for "in his illness he did not seek the Lord, but rather trusted in the skill of physicians." (*2 Par.* XVI. 12.) Far better did Ezekias act, who ascribed the cure of his disease neither to the figs, nor to him who caused them to be applied, but to God. But if medicines are of no avail, or if the physician does not thoroughly understand the violent nature of the disorder, or if, for some reason or other, an error is committed, and the health is not improved, let not blame immediately be laid on this or that person, but let all be ascribed to the Divine Providence and Will, and let there be no other thought than God wills not that I should be restored to health; or He wills that I should recover slowly.

Lyduvina, a very holy virgin, who was harassed by all sorts of pains, till she became a miserable object to look upon, and, as it were, the habitation of almost all diseases, nevertheless fixed her will so firmly on the Lord, that it pleased her to think and speak and do nothing with premeditation which she thought would be displeasing to God. It is related that she very often said with patient Job,—" 'And that this may be my comfort, that afflicting me with sorrow, He spare not, nor I contradict the words of the Holy One' (*Job* VI.

10), since the performance of His Will is to me the sweetest consolation."

That man has found a remedy of perfect efficacy, for all difficulties and calamities, who has ever yielded himself to the Divine Will.

BOOK V

CONCERNING THE AIDS IN CONFORMING THE HUMAN WILL TO THE DIVINE

"The Lord is with us, fear ye not." *Numb.* xiv. 9.

THE HELIOTROPIUM

BOOK V

CHAPTER I

THE oblation of self to the Divine Will will never
be perfect unless in all things we thoroughly
trust in God. For how can I be in agreement with another in all things, if I do not trust in him? And how
can I trust in him, if I do not believe that he will faithfully and diligently care for what belongs to me? I
must now, therefore, treat of placing Trust in God.

1. To one who desires to know what the Holy
Scriptures say about this virtue, an eminent writer
(Luiz of Granada) replies:—"Scarcely a single chap-
ter can be found in the Sacred Writings in which God
does not promise His help, and Grace, and Providence to those *who trust in Him.*" David, that holy
king, who is a most admirable instructor in this kind
of Trust, strenuously enforces this single virtue in
almost all the Psalms. "But let all them be glad that
hope in Thee: they shall rejoice forever and thou shalt

dwell in them." (*Ps.* v. 12.) "I will love Thee, O Lord, my strength: the Lord is my Firmament, my Refuge, and my Deliverer. My God is my Helper, and in Him will I put my trust. My Protector and the Horn of my salvation, and my Support." (*Ps.* XVII. 2, 3.) "The Lord is my Light and my Salvation, whom shall I fear? The Lord is the Protector of my life: of whom shall I be afraid? If armies in camp should stand together against me, my heart shall not fear. If a battle should rise up against me, in this will I be confident." (*Ps.* XXVI. 1-3.) "He that dwelleth in the aid of the Most High, shall abide under the protection of the God of Jacob." (*Ps.* XC. 1.) "They that put their trust in the Lord shall be as Mount Sion: he shall not be moved for ever." (*Ps.* CXXIV. 1.) "In Thee, O Lord, have I hoped, let me never be confounded: deliver me in Thy justice." (*Ps.* XXX. 2.)

The heart of this king was capacious, and very full of a mighty Trust in God. He gave forth, in truth, those Divine streams from which he had already drunk.

And this same Trust in God the wisest and holiest of men have ever commended very highly. Solomon, that prodigy of wisdom, says,—"Have confidence in the Lord with all thy heart." (*Prov.* III. 5.) It is not any kind of trust which he requires, but that which proceeds *from the entire heart.* And so also the chief of the Apostles,—"Casting all your care upon Him, for He hath care of you." (1 *Pet.* v. 7.) And the Psalmist,—"Cast thy care upon the Lord, and He shall sustain thee." (*Ps.* LIV. 23.) Solomon, too, gives this advice,—"In all thy ways think on Him, and He shall direct thy steps." (*Prov.* III. 6.) "It is good to confide in the Lord, rather than to have confidence in man." (*Ps.* CXVII. 8.) "Blessed be the man that trusteth in the Lord, and the Lord shall be his confidence. And he shall be as a tree that is planted by the waters, that spreadeth out its roots towards moisture: and it shall not fear when the heat cometh. And the leaf thereof shall be green, and in the time of drought it shall not be solicitous, neither shall it cease at any time to bring forth fruit." (*Jer.* XVII. 7, 8.) "And thus consider through all generations: that none that trust in Him fail in strength." (I *Mach.* II. 61.) "Blessed are all they that trust in Him." (*Ps.* II. 13.) For this Trust constrains God to do good to you if you put your Trust in Him. Therefore, trust in God, and abide in your own appointed place, contented with your lot. Cheerfully embrace your condition, however lowly, and refrain from stretching yourself beyond the measure of the rule which God has apportioned to you. Remember "that man liveth not by bread alone" (*Luke* IV. 4); "that God is able of these stones to raise up children to Abraham" (*Matt.* III. 9); and that "it is easy for the Lord to save either by many, or by few." (I *Kings* XIV. 6.)

2. Amasias, King of Juda, hired an army for a hundred talents of silver, by the payment of which sum he brought to his standard a hundred thousand men. And when he had done this,—"A man of God came to him, and said: O King, let not the army of Israel go

out with thee, for the Lord is not with Israel, and all
the children of Ephraim: And if thou think that
battles consist in strength of the army, God will make
thee to be overcome by the enemies: for it belongeth to
God to help, and to put to flight. And Amasias said
to the man of God: What will then become of the
hundred talents which I have given to the soldiers of
Israel? and the man of God answered him: The Lord
is rich enough to be able to give thee much more than
this." (2 *Par.* xxv. 7-9.) Amasias trusted in God
and obeyed, and slew twenty thousand of his enemies.
So great a thing is it to trust in God, and not in human
strength.

Sir Thomas More, a man of remarkable saintliness
and learning, when he was in prison replied to the
arguments of his daughter Margaret in nearly these
words:—"Nothing," he said, "can happen which God
does not will. Moreover, what He wills, however
much it may appear to us to be *evil,* is in reality the
best thing that can happen. I will not distrust the
Goodness of God, my Margaret, however weak and
frail I may feel myself to be. Yea, if I perceived
myself to be in such a state of terror and dread that I
should seem likely to fall immediately, still I would
remember that St. Peter through little faith began to
sink with a single blast of wind, and I would do what
he did, I would call upon Christ and say, 'Lord, save
me.' And I trust that He would stretch forth His
Hand and take hold of me, and would not suffer me
to sink. But if He should permit me even further to

enact the part of Peter, and to fall entirely, and to deny Him with oaths and curses, yet I still hope He would look upon me with the eye of His bounteous Mercy, and would raise me up again, so that I might confess the Truth afresh, unburden my conscience, and manfully endure the pain and shame of my former denial. In one word, I hold it as most certain that without my own fault God will not forsake me." And this was said like a wise and Christian man; for Divine Providence mingles itself with all things, and we know that while numberless people are restrained by it from falling, none are impelled by it to fall. "When he shall fall he shall not be bruised, for the Lord putteth His Hand under him." (*Ps.* XXXVI. 24.) And how can he be injured who falls upon so soft a couch? Wherefore, before all things we must trust in God.

3. And what does our Lord inculcate in so many ways, and urge upon us, but this very Trust in God? How variously does our Divine Master reason upon this subject from birds, and flowers, and the hairs of our head, to encourage us to this Trust. Thus, when bringing before us the ravens, and lilies, and sparrows, He says,—"Consider the ravens: for they sow not, neither do they reap; neither have they storehouse nor barn; and God feedeth them: how much are you more valuable than they? And which of you by taking thought can add to his stature one cubit? If then ye be not able to do so much as the least thing, why are you solicitous for the rest? Consider the lilies how

they grow : they labour not, neither do they spin; but I say to you, not even Solomon in all his glory was clothed like one of these. Now if God clothe in this manner the grass that is to-day in the field, and to-morrow is cast into the oven; how much more you, O ye of little faith?" (*Luke* xii. 24-28.) And by how many illustrations did our Lord urge His disciples, in order to teach them to trust entirely in God. Thus, too, when He was about to feed the five thousand in the wilderness, He inquired of Philip whence they can buy bread. "And this He said *to try him*." (*John* vi. 6.) And so also, when about to feed the four thousand, He called the disciples into council upon the same matter, and asked,—"How many loaves have ye?" But their Trust in Him was small, and so they replied,—"From whence can anyone fill them here with bread in the wilderness?" (*Mark* viii. 4.) Oh, Sirs, God can do it, who wills that in all things we should trust in Him without wavering. Divine Providence cannot be deceived, and it wills not to deceive any one. God will abide by His promises.

4. Tostatus, a bishop, and a prodigy of learning, discoursing on the Chronicles of the Kings, says,— "Such is the law of Adam, which man is bound to observe with God; viz., that when any one humbles himself before God, and worships Him to the utmost of his power, God also will show His care for him." For to whom do we cry,—"Our Father, who art in Heaven?" Surely this munificent Father will abundantly provide for all. "But if," says S. Jerome,

"small animals depart not from God, Who is their
Creator, and if His Providence is over all things, and
those among them which are destined to perish do not
perish without the Will of God, ought not you, who
are immortal, to fear because you live without regard
to the Providence of God? Why, then, do we not trust
in Him with all our strength, and excite feelings
worthy of so great a Father? Not even in the very fire
ought we to despair. Are we straitened in domestic
matters? We have a rich Master Who never suffers
those who belong to Him to die of hunger. Do hosts
of enemies rise against us, whether springing from the
earth, or excited by hell? We have a Leader of
greater power than these, Who with one blast will scatter the armies of the kingdom of darkness. Do slan-
derous tongues harass us, and load us with false accusations? Let us look at God, our Judge and Avenger, and we shall not fear earthly things; for God will
not suffer Himself to be vanquished by man, or his
bounty to be outdone by human trust. Does any one
dare to trust in Him? God will dare to give him
greater blessings. Does any one venture to hope for
much? God will overpass human hope, and from the
rich treasure-house of Heaven will bestow on him far
greater blessings than he thought of; so that, in order
to banish human need, it is enough to have placed one's
Trust in God, and to have had great hopes of his
bounty. For the greater the hope is, the greater are
the heavenly gifts. So that we may perceive that human hope and trust are not merely equalled by the

Divine bounty, but in numberless ways are surpassed by it. And a most glorious struggle is this! Man's great trust in God with the boundless liberality of God; entered upon, as it were, with prodigal rivalry, on both sides, of trust and munificence, just as if man *did not will* to be conquered, while God *is not able* to be conquered.

5. And here listen to S. Augustine, Bishop of Hippo, (*In Ps.* CXLV.), who argues most forcibly:—"God," he says, "made the heaven, and the earth, and the sea, and all that is in them; if, therefore, He made all that is in them, He made you also, sparrow, locust, and worm; there is none of these which He made not, and He has a care for them all. Forbear, therefore, to say, 'I belong not to God;' your soul belongs to God, and your body belongs to God, because God made both your soul and your body. You reply perhaps, 'God does not take account of me among such a great multitude.' What? God not take account of you, Who numbers even all the hairs of your head? 'But we are sometimes involved,' you say, 'in such misfortunes, and so are entirely stripped of all consolations and help, that it is not to be wondered at if our trust does sometimes falter.'" Here, also, S. Augustine shall answer for me. And I pray all you who read this, or hear it read, to treasure in your inmost heart the reply of that most holy man:—"Whatever, then," says Augustine (*In Ps.* CXLVII.), "happens to us here contrary to our will, you must understand that it does not happen except by the Will of God, by His Provi-

dence, by His Ordinance, by His Good-pleasure, by
His Laws. And if we understand not why anything
is done, let us ascribe it to His Providence, because
it is not done without cause." And that the matter
may be made the clearer by examples, the same holy
Father says (*In Ps.* CXLVII.) :—"Who hath arranged
the limbs of a flea and a gnat that they should have
their proper order, life, motion? Consider one little
creature, even the very smallest, whatever thou wilt.
If thou considerest the order of its limbs, and the ani-
mation of life whereby it moveth, how doth it shun
death, love life, seek pleasures, avoid pain, exert divers
senses, and vigorously use movements suitable to itself! Who gave its sting to the gnat for it to suck
blood with? How narrow is the pipe whereby it
sucketh! Who arranged all this? Who made all this?
Thou art amazed at the smallest things; praise Him
that is great." And so fear God as the Judge, hope
in Him as the Rewarder, and in none else; and thus,
rising superior to all human affairs, put your trust in
God alone, feeling sure that He is neither able nor
willing to deceive. "No one hath hoped in the Lord,
and hath been confounded." (*Ecclus.* II. 11.)
"Blessed are all they that trust in Him." (*Ps.* II. 13.)

CHAPTER II

HOW small is the knowledge which we wretched mortals have of God! Scarcely through a crevice even do we derive any Divine light. This much, indeed, we know, that God is the Supreme Good, and is so boundlessly supreme that we may not lawfully seek or wish for anything which we are not able to obtain from this so great Good. In His time we shall certainly obtain all we desire, only let us not meanwhile fail in courage, but standing firm, with perfect Trust in God, let us believe that,—"It is good to wait with silence for the salvation of God." (*Lam.* III. 26.) The Lord is good to those who hope in Him, and to the soul which seeks Him. But wherein this Trust in God chiefly consists we will now proceed to examine.

1. Trust is superior to hope in this way, that it is not hope of every kind, but that which is of the greatest vigour and perfection. Seneca (*Ep.* 16) well observes this distinction when he says,—"I have *hope* of you, but not *trust* as yet." Now it is necessary that this Trust in God should embrace all human actions, for under all circumstances, great and small

alike, and in all the affairs of life, we must trust in God with the utmost sincerity, believing that He will never fail those that put their trust in Him.

King David founded a school, and "commanded that they should teach the children of Juda the use of the bow, as it is written in the book of the just" (*2 Kings* I. 18) ; and in this art Jonathan, the king's son, greatly excelled, for so sure a marksman was he that he received this commendation from his beloved friend David,—"The arrow of Jonathan never turned back," (*2 Kings* I. 22;) for his arrows were wont not to strike lightly, or merely graze the surface, but to pierce through the armour of his enemies. And such a bow is Trust in God; it both hits and pierces the Heart of God with its arrows that never miss their mark. But of all the kings of Israel and Juda (there were thirty-nine in all) how many were able to use this bow? Three or four only out of the whole number; David, Ezekias, Josias, with whom Josaphat also might be reckoned, since he abolished the sacrifices in the high places. The heart of these kings was certainly perfect with God, and ever full to overflowing with entire Trust in Him.

When a vast army of Moabites and Ammonites was threatening King Josaphat, and he was utterly inferior in numbers to the enemy, with sure Trust he "betook himself wholly to pray to the Lord" (*2 Par.* xx. 3,) and when he had prayed at great length, he added to his prayer this most excellent clause, "but as we know not what to do, *we can only turn our eyes to Thee.*"

(Ver. 12.) "And Jahaziel was there, upon whom the Spirit of the Lord came in the midst of the multitude, and he said: Attend ye, all Juda, and you that dwell in Jerusalem, and thou King Josaphat: Thus saith the Lord to you: Fear ye not, and be not dismayed at this multitude: for the battle is not yours, but God's. It shall not be you that shall fight, but only stand with confidence, and you shall see the help of the Lord over you, O Juda, and Jerusalem: fear ye not, nor be you dismayed: to-morrow you shall go out against them, and the Lord will be with you." (Ver. 14, 15, 17.) Josaphat was greatly encouraged by these words, and led his army against the enemy; but, lest his soldiers should be afraid to engage so vast a host, like a careful general he fortified their courage and said,—"Believe in the Lord your God, and you shall be secure: believe His prophets, and all things shall succeed well." (Ver. 20.) And then, unlike what is usually done in battles, "he appointed the singing men of the Lord, to praise him by their companies, and to go before the army, and with one voice to say: Give glory to the Lord, for His mercy endureth for ever." (Ver. 21.) Behold, the King advancing with his army to battle, like a Bishop with his Priests going into the temple! It is an unheard-of thing in war, and one which would move ridicule, to post a band of singers, who cannot fight, in the van of the army. But God was with Josaphat, who was engaging in the battle with so sure a Trust in Him. And when they had begun, not indeed the soldiers to cast their darts, but the singers to sing psalms, the enemy turned one upon the other, and "they destroyed one another." (Ver. 23.) And as the army of Josaphat advanced they found the whole plain strewed with dead bodies, nor had one escaped. And in this great slaughter spoils were found so precious and abundant that not even three days sufficed for carrying them away. Behold, then, what power sincere Trust in God has! It can effect anything, and is invincible.

2. And although in all actions, as I have said, Trust in God is needful, yet specially is it so when either prayers are to be offered, or adversity is to be endured.

S. Bernard (*In Quad. Serm.* 4), discoursing on prayer, says that in the case of many it is either timid, or lukewarm, or presumptuous. "Timid prayer," he goes on to say, "does not reach to heaven, because unreasonable fear holds back the soul, so that the petition is not able, I will not say to ascend, but not so much as to make a start. Lukewarm prayer becomes languid as it rises, and fails, because it has no vigour. Presumptuous prayer ascends indeed, but rebounds, for it encounters resistance; and not merely does it not obtain grace, but it also earns offence. But prayer which is faithful, humble, and fervent, will without doubt reach to heaven, from whence it is certain that it cannot return empty." Before all things it is necessary that prayer should be trustful. How many are there who before they begin to *pray,* begin to *despair*. "God will not hear me," they say; "I shall not obtain what I seek; I shall cry to Him in vain." What a wretched ambassador! He has scarcely left home, when he faints through want of Trust. But our Lord instructs us how Trust is to be shown towards God in our prayers when He says,—"There was a judge in a certain city, who feared not God, nor regarded man; and there was a certain widow in that city; and she came to him, saying, Avenge me of my adversary. And he would not for a long time; but afterwards he said within himself, Though I fear not God, nor regard man; yet because this widow is troublesome to me, I will avenge her, lest continually coming she weary me." (*Luke* XVIII. 2-5.) See the sturdy and almost daring hope which instilled into the widow the feeling,—"To-day you shall have your suit decided." When to-day's hope had disappointed her, to-morrow's hope encouraged her,—"It will be done to-morrow, or the day after to-morrow. This week, this month, or certainly this year, judgment will be delivered." Her persevering trust at length prevailed; and this our Lord uses as an argument in the following way:—If prayer can effect so much even with a man utterly void of justice, of how great power will it be with Him Who is Mercy itself? Our mind, like the widow, reckons up its adversaries in overwhelming numbers. Why, then, does it delay to appeal to the Judge Who is perfect in Justice, and commit its entire cause to Him with unfaltering Trust? "Will not God revenge His elect, who cry to Him day and night; and will He have patience in their regard?" (*Luke* XVIII. 7.) Blessed David, commending this Trust above all things, says,

—"Commit thy way to the Lord, and trust in Him, and He will do it." (*Ps.* xxxvi. 5.) Why, then, do you stand shivering with fear? Why are you distrustful, O most faint-hearted of mortals? Does any one assail you with curses or injuries? Complain of it to God, "*and He will do it.*" Is your flesh full of sin? Pray to God, "*and He will do it.*" Does the evil spirit move against you various engines of hell? Call God to your aid, "*and He will do it.*" Whatever you do, trust in God, "*and He will do it.*"

3. And have you forgotten, O man of small faith, what our Lord relates for our instruction in this matter? "Which of you," He says, "shall have a friend, and shall go to him at midnight, and shall say to him, Friend, lend me three loaves; because a friend of mine is come off his journey to me, and I have not what to set before him? And he from within should answer and say, Trouble me not: the door is now shut, and my children are with me in bed; I cannot rise and give thee. I say to you, although he will not rise and give him, because he is his friend; yet because of his importunity he will rise, and give him as many as he needeth. And I say to you, Ask, and it shall be given you; seek, and you shall find; knock, and it shall be opened to you. For every one that asketh receiveth; and he that seeketh findeth; and to him that knocketh it shall be opened." (*Luke* xi. 5-10.) There is nothing more pleasing to God than that we should address Him with as great confidence as a friend does a friend. Nor will any one ever address God unseasonably. Look

at the beggar, who for a single penny, or a crust of bread, waits patiently before a house, or runs after the carriages as they roll by. And what is it fitting that *we* should do when we are suitors for the bounty of the wealthiest of Kings? Is there not need here of the most patient Trust? John, the beloved Apostle, says,—"And this is the confidence which we have towards Him, that whatsoever we shall ask according to His Will, He heareth us: and we know that He heareth us whatsoever we ask; we know that we have the petitions which we request of Him." (1 *John* v. 14, 15.) "And which of you if he ask his father bread, will he give him a stone? Or a fish, will he for a fish give him a serpent? Or if he shall ask an egg, will he reach him a scorpion? If you then," says Christ, "being evil, know how to give good gifts to your children: how much more will your Father from Heaven give the good Spirit to them that ask Him?" (*Luke* XI. 11-13.) But it very often happens that we, in our miserable ignorance, ask not for bread, but for a stone; not for a fish, but for a serpent; for "we know not what we should pray for as we ought" (*Rom.* VIII. 26); and when God denies us that which would be for our harm, we are angry with our most Benignant Father, and complain, with anger, that our prayers are not heard. Madmen that we are! do not parents often refuse an apple or a pear to a little child from whom a vast inheritance of money will not be withheld? Paul of Tarsus, when praying for the removal of the "sting in the flesh," thought he was offering a

most reasonable petition; but God did not grant his
prayers.   And as often as this happens it ought to be
clear to us that what we pray for is not granted for
our advantage, or that it is rightly deferred, in order
to be granted at some far more fitting time, and that,
meanwhile, we may win God's favour by our persevering trust.   "God," says S. Isidore, "very often does
not hear our prayers according to our will, but according to our salvation."   Eternal Providence cannot
but know what most conduces to our welfare; nor can
Eternal Benevolence not will to grant what it knows
is for our good.   Most accurately does it know the
proper time when it ought to help each person.   And
so nothing should ever be asked from God without
perfect subjection or resignation of the will; for *"whatever we shall ask according to His Will, He heareth
us."*   And therefore to all our prayers these words
of our Lord must be appended,—*"Nevertheless, not
My Will, but Thine be done."*   But, if we obstinately
strive to wrest anything from God, it is to be feared
lest what, as a most merciful Father, He has denied,
He may, as a severe Judge, permit for our evil: and
thus our *"prayer be turned to sin."*   (*Ps.* cviii. 7.)
Let this be held by us as a most infallible truth, that no
prayers offered with fitting resignation of will are
vain, absolutely none; for either that which is sought
will be obtained, or something better.   And this it is
which wonderfully inflames the confidence of every
one who prays, because, *"Whatsoever we shall ask according to His Will, He heareth us."*

CHAPTER III

IN WHAT WAY TRUST IN GOD IS TO BE CONFIRMED AND ENCOURAGED IN ADVERSITY

LOOK at a pilot in a storm, a soldier on the field of battle, an athlete in the arena. No one can tell what you are capable of, no, not even your ownself, unless you are exercised with afflictions of various kinds. There is need of trial in order to become acquainted with oneself. *No one has ever learnt what he could do except by trying.* Great men rejoice at times in adversity, just as brave soldiers exult in battle. Virtue is greedy of danger, and thinks of whither it is advancing, not of what it will have to endure, since whatever it endures is a part of its glory. How can I tell what advance you have made in Trust towards God, if all things turn out as you desire? How can I tell what courage you have to bear poverty, if you are rolling in riches? How can I tell what constancy you have to endure ignominy, and disgrace, and universal hatred, if you reach old age amid the approbation of all, and pass your life without an enemy? In good truth, *there is need of trial for the knowledge of self.* There is no great difficulty in saying in prosperity,—"The Lord is my Firmament, my Refuge, and my Deliverer." If a beggar begins for the first time to say,—"I am now easy in my mind; this week, at least, I shall not be starved," when he has a bag bursting with bread, he shows that he is a man destitute of hope. "Hope that is seen is not hope; for what a man seeth, why doth he hope for? But if we hope for that which we see not, we wait for it with patience." (*Rom.* VIII. 24, 25.) Our Trust, therefore, shines most conspicuously at that time when flowing blood proclaims wounds, when waves beat into the frail ship, when we are enclosed in difficulties; this is the place, and this is the time for Trust. In what way, however, Trust can best be shown in the midst of misfortunes we will now proceed to show.

1. And here two points are to be laid down as a fundamental principle. In the first place, let us be thoroughly assured that everywhere, and in every rank of life, there are miseries and calamities in abundance; for that life is made up of these our Lord Himself proclaimed,—"In the world you shall have distress; but have confidence, I have overcome the world." (*John* XVI. 33.) "All that will live godly in CHRIST JESUS shall suffer persecution." (2 *Tim.* III. 12.) Secondly, let us remember the declaration of S. Paul, —"Let no temptation take hold on you, but such as is human; and God is faithful, Who will not suffer you to be tempted above that which you are able; but will make also with temptation issue, that you may be able to bear it." (1 *Cor.* X. 13.)

And now that this two-fold foundation has been

laid, S. Cyprian (*Orat.* 3, *cont. Judæos*) is the first to come and teach us Trust in God in adversity, as follows:—"Your servant, perchance, has committed an offence against you, and deserves to be struck either with a hand or stick. You strike the fellow with the lightest possible hand, when he at once begins to rave, refuses to serve you any longer, runs out of the house, and complains to your enemy of I know not what injuries. Now suppose I should be inclined to plead this man's cause, should I meet with a favourable reception from you? 'This servant,' you would say, 'has, in good truth, offended grievously in more than one particular. He deserved to be beaten, and severely too; but he has shown resistance under correction, and has rushed from the house, which is a capital offence. If, however, he had sought for friends to plead for him, he might have seemed to have been angry with some reason; but to hurry off to enemies, and to give vent in their presence to numberless complaints against his master; this, indeed, is an act which well deserves capital punishment.' "

And now, my Christian friend, behold yourself under this figure of the slave! If you are punished by God, and far more gently indeed (for this is the way of God) than you deserve, why do you refuse to submit to the punishment? And why do you give utterance to such unbecoming words as,—"Well, then, I will commit some offence worthy of transportation or imprisonment; I will drink myself drunk to drown my cares? Why should I not occasionally indulge my tastes, since I am weighted down with so many evils from God?" This, my friends, is to hurry off to the enemies of God. Why do you not rather go to His friends, and hope for pardon from their intercession? Trust in God, and begin afresh to show yourself a good servant. Where there is Trust in God, the will is united to God. It is most disgraceful that when a Master, Who is so good, desires to punish a servant, who is so bad, he should yet dare to say,—"I will not be punished; I have done nothing to deserve punishment, or at least so heavy a one." Away with all such speeches as these! Trust in God; and abide in your own proper place. S. Jerome (*Ad Fabiolam*), encouraging to this Trust, says,—"Many are the wiles and snares which surround us; but let us say, Though I walk in the midst of the shadow of death I will not fear, for Thou art with me. If the armies of all the devils in hell are confederate against me, yet shall not my heart be afraid; and though there rose up war of all the wicked men in the world against me, yet will I put my trust in Him. But if hosts of devils trouble you, and you begin to be inflamed towards different sins, and your thoughts say to you, 'What shall we do?' Eliseus shall answer, 'Fear not: for there are more with us than with them.'" (4 *Kings* vi. 16.) Well does S. Ambrose (*De Joseph.* 5) say,—"There is *most help* where there is *most danger;* for God is a Helper as necessity arises, and in tribulation." It is God Who turned the rock into a storehouse of honey and oil that the people of Israel might "suck honey out of the rock, and oil out of the hardest stone." (*Deut.* XXXII. 13.) He refreshed so many hundred thousand men with a stream of the purest water, where not even a sparrow would have found enough to satisfy its thirst. God has winged messengers so swift that they even outstrip the wind, and such succour as this does He send to His people. Let us, then, trust in God with all our heart, since the Lord is with us. But still, is it not often our wish to inquire, as Gedeon asked of the Angel,—"If the Lord be with us, why have these evils fallen upon us? Where are His miracles, which our fathers have told us of?" (*Judges* VI. 13.) Wonderful things are told us concerning God's providential care over us; we are commanded to trust in Him in all things, but meanwhile we are tossed about hither and thither by the waves of manifold calamities. If, then, say we, *the Lord is with us,* how is it that we are encountered by so many misfortunes, and are pressed down with so many ills?

2. To this question S. Bernard will well reply. When endeavouring to console the Abbot of S. Nicasius at Reims on account of the departure of Drogo from his monastery, he says (*Ep.* 32),—"Let not this tempest, terrible as it is, drown you. Let your humble prudence anxiously study not to be overcome by evil, but to overcome evil by good. You will overcome by bravely fixing your hope in God, and by patiently waiting for the end of this business. It is good for you to be humbled beneath the mighty Hand of God, and to desire on no account to resist His Supreme

Disposal." Let the devil indeed rage as he will, he hurts no one without Divine Permission, for he does not dare to touch even the swine until Christ gives him leave. (*Luke* VIII. 32.) How, then, will he assault you, or touch you, or harass you, if Christ does not permit him? Why, therefore, do we fear Cerberus, who is now bound with a chain, and does no harm to anyone unless one comes too near him?

In order that the Apostles might make proof of themselves and their Trust in God, our Lord led them with Himself into a ship, and gave permission to the winds to stir up the troubled sea. During the storm the disciples thought that they were now being swallowed up by the waves, and, which was worse, "He was asleep." (*Matt.* VIII. 24.) And so they cry out,— "Lord, save us; we perish." To whom Christ replied, —"Why are ye fearful, O ye of little faith?" Why are you disturbed by so much dread? Where is your Trust in me? What matters it that Man sleeps, if only God, who never sleeps, watches for you?

And from this we clearly gather that Trust in God nowhere shines out more conspicuously than in the midst of dangers, and when all things are in direct confusion. In the midst of what storms and ruin did Job himself stand perfectly erect! His enemies drove away all his cattle, and upon that which remained fire fell from Heaven and consumed. One great ruin buried all his children beneath it; and Job himself, not so much covered with wounds as reduced to one great sore, and bitterly assailed also by the tongue of his

kindred and wife, lost everything except his noble
Trust in God. And so now banished to the dunghill,
seated amid worms which burst out on all sides, and
wiping off the corruption which ran down from himself, not with a cloth but with a potsherd, he still, like
a triumphant wrestler, cried out,—"Although He
should kill me, I will trust in Him: and He shall be
my Saviour." (*Job* XIII. 15, 16.) And this most destructive tempest was followed by a profound calm and
joyful tranquillity. Oh how often "does happier fortune follow on a beginning full of tears!" If, therefore, calamity assails anyone, let him increase his
Trust in God. For what, I would ask, are you accustomed to do, my good friend, when a sudden shower
of rain overtakes you? In the town I suppose you
would enter some house; but if you are caught in the
open country, you look round for some spreading tree
under which you might shelter yourself from the rain.
Behold, then, your roof, your tree, your secure refuge,
is Trust in God; nor can there ever be so opportune
a shelter in solitude, a roof in a storm, a fire or bath
in time of cold, as will be to you in all adversity this
Trust in the Lord of the Universe! In one word,
whatever storms descend upon you, you will stand
perfectly secure beneath this well-roofed covering.
Trust in God, then, and as sailors make all preparations for their voyage, but wait for a wind from God,
so, if you do not fail in your duty, God will take care
of the rest.

3. But you may say, it is an evil greater than man

be supposed, to be harassed, not merely by the wicked, but also by those who are thought to be good: this it is which afflicts and disquiets one. But there is nothing new here, my good friend. Even in the time of the Apostles it was a common and well-known form of sin to bring forward a spurious kind of law, and to adjust on Fraud the mantle of Justice; nor was it at all unusual to receive injuries from friends and relatives, and from those to whom one had done the greatest acts of kindness. Nay, things were even worse than this, for kindnesses were turned into crime, and the blood of those for whom blood ought to be poured out was not spared. Not only did Achitophel, who was one of the counsellors of David, persecute him to the death, nor only Saul his father-in-law, but Absalom also, his son. And by whom was our Lord put to death? Not only by impious idolaters, but also by His Own chosen people. By these "was I wounded *in the house of them that loved me." (Zach.* XIII. 6.) What injuries, too, did not our Lord receive from His Own disciples? Iscariot, whose feet a few hours before He had washed, and to whom He had given His Body to eat, sold his Lord, most ungrateful bearer of the purse that he was, while Peter, so full of love, denied Him, and the rest forsook Him. And why do we wonder? "A man's enemies shall be they of his own household." (*Matt.* X. 36.) But the man who trusts in God gains an easy victory over all such things.

But you may ask how is this Trust in God, in time

of adversity, to be stimulated? See, then, I will set before you briefly six examples.

First of all, when things go wrong with you, turn to God as soon as possible, and at the very moment, and complain to him of whatever is troubling you. And here nearly all of us err grievously; when adversity presses upon us we fill the ears of many of our friends with numberless complaints: but God is the last of all Whose help we implore, utterly inverting the order of things. But far otherwise did King David act:—"I have lifted up my eyes to the mountains," he says, "from whence Help shall come to me. My Help is from the Lord, Who made heaven and earth." (*Ps.* cxx. 1, 2.) He who does not do this at the beginning of every calamity is so overcome by anger, grief, or a sense of injury, as to be unable to control himself. As soon, therefore, as you feel that you are troubled, say,—"Lord, what wilt Thou have me to do?" And the interpreter of the Divine Will will answer you,—"Expect the Lord, do manfully, and let thy heart take courage, and wait thou for the Lord." (*Ps.* xxvi. 14.)

Secondly, keep silence and bridle, at least, your mouth and tongue; if you cannot restrain your mind. Receive this counsel from the wisest of kings,—"I said: I will take heed to my ways; that I sin not with my tongue. I have set a guard to my mouth, when the sinner stood against me. I was dumb, and was humbled, and kept silence from good things." (*Ps.* xxxviii. 1-3.) Keep silence, therefore, for if in the midst of troubles and injuries you give rein to your tongue, know for a certainty that you will be hurried away headlong; scarcely will you begin to *speak* but you will *offend;* therefore, keep silence, and specially about your enemies. You are not able to speak well about them; then at least do not speak ill. Let your conscience be your comforter, and God that most just Judge, Whose eyes neither your adversaries nor their machinations can escape. Trust in God, I say, and keep silence.

Thirdly, when you have turned to God and have begun to keep silence, next surrender yourself wholly to the power of the Divine Will. Unite and devote your entire self as closely as possible to it; but give thanks also to God, because He thinks you worthy to suffer innocently, or, if you are guilty, that you may still regain your innocence by patience. In this embrace of the Divine will, let man hold God in his arms, as it were, and say with Jacob when wrestling with the angel,—"I will not let Thee go except Thou bless me." (*Gen.* XXXII. 26.) If, when a ship is in peril on the water, two persons, through fear of the impending danger, should so embrace as that each should fold the other in his arms, they would necessarily perish together if the ship were to be lost, for, in proportion as the peril is greater, the closer does their embrace become. And just in the same way must the Divine Will be embraced, so that man may cleave to God with an indissoluble bond of union, and say,—"I will not let Thee go, O my God; I will drag Thee with me under the very waters; we must sink together; even in the waves I will embrace Thee, the more trusting in Thee, the less I trust in myself."

4. Fourthly, when the storm has a little subsided, compose yourself to prayer, call upon Christ to plead your cause, and commend all your affairs to him, and do not think it enough to have done this once, or twice, but do it again and again, if need be, for many days and years. And do not cease till, by firm trust and constant prayer, you open the Hand which God, like a man of prodigious strength, shows to you shut, with the fingers firmly pressed together. When King Ezechias had received the impious letter of Sennacherib he "went up to the House of the Lord, and spread it before the Lord." (4 *Kings* XIX. 14.) And do you too, whoever you be, that are afflicted, spread your letter also before God, and whatever complaints you have, lay them down before this most Just Judge and Benignant Parent. If, however, you do not obtain what you seek, acknowledge the secret Judgments of God and His Providence, which has been firmly fixed from eternity, and commend yourself entirely to it. You have done what lay in your power, and the Good God will take care of the rest.

Fifthly, avail yourself of the advice of a prudent and upright man. The son of Sirach says,—"*Do thou nothing without counsel,* and thou shalt not repent when thou hast done." (*Ecclus.* XXXII. 24.) Take the greatest care also that you follow not your own feelings, and the impulse of your own mind.

You have at once lost meekness, you have lost all patience, if you admit as counsellors feeling and impulse, for the worst of all counsellors without doubt are they. God began this web which excites your wonder, and He knows best of all, in what way the weaving is to be carried out; but if you unseasonably interfere, and repeat,—"So I will, and so I command, let my will stand for reason" (Juv. *Sat.* vi. 222); you will, as far as lies in your power, disturb the sweet arrangement of God, and, therefore, to no one but yourself must you attribute the evil result.

Every misfortune arises from that which Baruch mourns over when he says,—"We have sinned before the Lord our God: and we were not obedient to Him, and we have not hearkened to the voice of the Lord our God, to walk in His commandments, which he hath given us." (*Baruch* i. 17, 18.) Therefore, have Trust in God, for so much the securer will you be against every enemy in proportion as your Trust in Him is stronger.

Sixthly, but if you have used all diligence, and yet nothing turns out according to your wishes, do not direct your anger against God, or against any creature, but rather reflect that God accurately knows all that you have suffered, or that you will have to suffer, and that He wills that these sufferings should be the trial of your constancy. And for this reason let whatever pleases God, please you also. "We are happy, O Israel: because the things that are pleasing to God, are made known unto us." (*Baruch* iv. 4.)

5. But if God should not cease to chasten His children, and should exercise them first with one kind of calamity and then another, He is only doing that which every good father and mother do. When parents chastise their children, every now and then they ask, after one or two blows,—"Will you do it again?" If the child is silent when beaten, the father continues to beat him, and if he still refuses to answer, through obstinacy, the father continues the punishment, still asking, every now and then,—"Will you do it again?" And so he goes on till the child says,—"I will not do it any more." Then the father replies,—"Go, then, and take care that you do not do this again." And in this way God also is wont to punish us, and inquire,—"Are you ready to submit yourself entirely to My Will, and to trust in Me in all things?" And then, because we are either silent through obstinacy, or do not reply in earnest that we will obey the Divine Will, God oftentimes continues the chastisement, only waiting, however, till we say from our hearts,—"I am ready, O my Father, I am ready to obey Thy Will in all things. What wilt Thou have me to do?"

But this Trust in God, of which I am speaking, will not long abide unless patience and perseverance strengthen it. In the temple of Solomon there were two pillars, one of which was called Jachin, and the other Booz (3 *Kings* VII. 21); and to these two columns patience and perseverance are well compared. On these pillars Trust must be supported. Patience represses excessive sadness, while to perseverance nothing seems too long, however slowly time may pass. And springing from these columns Trust in God is "as Mount Sion: he shall not be moved for ever." (*Ps.* cxxiv. i.)

CHAPTER IV

HOW GREAT TRUST IN GOD WAS EXHIBITED BY ALL THE SAINTS

I WILL not speak of Abraham, who trusting in God "against hope, believed in hope. In the promise also of God he staggered not by distrust; but was strengthened in faith, giving glory to God; most fully knowing that whatsoever He has promised He is able also to perform." (*Rom.* IV. 18-21.) He it was who refused not to offer up his only son as a sacrifice to God, and who with three hundred and eighteen servants attacked and vanquished four kings through his surpassing Trust in God. (*Gen.* XIV. 14-16.) Neither will I speak of Joseph, the governor of Egypt, who, though so often brought to extremity, yet did not lose his courage, for his heart trusted in the Lord. What miracles did not Moses, who trusted in God, perform? He enclosed all the hosts of Egypt in one vast sepulchre in the sea. In the war with Amalec he held a rod in his hand, instead of any weapon such as generals use, and thus he addressed the captain of the host:—"Choose out men: and go out and fight against Amalec; tomorrow I will stand on the top of the hill having the rod of God in my

hand." (*Exodus* XVII. 9.) Wonderful indeed!
Moses, standing like an idle spectator, lays whole
armies in the dust. His panoply was the rod of God,
and Trust in Him. Josue, too, the leader of the hosts
of Israel, prevailing through his incredible Trust in
God, dared to command the sun, and say,—"Move
not, O Sun, toward Gabaon, nor thou, O Moon, toward the valley of Ajalon. So the sun stood still in
the midst of heaven, and hasted not to go down the
space of one day. There was not before nor after
so long a day, the Lord obeying the voice of man,
and fighting for Israel." (*Jos.* x. 12-14.) And so,
in a short time, all the kings of Chanaan were conquered. And what is the lesson from this? to admonish all those who exercise authority over others
that they place their trust in God alone, Who directs
the hearts of men, and commands alike the highest
and the lowest to stand still in mid-career. Or why
should I speak of Caleb, who had such Trust in God,
that, when so many hundred thousand men were
tumultuously gathered together he alone resisted them,
and exclaimed,—"Be not rebellious against the Lord:
and fear ye not the people of this land, for we are
able to eat them up as bread. All aid is gone from
them: the Lord is with us, fear ye not." (*Num.*
XIV. 9.) And how great was the trust of Gedeon,
who was educated rather for agriculture than warfare, and who with three hundred men (*Judges* VII.
8) dared to attack so many thousands of the enemy,
and overcame them. King Ezechias, too, abounding

in Trust in God, not merely obtained the addition of fifteen years to his life, but, as a pledge of it, was permitted to recall the shadow of the sun ten degrees. (*Isai.* XXXVIII. 8.) As, therefore, Josue caused the sun to stand still, so Ezechias made it go back over an immense part of its orbit. And thus, in good truth, the soul which trusts in God impels Him to disturb the course of the world, and to change the order of nature. Ezechias, then, was able to work this miracle by his Trust in God, which when Sennacherib was threatening Jerusalem, induced him to put on sackcloth, rather than armour; clad in which he, first of all, entered the temple, and exhorted the people to prayer, and to renew their Trust in God, saying,— "Behave like men and take courage: be not afraid nor dismayed for the king of the Assyrians, nor for all the multitude that is with him: for there are many more with us than with him. For with him is an arm of flesh: with us the Lord our God, who is our helper, and fighteth for us." (*2 Par.* XXXII. 7, 8.) How full of Trust in God was this exhortation! But how did it happen that the wretched Zedecias did not do the like, when all the while his army was larger than that of Ezechias? It was this which ruined that king; he trusted too much in his own strength, and perished, trusting "upon this broken staff of a reed: upon which if a man lean, it will go into his hand, and pierce it." (*Isai.* XXXVI. 6.)

2. The same thing also caused the ruin of that most excellent King Asa. For thirty-six years he lived an

admirable life, and was on this account beloved of God; but at length he forfeited all the favour which he had acquired on account of this one sin, *that he trusted in human strength.* But although this was the conduct of Asa yet, if it is measured by the rule of human reason, it may seem little deserving of condemnation; for what was the nature of his sin? He surrendered his gold to Benadad, King of Syria, and alleged, as a reason for the act,—"There is a league between me and thee, as there was between my father and thy father, wherefore I have sent the silver and gold, that thou mayst break thy league with Baasa, King of Israel, and make him depart from me." (2 *Par.* XVI. 3.) And what was there wrong here, I would ask? Nevertheless Hanani the Seer severely rebuked Asa, and said,—"Because thou hast had confidence in the King of Syria, and not in the Lord thy God, therefore hath the army of the King of Syria escaped out of thy hand. For the eyes of the Lord behold all the earth, and give strength to those who with a perfect heart trust in Him. Wherefore thou hast done foolishly, and for this cause from this time wars shall arise against thee." (2 *Par.* XVI. 7-9.)

And so Job says,—"If I beheld the sun when it shined, and the moon going in brightness: and my heart in secret hath rejoiced, and I have kissed my hand with my mouth." (*Job* XXX. 26, 27.) "The good," says S. Gregory, "which he did he thus relates, that he may ascribe it all to God. Job was not wont to praise his own diligence, or to kiss his hands; for not in himself, and in his own power, but in God did he place all his trust. Thus, too, the Emperor Charles V, who was really 'pious' and truly 'happy,' was accustomed to say,—'I came, I saw, but God conquered.' "

Jonas, when enclosed in the belly of the whale, and now reduced to the last extremity, was still able to betake himself to prayer, as though he were in perfect safety in a ship, and never, and in no place, could he better exercise the virtue of Trust in God;—"And Jonas prayed to the Lord his God out of the belly of the fish." (*Jonas* II. 2.) Everywhere there is place for prayer and vows. And what was his prayer?— "The waters compassed me about even to the soul: the deep hath closed me around about, the sea hath covered my head. When my soul was in distress within me, I remembered the Lord: that my prayer may come to Thee, unto Thy holy Temple." (Ver. 6, 8.) See his great Trust in God! And so, too, Daniel in the midst of the hungry lions, and the three Hebrew Children in the flames at Babylon, dispatched as ambassadors to God prayers full of Trust in Him.

And how greatly did Paul of Tarsus excel in this virtue, who, though often burying himself, as it were, could yet say,—"I know Whom I have believed, and I am certain that He is able to keep that which I have committed unto Him against that day." (2 *Tim.* I. 12.) And armed with this Trust in God he feared no labour or danger, but hurried through showers of stones, and swords, and darts, and flames, relying on the Divine Aid, and by the help of his God he often passed over even walls of iron.

3. Among women Judith excelled most admirably in this virtue, daring to do a deed which had never been heard of before. For when she had conceived the design of killing Holofernes, she inflamed her Trust in God with fervent prayer, and said,—"Assist, I beseech thee, O Lord God, me a widow. For Thou hast done the things of old, and hast devised one thing after another : and what Thou hast designed hath been done. For all Thy ways are prepared, and in Thy providence Thou hast placed Thy judgments. For Thy power, O Lord, is not in a multitude, nor is Thy pleasure in the strength of horses, nor from the beginning have the proud been acceptable to Thee : but the prayer of the humble and the meek hath always pleased Thee." (*Judith* IX. 3, and fol.) And through the same amazing Trust in God she replied to Holofernes,—"As thy soul liveth, my Lord, Thy handmaid shall not spend all these things till God do by my hand that which I have purposed." (Chap. XII. 4.) And when she was now standing by the bed of Holofernes in his drunkenness, she said, while she silently poured forth tears and prayers,—"Strengthen me, O Lord God of Israel." (Chap. XIII. 7.) With great success did she perform her design, and when received again within the gates of Bethulia, these were the first words with which she burst forth,— "Praise ye the Lord our God, who hath not forsaken

them that hope in Him. And by me His handmaid He hath fulfilled His mercy, which He promised to the house of Israel: and He hath killed the enemy of His people by my hand this night." (Chap. XIII. 17, 18.)

And to her Susanna may be justly added, a noble example of Modesty and Trustfulness. When she was being led away to be put to death, "she weeping looked up to heaven: for *her heart had confidence in the Lord.*" (Dan. XIII. 35.) Nor did she trust in vain, for by the unanimous voice of all, Daniel acting as her judge, she was acquitted of every charge.

Nor was Esther inferior to her, for she in like manner undertook a task of great danger through her Trust in God. It was a law in the palace of Assuerus that if any one came into the presence of the king without being summoned he should be put to death, unless the king should stretch out his golden sceptre as a sign of clemency. (*Esther* IV. 11.) But when Mardochai on the one side was urging Esther with constant entreaties to approach the king, and on the other the law stood in the way and terrified her, she at length determined upon this plan. All the Jews were bidden to give themselves to prayer and fasting for three whole days, and Esther with her maidens did the like. And when three days had been spent in this way, the queen, conceiving within herself unbounded Trust in God, entered into the king's presence to beg his favour for her people. And everything turned out according to her desire.

4. It may be affirmed generally of all men and women who have been remarkable for saintliness of life, that *their heart had confidence in the Lord.* This was singularly the case with S. Catherine of Siena. Although at all other times she was exceedingly sparing of her words, yet, whenever she engaged in conversation about Trust in God, she could scarcely find any limit for her speaking, or, if she heard others talking of this virtue, she never could hear enough.

S. Bernard, when he was afflicted with a grievous disease, and was almost drawing his last breath, thought that he was standing before the Judgment-seat of God. Satan, too, was there as an adversary, and assailed him with shameful accusations. When the accuser had finished, and Bernard had now to speak for himself, he thus began his address with great confidence:—"I confess that heaven is due neither to myself, nor to my actions. Of so great a reward I am utterly unworthy. But my Lord has obtained it for me by a twofold right—by inheritance from His Father, and by the suffering of the Cross. Through this gift I am confident that I too shall be an heir of that kingdom." At these words the adversary was put to shame, and, the conference ending, Bernard came to himself.

S. Hugh, Bishop of Lincoln, a man of the greatest integrity, was one night haunted with grievous anxieties, and when he could not shake them off, he began to be disturbed in mind; but with early morning he came to himself, and sighing deeply said,—"Alas! I have greatly sinned, because I have not, as becomes a Christian man, *cast all my care upon the Lord,* according to the command of the prophet!"

Frederick II, Duke of Saxony, surnamed "the Placid," died in the year 1464. Several years before his death this prince stirred up a quarrel with Frederick, Bishop of Magdeburg, and from that proceeded to war. And that he might carry it on with the greater prudence, and in order to secure success, he sent a spy to gain full information about the preparations and plans of the enemy. This was done; and when an examination had been made at all points, word was brought back to Frederick that there were no preparations at all for war, and that not even a single soldier had been called out, and furthermore that the Bishop had said that he should commend his cause to God, Who would take up arms for His servant. As soon as the Elector heard this he said,— "Let some one else show his madness, if he will, and wage war against a man who is confident of gaining the victory through the help of God." And here the bishop is worthy of praise for relying on the protection of God, and so, too, is the prince for laying aside his arms, and fearing to have God as an Adversary.

5. And this is the counsel of the wise man,—"Have confidence in the Lord with all thy heart." (*Prov.* III. 5.) But they who are destitute of such Trust look at human things alone, and measure all things by human strength. And it often happens that God for-

sakes such people as these in the execution of their devices, so that fruitlessly and with vain endeavours they look for great results, and drag along their languishing mind in a wretched state of expectation, and often close these human thoughts of theirs by some untoward event. But, on the other hand, our Trust in God most effectually conciliates on our behalf the Divine Beneficence. God rejoices to confer benefits, and showers the gifts of His munificence on those especially who elevate themselves to great Trust in Him. But if He keeps His bounteous Hand fast closed, and does not spread out the cloud of His Liberality, or only causes it to rain down upon us with very gentle drops, let us silently reflect Who it is that has dried up that heavenly cloud, which hangs suspended in the air, ever ready to descend in showers, and has caused it to cease from falling; let each person, I say, reflect on this, and accuse his sins, his lukewarmness and languor, and specially his want of Trust in God, and let him rouse himself to fresh Trust and hope for showers instead of drops. For when hindrances have been removed these clouds are ever ready to rain, and not merely now with such showers as were expected, but whole rivers and seas will, as it were, be cast down from heaven that they may overwhelm in the waters of their abundance the heart which pants after them, and is strong in Trust. For God is not so rich in promises as in deeds. He has promised that even mountains may be removed, and the dead raised to life again.

"Blessed be the man that trusteth in the Lord, and the Lord shall be his confidence." (*Jer.* XVII. 7.) None ever trusted in the Lord, and was confounded.

CHAPTER V

A HELMET on the head does good service to many, and so does a breastplate on the chest, and an anchor in the sea; and yet many who are defended with a helmet are struck down, many covered with a breastplate are pierced through, many furnished with an anchor are drowned; but "they that trust in the Lord shall be as Mount Sion: he shall not be moved for ever." (*Ps.* cxxiv. 1.) For as no assault of tempests and no violence of waves can move the rock of Sion from its place, not merely because it is a Mount, but because it is the holy Mount of God, so no assault of troubles will overthrow the man who really trusts in God, and desires to be obedient to the Divine Will in all things. This Trust in God is a helmet which can be cleft by no stroke, a breastplate which can be pierced by no weapon, an anchor which is liable to no shipwreck. "Which hope we have as an anchor of the soul, sure and firm." (*Heb.* vi. 19.)

1. S. Paul, that world-wide Preacher, observed that the Trust of certain of his converts was wavering, as if they had been fed with vain hope. Think-

ing that these over-timid brethren should be instructed aright, he said,—"Do not therefore lose your confidence, which hath a great reward. For patience is necessary for you, that doing the Will of God, you may receive the promise." (*Heb.* x. 35, 36.)

And the first reward of such a Trust is that it deceives no one, or makes him ashamed. (*Rom.* v. 5.) But that fallacious trust in human things deceives ten thousand times, and yet it does not make the deceived at all more cautious. In the year 1084, Archbishop Otho, brother of William, King of England, under the influence of certain predictions, believed that he should be the next Pope after Gregory VII, and, in order to pave the way to the Chair with steps of silver, he collected money on all sides by nefarious means; and when he was on the point of approaching the height of greatness in expectation, he was thrown into prison by his brother William, where he spent three years, and this was the throne which was the reward of his hope: nor did he ever wear the Roman tiara. And so in the case of many others, their hope has turned to disgrace and loss. "For the hope of the wicked is as dust, which is blown away with the wind, and as a thin froth which is dispersed by the storm: and a smoke that is scattered abroad by the wind: and as the remembrance of a guest of one day that passeth by." (*Wisdom* v. 15.) But Hope and Trust in God bring disgrace to no one. "Hope confoundeth not." (*Rom.* v. 5.) "No one hath hoped in the Lord, and hath been confounded.

For who hath continued in His commandment, and hath been forsaken? or who hath called upon Him, and He despised him?" (*Ecclus.* II. 11, 12.)

And here, I pray you, consider how the Trust which Moses placed in God did not confound him. When the Israelites went out of Egypt they were enclosed within a narrow compass, for behind them was their enemy Pharao, and in front of them mountains and the sea forbade all further flight. Whereupon Moses is said to have poured forth this prayer, (JOSEPH. *Antiq.* II. 16) :—"Thine, O Lord, is this sea; Thine too is this mountain which shuts us in; and this can at Thy command either be cleft in sunder, or turned into level ground, and the sea can be made dry land. Nay, we might escape by a flight through the air, if it should please Thee that we should be thus preserved." And when he had thus prayed, he struck the sea with his rod; which suddenly parted with the blow, showed a path for them to pass over straight before them. "Hope confoundeth not." Therefore, the first prerogative of Trust in God is *not to deceive*.

2. A second reward of the same Trust is *entire tranquillity of life.* He who really trusts in God performs his duties without excitement, however widely they may extend, being joyful even in the midst of adversity. "Let all them be glad that hope in Thee : they shall rejoice for ever." (*Ps.* v. 12;) "for we are saved by hope." (*Rom.* VIII. 24.) "Blessed are all they that trust in Him. (*Ps.* II. 12.) Most beau-

tifully, according to his wont, does S. Augustine say on the words of the Psalm cxxvii. 2,—"Thou shalt eat the labours of thy hands (fruits) : blessed art thou, and it shall be well with thee."—"He seemeth to speak perversely to those who understand not, for he should have said, 'Thou shalt eat the fruit of thy labours.' For many eat the fruit of their labour. They labour in the vineyard, they eat not the toil itself, but what ariseth from their labour they eat. What meaneth 'thou shalt eat the labours of thy fruits?' At present we have toils; the fruits will come afterwards. But since their labours themselves are not without joy, on account of the hope (whereof we have a little before spoken, 'Rejoicing in hope, patient in tribulation'), at present those very labours delight us, and make us joyful in hope. If, therefore, our toil has been what could be eaten and could also delight us, what will be the fruit of our labour when eaten?"

There is an old saying of the Germans, and one which is very often inscribed on walls, to the effect that he who has commended all things to God will be tranquil on one side, and blessed on the other. And it really is so, for always to commend all things to God obtains in this life tranquillity, and in the life to come Beatitude. But all things are to be commended to God, and are all alike to be received from the hand of God in such a way as that this rule should admit of no exception. And most admirably does a pious writer say that this rule, of receiving all things from the Hand of God, is so universal in its obligation as that no departure whatever from it is to be allowed. So that not only crosses, and external afflictions coming from the world and one's neighbour, ought to be received as from God, but also those internal sufferings which take their rise from our imperfections; since all things work together for good for them that love God. (*Rom.* VIII. 28.)

3. The third reward is *strength in adversity,* and a soul that cannot be subdued by calamity. "The just is as an everlasting foundation. The just shall never be moved." (*Prov.* x. 25, 30.) David, that most courageous king, exclaims,—"I have put my trust in the Lord, and shall not be weakened." (*Ps.* XXV. 1.) Admirably does Theodoret say,—"Have God as your Pilot and Charioteer, and let all that belongs to you hang on His Providence, for in this way will you remain unshaken and unchangeable." Such was the way in which the army of holy Martyrs bore themselves. It is a new and rare sight to be suspended on "the Horse,"* and to have the ribs burnt, and yet all the while to laugh and jest. It is nothing new that there should be a great concourse of the people when sweetmeats are scattered about, or when gifts and doles are bestowed. But when heads are struck off, when gridirons, and wheels, and crosses are brought forward, and when tortures of all kinds are called into play, that people should still be found to run to meet them, and vie with one another as to

* An instrument of torture.

who should be the first to die, this is indeed a novelty, this was never heard of before. "And yet this," says *Eusebius*, "I have witnessed with my own eyes. I have seen numberless people in Egypt led outside the city walls into the open country without being fettered, one striving to get before another in stretching out their necks. The executioners and their swords were wearied out; they sat down tired, and others took their place; the swords were exchanged for fresh ones; the day was not long enough for the work; and yet none of them, not even a little child, was terrified by death." Behold these invincible heroes and heroines! Like Mount Sion, they could not be moved. And here S. Chrysostom (*In Ps.* cxxiv. i.) appositely remarks,—"By Mount Sion he means Trust in God, which is immutable, firm, constant, invincible, and impregnable. For just as if anyone were to employ innumerable engines, he would be able neither to root up a mountain nor cause it to totter, so also whoever attacks the man who has placed his Trust in God will labour to no purpose. But why said he not absolutely, 'as a mountain,' but makes mention of Mount Sion? It is to teach us that we ought not to despond in afflictions, nor be overwhelmed with them, but hanging on. God, with trust in Him, bravely bear all things, whether they be wars, or conflicts, or tumults. For as this Mountain, which was once upon a time desolate, and abandoned by its inhabitants, returned to its former prosperity when its inhabitants had come back, and wonders were again shown there, so a man of brave and generous spirit, although assailed by numberless calamities, is nevertheless not moved in even the least degree. They who trust in the Lord shall change their courage from human into Divine, "they shall take wings as eagles, they shall run and not be weary, they shall walk and not faint." (*Isai.* XL. 31.) "Blessed are all they that trust in Him." (*Ps.* II. 12.) Therefore, "do ye manfully, and let your heart be strengthened, all ye that hope in the Lord." (*Ps.* XXX. 25.)

4. The fourth reward is *freedom from many sins.* "And none of them that trust in Him shall offend." (*Ps.* XXXIII. 23.) On the testimony of S. Bernard (*De Grat. et Lib. Arbit.*) :—"True conversion consists in not being pleased with anything but that which is proper and lawful; and the will then at length will be perfect when it is fully good and goodly full."* But that man may be thought to possess this "fully good and goodly full" will, who no longer follows his own will, but embraces the Divine Will instead, and transfuses his whole self into it with the most devout submission. And he it is who trusts in God in all things. But whoever is skilled in this happiest of arts, and makes a real and entire surrender of himself both to the Providence of God and His Will, fears not the grievous assaults of sins. True Trust in God removes not only the disquietude of a troubled breast, but also that torpor of mind and listlessness

* "Et tunc demum perfecta erit voluntas, cum plene fuerit bona, et bene plena."

which is the opposite of it. Learn, therefore, to trust in God, even if all things are adverse. Learn against hope to believe in hope (*Rom.* IV. 18), and the Will of the Lord shall prosper in your hand. (*Isai.* LIII. 10.)

5. The fifth reward. By a true Trust in God *we are made as it were omnipotent.* S. Paul fearlessly exclaims,—*"I can do all things* in Him Who strengtheneth me." (*Phil.* IV. 13.) But what need have we of further evidence? Our Lord Himself has said most clearly,—"If thou canst believe, ALL THINGS *are possible* to him that believeth." (*Mark* IX. 22.) Upon which words of our Lord S. Bernard (*Serm.* 85 *in Cant.*) beautifully says,—"Why should not *all things be possible* to the man who leans on Him Who can do all things? Nothing more clearly shows the Omnipotence of God *than that He makes all those omnipotent who trust in Him.* For is not he *omnipotent* to whom *all things are possible?"*

When the Apostles asked our Lord privately why they could not heal the child who was a lunatic, and possessed of an evil spirit, He ascribed the entire reason to their want of Trust in Him, saying,—"Because of your unbelief; for amen I say to you, If you have faith as a grain of mustard-seed, you shall say to this mountain, Remove from hence hither; and it shall remove; and nothing shall be impossible to you." (*Matt.* XVII. 19.) And not only is Christian Faith commended, but also that Trust which so invests itself with Divine Omnipotence as to attempt things however difficult, and perform wonders. Although Christ said not, *"Work miracles,"* but, *"Have faith in God,"* yet leave off your complaints against the ordinance of God; master your cowardice which trembles before difficulties; drive out from yourselves all want of Trust. If you are not able to tread upon serpents and dragons, trample under foot your pride; if you cannot subdue fire at your word, extinguish the flames of your lusts; if you cannot tame lions, and subdue leopards and tigers, restrain your anger; if you cannot raise the dead to life again, kill envy, which is endued with marvellous vitality through your evil doings; if you cannot clothe dead trees with fresh foliage, yet furnish with a rich gift your hand which has hitherto been niggardly. It is this which Christ requires—*"Have faith in God."* And he who has this elicits some good from all evils; from every lump of lead he collects some silver and gold. And this is Divine workmanship; for, as Boethius says, "that alone is Divine power to which even evils are good, when, by handling them aright it elicits from them some good results."

CHAPTER VI

THAT TRUST IN GOD WITHOUT KNOWLEDGE OF DIVINE PROVIDENCE IS WEAK AND UNCERTAIN

DURING that sorrowful journey of Abraham to Mount Moriah, where his son was to be slain, when the third day was now dawning and the mountain lay before them, Isaac, who was carrying the wood on his shoulders, addressed his father, whom he saw furnished with a knife, and said,—"My father, behold fire and wood: where is the victim for the holocaust? And Abraham said: God will provide himself a victim for an holocaust, my son. So they went on together." (*Gen.* XXII. 7, 8.) And would that *we* also, especially when difficulties press upon us, and we find no way of escape, would constantly repeat in our mind this single sentence,—"*God will provide.*"

And with what marvellous Trust in God did Abraham endeavour to carry out the command which, as it appeared, was directly contrary to the Divine promises. It cannot be told what acts of Trust he made during those three days in which he was journeying to the mountain which God had told him of, while he constantly repeated to himself these words,—"*God will provide;* He will surely provide in some wonder-fur way." "For the father," as S. Chrysostom says, "sacrificed the son, offered himself as a victim, God accepted both, and yet the life of the victim remained." And so Abraham, thoroughly trusting in God, came to the mount, to the altar, to the knife, and to the slaying of his son. In good truth that holy man had deeply drunk into his soul that saying which is ever most infallible,—*"The Lord will provide."*

Whoever desires to receive this Divine form of speech will learn it best by using it every day, and both in his own case and in that of others will discover marvellous traces of Divine Providence. And let us, I pray, briefly review our former life. Through how many turns and windings has Divine Providence safely guided us! From how many and how great perils has it sweetly delivered us! Every one of us may truly say,—"He sent from on high, and took me, and drew me out of many waters. He prevented me in the day of my affliction, and the Lord became my stay. And He brought me forth into a large place, He delivered me, because I pleased Him." (2 *Kings* XXII. 17-20.) And into what great dangers of life, and body, and soul have I not run, but have escaped! *"The Lord will provide."* Let us, then, trust in God. But to this confidence in God only he will attain who rightly recognizes also His Providence. Whether there is such a thing as providence is a subject upon which I decline to enter, for Clemens Alexandrinus (*Strom.* 5.) rightly says, there are certain questions which are worthy of punishment, of which sort is it to ask for proofs whether there be a Providence.

1. But what is Providence? Damascene (*De Fide Orthod.* II. 29.) well says,—"Providence is the Will of God, by which all things are fitly and harmoniously governed." We will state the case thus,—God foresaw from all eternity in what way each created thing could fulfil its own end, and at the same time He also foresaw all the difficulties which would occur in attaining this end. Therefore, God, by His most holy Will, decreed that such aid should be ministered as that by it all men should have the very best guidance to their own end. And this, from the very creation of the world, He purposed and carried into effect by His boundless power; so that, in this way, Divine Providence, as Dorotheus says, is the source of all good things. And this Providence of His, God from the very beginning brought before people's eyes, by means of the Deluge, by the burning of Sodom, by the plagues of Egypt, and by the sustenance sent down from heaven for so many hundred thousand Israelites, in whose presence, moreover, He framed laws, manifested His glory, appointed as a guide of their journey a bright and fiery pillar, sent abundant showers of birds, and gave wonderful victories. God exercises this Providence over all created things; a truth which is most certain. Wisdom exclaims,—"He made the little and the great, and He hath equally care of all." (Chap. VI. 8.)

But, in order that we may fix the knowledge of

Divine Providence deep in our inmost mind, it is necessary to lay down this fundamental truth, that nothing is anywhere done in the whole world *by accident or chance.* If we examine the question with regard only to *our own* forethought or knowledge, we shall come to the conclusion that many things happen by a kind of chance and fortune, but if with regard to the *Divine Intelligence,* that nothing at all is done by chance; for the Divine Intelligence is infinite, and extends without any effort to everything which can be understood. God, in a single moment of time, and with one and the same glance of His Eye, if I may so speak, penetrates and sees through all the most secret places and depths of heaven, and earth, and sea, and hell. He from all eternity has "ordered all things in measure, and number, and weight." (*Wisd.* XI. 21.)

2. Most wisely does S. Augustine (*In Ps.* IX.) remark,—"And in this way let all things be referred to the guidance of Divine Providence, which fools think happen by chance, as it were, and accident, and not by Divine Disposal." This will appear by an example:—A master sends two of his servants, who are entirely ignorant of his intention, by different roads to the same place. That one should meet the other there is a chance, not indeed to *the master,* but to *the servants.* And in the same way, that a treasure should be found by a poor man when digging is a chance indeed to that poor man, but not to God, Who willed that the money should be hidden there

so that a hireling should dig, and find it, and become rich, not by chance, but the fatherly Providence of God.

It was not by accident, in a case which seemed to be entirely one of chance, that the dead body should be cast into the sepulchre of Eliseus, so that, "when it had touched the bones of Eliseus, the man came to life, and stood upon his feet." (2 *Kings* XIII. 21.) It was not by chance that Moses, when exposed in the cradle of bulrushes, was found by the daughter of Pharao and adopted for her son. (*Exod.* II. 5.) It was not by chance that Achab was wounded between the joints of his armour, although "one of the people shot an arrow at a venture." (2 *Par.* XVIII. 33.) This arrow was sped by the unerring Hand of God, just as was that also which pierced Julian the Apostate. It was only to the archer who shot the arrow that the effect was uncertain. It was not by chance or accident that the sparrows flew about the house of Tobias, and deprived that excellent man of his eye-sight, (*Tobias* II. 11;) but God permitted this trial to fall upon him that an example of patience might thus be furnished for posterity. *Nothing happens by chance;* and so it was no accident that, when our Lord was about to be born, the whole world should be taxed by Augustus. (*Luke* II. 1.) It was not by chance that He sat down by the well of Sichar, when about to converse with the woman of Samaria. (*John* IV. 5.) All these things were noted from all eternity in the book of Divine Providence.

3. But why does God permit so great and such frequent evils? Here even Plato bids us hold our peace. The Judgments of God are a great deep! Admirably does S. Augustine (*In Ps.* xxv.) say,— "The storms of this deep arise; you see the wicked flourishing, and the good suffering. There is temptation, there is a surging wave, and your soul cries out, O God, is this Thy Justice, that the wicked should flourish and the good suffer? And God replies to you, And is this your *Faith?* Have I promised you this? Or were you made a Christian for this end, that you might flourish in the world?"

Let us, therefore, compose our minds, and yield ourselves to the Providence of God, even though we see the wicked in power, the good oppressed, religion overthrown, and justice extinguished; for none of these things would take place *if God did not specially permit it,* and He would not permit it unless He had the most just grounds for it, and if it were not better thus to *permit* than to *hinder.* Nor is it of any consequence that the secret Government of God is not now made manifest. At the last day there will be seen, as in a mirror, the whole course of the human race, and the entire disposal of Divine Providence which God has exercised in the case of separate kingdoms, towns, and families, and in dealing with each individual man, so that it may appear how kind He was to sinners, and how every one of them is more or less inexcusable; in a word, how the form of government which God employed was accurately adapted both to the varying nature of things, and to show forth His glory.

4. Once upon a time Theodore, who was suffering from violent pain in the head, came to Pachomius and asked him to drive away this suffering by prayer. To whom Pachomius replied,—"Do you think that this pain in your head, or any similar complaint, befalls you without the Permission and Will of God? Bear it; and when God pleases it will be cured. Abstinence from food is good, and so is liberality towards the poor; but the sick man is a far greater gainer when he patiently and perseveringly waits on the Divine Will." And from this we can understand how that man will know little about tranquillity of mind who is not entirely resting on Divine Providence as his foundation. But he cannot long be unhappy who, by means of a living faith, has penetrated into this secret abode of Divine Providence. "Many are the afflictions of the just; but out of them all will the Lord deliver them. The Lord keepeth all their bones, not one of them shall be broken." (*Ps.* xxxiii. 20, 21.) God is not like an architect who when he has built a house leaves it. He is not only present with His work every moment, but *dwells* in it continually.

5. A writing-master, who teaches little boys to form their letters, sometimes guides the hand of one while he pays no attention to another; and why is this? One boy is of a good disposition, ingenious, docile, and well-behaved; while the other is rude, disobedient, and intractable. And in this way God fulfils the will

of those who fear Him, and so protects and governs them under all circumstances, and at all times, that all things turn out for their good; whereas in the case of stubborn and rebellious children it is said,—"When you multiply prayer, I will not hear." (*Isai.* I. 15.) But why is it, they say, that God does not protect and guide us in the same way as He does this or that person? You yourselves are to blame:—"The eyes of the Lord are upon the just: and His ears unto their prayers. But the countenance of the Lord (*i. e.,* His countenance full of indignation) is against them that do evil things: to cut off the remembrance of them from the earth." (*Ps.* XXXIII. 16-17.) To those obedient children God promises:—"When thou shalt pass through the waters, I will be with thee, and the rivers shall not cover thee: when thou shalt walk in the fire, thou shalt not be burnt, and the flames shall not burn in thee." (*Isai.* XLIII. 2.) "I will be to it, saith the Lord, a wall of fire round about: and I will be in glory in the midst thereof." (*Zach.* II. 5.) The soul of a man who conforms himself to the Will of God, He occupies as His Throne, and reigns there as a King. Let those approach, if they can, who wish to do it harm when God does not give them leave. Jacob, when questioned by his brother Esau about the company that was with him, said,—"They are the children which God hath given to me thy servant." (*Gen.* XXXIII. 5.) And so he quietly taught him, as S. Chrysostom says, how great was God's Providence towards him.

This marvellous Providence of God is like the ladder which Jacob, when sleeping in the open air, saw reaching from earth to heaven. (*Gen.* XXVIII. 12.) God, Who is supreme in Providence, had before Him, from all eternity, all things which should ever happen in heaven and earth. For His Wisdom "reacheth therefore from end to end mightily, and ordereth all things sweetly." (*Wisd.* VIII. I.) And such is the Power of His Providence that it cannot be hindered, or deceived, or baffled, or turned aside by anything; yet such is its sweetness that it does nothing contrary to the nature of any creature, most mightily and sweetly foreseeing and disposing all things. It is like the fable of the ancients, who said that there was a golden chain which was let down from heaven to earth, and that when it had encircled all things it was again drawn up to heaven. Let us, therefore, day by day, take refuge in the infinite Providence of God; and when we see that the whole world is filled with so many and so great acts of wickedness, this also will come into our thoughts,—"The Lord shall laugh at him: for he foreseeth that his day shall come." (*Ps.* XXXVI. 13.) If we withdraw our eyes from the world at large, and fix them on our home and ourselves, we shall see about us a Providence so watchful and so full of love, that not even a single hair can fall from our head without its knowledge or permission. And so S. Augustine exclaims,—"What will be wanting to me, even if my enemy tears me limb from limb, since God numbers all my hairs?"

CHAPTER VII

HOW GREAT THE PROVIDENCE OF GOD IS IN REFERENCE TO THE NECESSARIES OF LIFE

ALL things, it is true, are in the Hand of God, and yet a certain person has not said amiss that He has three keys in His Own keeping, which He entrusts to no one. One key is that which lets out rain, wind, snow, and such-like influences of the sky. Another is that which opens the graves, and calls the dead to life again. The third is that which belongs to food and everything necessary to the support of life. But if God were to close these receptacles whence our supplies are derived, who could open them? Therefore He is the Storekeeper and Dispenser of all things; and whatever is needful for the support of life must be sought from Him.

1. Mark the Anchorite used to say,—"If a man trusts not in God in these transitory things, how much less will he trust in Him in those things which relate to eternity!" And the first argument which our Lord uses to shame our want of Trust in Him, is,—"Is not the life more than the meat, and the body more than the raiment?" (*Matt.* vi. 25.) Here, then, by the most cogent arguments, He removes from the mind

that pernicious solicitude about food and clothing, and teaches us that we should trust alone in the benign Providence of God. For if God is so provident and bountiful in those things which seem to be more weighty, why do we charge Him with forgetfulness, or want of care, in other things which are of lesser moment? If He gave us the body, why should he refuse us clothing? If He bestows on us a horse, why should He withhold the bridle? Is not the life itself more precious than that by which it is supported? And is not the body of more consequence than that with which it is covered? Most undoubtedly. He, therefore, Who gave life and a body to us, without any solicitude on our part, or rather when as yet we had no existence at all, will without doubt also give things for the support of the life and body, especially since He Himself wills that our life and body shall stand in need of such things. If then He of His Own free will gave that which is greater, He proclaimed that He was both able and willing also to give that which is less. He will not, however, give to us while we are in a state of *idleness,* since He did not create us for this; but He will give to us when we are free from *anxious care,* for He wills that this should be cast on Himself. God when challenging Job, inquires,—"Who provideth food for the raven, when her young ones cry to God, wandering about, because they have no meat?" (*Job* xxxviii, 41.) And this same argument derived from birds our Lord enforces when He says,—"Consider the ravens: for they sow not, neither do they reap; neither have they storehouse nor barn; and God feedeth them: how much are you more valuable than they?" (*Luke* XII. 24.) And often inculcating the same truth, our Divine Master says,—"Are not two sparrows sold for a farthing? And not one of them shall fall on the ground without your Father. But the very hairs of your head are all numbered. Fear not therefore, better are you than many sparrows." (*Matt.* x. 29-31.) And in order to make this as clear as possible He does not bring forward the children of Israel, who were fed in the wilderness for forty years, neither does He commend to us Elias, who was sustained by ravens, nor yet does He set before us lions, or bears, or elephants, or any large beasts of that kind, although these also are fed by Divine Providence, but the most insignificant of living things, those little birds which, since they are chiefly occupied in singing, and only take their food in the intervals, seem to be most especially free from all anxious care. And should man, who is of more value than countless birds, and who acknowledges God not only as his Lord, but as his Father, be thus distracted in mind?

And after pointing out the Providence of God in the case of birds, and the hairs of our head, our Lord proceeds to set forth how it is shown in the case of flowers. "Consider," He says, "the lilies of the field, how they grow; they labour not, neither do they spin: but I say to you, that not even Solomon in all his glory was arrayed as one of these. And if the grass of the field, which is to-day, and to-morrow is cast into the oven, God doth so clothe; how much more you, O ye of little faith?" (*Matt.* VI. 28-30.) See, then, how entirely free from anxiety are the flowers of the field about that clothing in which they glory, for all their beauty they acknowledge to be received from God alone, openly declaring that they owe nothing to human care. Now the nature of things, which is derived from the Providence of God, the industry and skill of man may imitate, but cannot rival; and so the robe of Solomon, which was exquisite in fabric, and ornamented even to a miracle, did yet in no way equal the elegance of the most insignificant flower. And do you now judge, if God clothes with such beauty the commonest flowers, which will be cut down and thrown into the fire, how much more will He clothe you who were formed by Him for immortality, and provide what is necessary not merely for covering the body, but also, if need be, for adorning it.

And to these arguments our Lord joins also a third one:—"Which of you, by taking thought, can add to his stature one cubit?" (*Luke* XII. 25.) Nay, rather he will diminish it by anxiety, for here the diligence of no one will profit him: "If then ye be not able to do so much as the least thing why take ye thought for the rest?" (*Luke* XII. 26.) If the greatest anxiety you can show does not advance so trifling a thing as that the stature of your body should increase, how will an abundance of corn and riches heaped together be able to preserve your body in life, unless the Providence of God grants a blessing? Empty and fruitless is all your labour unless God prospers it. To Him, therefore, commit the care of nourishing your body, to Him, too, the care of causing it to grow, for this He will do most fittingly and sweetly, without any assistance from your anxiety. He openeth His Hand, and filleth all living things with blessing. (*Ps.* cxliv. 16.)

2. Since God, therefore, provides for all things which are necessary to support life, for "He hath equally care of all," (*Wisd.* vi. 8) how comes it that there is so great a number of people in every place who suffer from the extremity of want? Truly does S. Chrysostom (*Orat.* 5, *de Div. et Paup.*) say,—"Not only do poor men stand in need of the rich, but the rich need the poor, and more so than the poor need the rich." And let us imagine two cities, in one of which rich men alone live, and in the other only poor: there can be no dealings between them; for in the former there will be no mechanics or tradesmen, no tailor, baker, smith, woollen-draper, or labourer. For such callings as these the rich are not adapted. There will be no menservants or maids here; and what sort of city, then, will it be if deprived of external help? In the other there will be an abundance of those who mend shoes, make clothes, and cultivate the fields; plenty of people, in a word, who are satisfied with moderate means. But if the necessaries of life were supplied to all in abundance, what would follow?

The destruction of all trades, mechanics' works and crafts of all kinds. Building, navigation, bird-catching, fishing, and trading of all sorts would go to ruin; and who would be masters, if there were none who would offer themselves as servants? Poverty, therefore, preserves the human race, and adorns it. Poverty makes men diligent and industrious. Poverty stimulates the arts. Let Poverty be banished from the world, and at the same time good manners, and nearly all virtues will be banished with it. To eat, drink, sport, act the glutton, or the wanton, and more than act the wanton, will be the chief busines, of life; riot will attend upon extravagance, vice upon riches. Where there is abundance of all things, there is generally no lack of vices also. Years of plenty prove this, in which the taverns are full of drunkards and overflow with all kinds of filthiness and infamy. The Deluge is an evidence of this; its beginnings were ease and luxury; and so the life of all men was lost to every feeling of shame, and was brimming over with lusts. See, then, how great is the Providence of God, which by means of poverty draws men from wantonness to toil. Labour stimulates the best of men. Whatever object of beauty we anywhere behold was laboriously fashioned by those who were ill supplied with money, and who therefore were obliged to sell their labours.

With how great Providence, moreover, does God come to our aid in poverty! "The Lord will not afflict the soul of the just with famine." (*Prov.* x. 3.) S.

Francis, when standing before the Bishop of Assisi, with nothing but a common piece of linen wrapped round him, exclaimed,—"Now can I say with perfect freedom, 'Our Father Who art in Heaven.'" He used also to give to his followers, as provision for their journey, those words of the Psalmist,—"Cast thy care upon the Lord, and He shall sustain thee." (*Ps.* LIV. 23.) When the Roman pontiff also was inquiring about their means of support, he replied,—"We have a poor Mother indeed, Religion, but a very rich Father." And so it is, this Father embraces His Children with such care and Providence that, when human aid fails, He ministers Divine.

S. Dominic, when founding his order, sent out two of his followers to preach. One evening they were tired, and hungry, and were sorrowfully complaining that they were among strangers, and had descended to the lowest depths of poverty in a place where no help could be expected, whereupon a certain person met them, and discovering the cause of their sorrow, addressed them as follows:—"You have forsaken all for the love of God, and so have showed great trust in Him, and are you now full of fear, as if you were bereft of all hope? God feeds the cattle, and will He suffer His children to perish with hunger?" Having said this he left them. They then entered a city, and after they had said their prayers in the church they were invited to supper by the curate. But another person also came up and showed great eagerness that they should become his guests; whereupon a friendly contest began between the two; and this was put an end to by a third person, a man high in authority in that place, who carried them off with him to his house as well as the curate and the other who was offering hospitality, and entertained them all sumptuously. And so our Lord says to His Own people, when they have toiled all the night,—"Come and dine." (*John* xxi. 12.) And yet there are times when these examples do not root out our want of Trust in God. Whatever He supplies we still fear want; in the very midst of water we are apprehensive of drought, and, unless a great abundance of everything surrounds us, we believe that much is wanting. And so the wicked thought ever and anon disturbs us,—Where is that which you hope for? To which S. Augustine well replies,—"Hope is not yet come to its fulfilment. An egg is something, but it is not yet a chicken."

4. The story goes that there was once upon a time a beggar, who, when he saw his wallet full, and completely stuffed out with bread, used to say,—"*Now I hope!*" And we are very like this beggar, for we, in sooth, hope when we believe that there is a prospect of our living sumptuously for many a year to come. We, in fact, conceive hope in exact proportion to our possessions at the time.

S. Amatus was a noble mirror for all such to look into as either show impatience against Divine Providence, or silently accuse it. After he had spent thirty years in a monastery he passed a life of perfect contentment on a solitary rock, for Berinus, who was assigned as a companion to him by the brotherhood, only brought him every third day a barley loaf and a pitcher of water. This was the rule both of his food and obedience. But the evil spirit was exasperated by this abstinence. And so upon a favourable occasion, when the holy man was on his knees, wrestling in prayer with God, a raven flew to him, and upset the pitcher and carried off the bread; and so all the three days' stock of provisions was lost. And what did Amatus then do? Perhaps he was enraged against the raven, and cursed the greedy bird with direful imprecations, and gave vent to fierce complaints about the Providence of God, and cursed these devices of the devil? He did nothing of the kind. This is *our* accustomed way of talking. Raising his hands and his soul towards heaven, he said,—"I give Thee thanks, O Lord JESU, because it is pleasing to Thy most Holy Will to discipline me with a longer fast. I know that this will be good for me, since nothing happens in the world without Thy Providence." Listen to this, ye querulous and unbelieving ones! Nothing is done in the world without Divine Providence, apart from which not even a leaf falls from a tree. And do you imagine that houses are burnt down, ships sunk, fortunes lost, good names blasted, while this Providence is lulled to sleep?

Theodoret relates that S. Mæsimas had two barrels, one full of wheat, and the other of oil. From these he used to give very liberally to the poor, and yet the tubs did not become empty. And God likewise has two barrels, the one full of corn and all things needful to support life, the other brimful and running over with mercy, liberality, and providence; and neither of them can be exhausted. To these two depositories must we run when our little vessels begin to be dry. Only let us thoroughly learn this one thing, TO TRUST IN GOD, and to commend ourselves afresh to His most Holy Will.

There is an old saying among the Germans, that if we did what we ought, God would do what we wished.*

> * Wann wir thaten was wir solten,
> So that Gott was wir wolten.

CHAPTER VIII

HOW GREAT IS THE PROVIDENCE OF GOD TOWARDS HIS FRIENDS

IT is a glorious declaration, "He that toucheth you, toucheth the apple of My Eye." (*Zach.* ii. 8.) And with how great care did God follow the steps of that young harper (David), and with what a manifold Providence did He preserve him in such great perils, just as if this was the only man whom He had taken into His care! He himself testifies,—"Lord, Thou hast proved me, and known me: Thou hast known my sitting-down, and my rising-up. Thou hast understood my thoughts afar off: my path and my line Thou hast searched out." (*Ps.* cxxxviii. 2, 3.) All that pertains to me, O Lord, has been weighed by Thee from all eternity, even to the smallest tittle.

1. Saul fought for the blood and life of David with perpetual snares, but to no purpose, for God protected him. But when David was lying hid in the wilderness of Maon, Saul came there and with "his men encompassed David and his men round about to take them." (1 *Kings* xxiii. 26.) And so effectually did he hem him in that there was no room for escape, or for hope. He was like a wild beast surrounded

with nets and dogs. Here, then, the situation of David seemed to have come to a desperate pass. Saul, who had all but gained the victory, was close at hand, threatening his life; the lion thought it was already holding the prey in its jaws. But this also was in vain, for God delivered him. A sorrowful messenger came to Saul to say that the Philistines had invaded the land, and that therefore he must hasten to drive the enemy from his borders. And so David, when matters had come to this hopeless state, and when he was all but within the claws, as it were, of a ferocious wild beast, was on a sudden released. God protected him; and so, by Divine Providence, he most happily escaped all the snares of the wicked king. But it is no marvel that David should have been thus kept by God as the apple of His Eye; for He knew with most perfect exactitude how to conform himself to Divine Providence. And behold a noble example of this! When he was flying from his rebellious son Absalom, Semei met him in the way, and assailed him with cruel curses. "Come out," he said, "come out, thou man of blood, and thou man of Belial. The Lord hath repaid thee for all the blood of the house of Saul: because thou hast usurped the kingdom in his stead, and the Lord hath given the kingdom into the hand of Absalom thy son: and behold thy evils press upon thee, because thou art a man of blood." (2 *Kings* xvi. 7, 8.) Behold the monstrous wickedness of the man! Feeling no reverence either for the Divine Law, or for the Prince of the people, or his King,

he called him contemptuously, and to his face, a mur-
derer, a tyrant, and a usurper. What a shameful
deed! Nor was it enough to assail with such insults
a prince who was the gentlest of men, and was tenderly beloved by his subjects, and who was afflicted besides with extreme calamity, and was wellnigh prostrate beneath it. Wicked Semei dared a still more
dastardly deed. King David, who was now changed
from a happy to a miserable man (than which change
nothing can be more deplorable), was walking bare-
footed, and with his face covered with tears, and yet
Semei attacked him with stones, as if he were a
mad dog, and instead of flowers cast dust upon him!
And here see the remarkable endurance of David!
worthy of admiration for all generations, by means
of which he bore himself with most entire submission
to Divine Providence, and recognized this grievous
injury as if it had been commanded by God. Abisai,
the brother of Joab, had said,—"Why should this dead
dog curse my Lord the king? I will go, and cut off
his head." (Ver. 9.) And then that devout prince,
who three times had been chosen king, although so
bitterly assailed by a person of impure life, who was
also his subject, and whom he had never harmed by
word or deed, not merely did not give way to anger
and fury, nor thought of vengeance and throwing
back his stones, but became the defender of his assail-
ant, warded off the violence of his soldiers from him,
extenuated the sin which he had committed though
guilty of violence to his majesty, recognized an instru-

ment of Divine Providence, acknowledged that God was the Author of all that had befallen him, and at length gave this command,—"Let him alone and let him curse: for the Lord hath bid him curse David: and who is he that shall dare say, why hath he done so?" (2 *Kings* XVI. 10.) Although, therefore, Semei committed a most heinous sin when he cursed, yet it is so far said that it was commanded him to curse, since God employed Semei's wicked will, which, however, He had not made, for the salutary correction of David.

And the same rule applies in all the trials and injuries in which God uses the will of wicked men, either to exercise the innocent, or to punish the guilty. These are to us as a whip when we have sinned, and a bridle lest we should sin; and, therefore, let anyone who is unjustly troubled by others exclaim with David,—"The Lord be merciful unto me, that I extend not my hand upon the Lord's anointed. As the Lord liveth, unless the Lord shall strike him,—or his day shall come to die, or he shall go down to battle and perish." (1 *Kings* XXVI. 10, 11.)

2. Think of Joseph, I pray, the governor of Egypt. Through what by-paths and difficulties was he led, until he came to that crowning point of honour! And the beginning of this so great glory was *the hatred of his brethren.* Nor was the progress of evils arrested here; for a monstrous act of wickedness followed upon this ill-will which had arisen at home. Joseph was sold as a slave to the Ismaelites, and was carried

into Egypt. Nor did a gentler lot await him there. The favour of his mistress was as destructive to that most virtuous of young men as the hatred of his brethren had been before. For when he allowed the daily blandishments of his mistress to fall upon unheeding ears, he was falsely accused to his master, and having been thrown into prison was kept there, innocent as he was, for the space of three years. It was not, of a truth, immediately upon his arrival in Egypt that he was placed in a chariot of triumph. By various vicissitudes and through many dangers he at length arrived at this pre-eminence. And all that befell him was done at the command of Divine Providence. Joseph himself most abundantly testifies to this when, speaking to his brothers about this same Divine Ordinance, he said,—"Not by your counsel was I sent hither, but by the will of God." (*Gen.* XLV. 8.) "Fear not: can we resist the will of God? You thought evil against me: but God turned it into good." (*Gen.* L. 19, 20.) "And let us," says S. Chrysostom, "not only listen to this, but imitate it also, and comfort in this way those who have afflicted us, not imputing to them the evils which they have committed against us, but bearing everything with perfect goodwill." For God, in His Supreme Providence, is thus wont to transform the worst events which befall His friends into joyful success. Often has an injury paved the way for blessings; many have fallen that they might rise the higher, and to greater things. Divine Providence is wont to use not only things which are rightly done, but sins also, to work out its own De-crees. Have you considered Joseph? Take away the wickedness of his brethren, take away their jeal-ousy, take away the story of their brother's death, which they so cruelly invented, and you have, at the same time, taken away those very things on which the safety of Egypt rested. There would have been no interpretation of the king's dream, no gathering-in of corn for seven years; but Egypt would have per-ished with famine, and neighboring nations would have perished also. Do you wish for a clearer ex-ample? Take away the covetousness of Iscariot, and the envy of the Jews, and at the same time you will have taken away the Ransom of the human race, the Blood and Death of Christ. Take away devils and conflicts, and then victories and rewards will al-most entirely cease. Take away tyrants, and where will martyrs be? It is the custom of Divine Provi-dence not only to use the good for good, but the evil also. The selling of Joseph was, without doubt, effi-ciently from God, if you regard the nature of the action, but the wickedness which was covered by this action arose from the corrupt will of his brethren. And here S. Gregory (*Mor.* VI. 14.) well remarks,— "Behold, how the Divine Power takes the wise in their own wisdom! On this account was Joseph sold that he might not be made much of; and therefore was he made much of, because he was sold."

3. Charito, when travelling to Jerusalem, was in-tercepted by an ambush of robbers, and was dragged

into their cave, and bound with chains. When the robbers had gone elsewhere, in search of booty, Charito did nothing else but extol God and Divine Providence with the loudest praises, and meditate upon this unexpected Permission of His, and thank his most loving Father for it, earnestly commending himself to Him, and desiring nothing else than that the Divine Will should be fulfilled in him. While his thoughts were thus occupied a serpent crept from its hiding-place to a can full of milk, from which it drank largely, although an uninvited guest; and, as his share of the entertainment, he, as ungrateful people are wont to do, poured in poison, instead of the milk which he had taken. When the robbers returned to their accustomed den their first act was to quench their thirst with a draught of milk. They drank more freely than the serpent, but so that they never drank again, for shortly afterwards the poison penetrated into their veins, and they all expired. Charito, therefore, who was now the heir of the robbers, and the sole proprietor of the vile den, commended himself more earnestly than ever to God's Will, and not in vain, for his chains having been loosened by Divine aid, in place of his wretched prison, he found a wealthy habitation, and the money which he discovered there he employed partly in relieving the poor, and partly in building a monastery. The cave of the robbers itself he turned into a church, where both Jews and heathens are now baptized. Oh! marvellous designs of God's Providence.

S. Monegundis would never have attained to such sanctity of life unless Divine Providence had guided her to it through manifold difficulties. She had two daughters, young girls of remarkable beauty, on whom the fond mother lavished all her care and love, herself at that time having but little thought for religion. It pleased Divine Providence to remove this enticement to sin; and so both daughters were carried off by a sudden death. The mother, just as if she herself had survived her own death, began to hate life, to pluck out her hair, to tear her cheeks, to refuse all consolation for her grief, and to desire nothing else than to die at once, and follow her daughters. After her grief had somewhat spent itself in tears her lamentation abated, and becoming more composed she exclaimed,—"Am I not utterly mad for so obstinately crying out against Providence? What am I doing? Have I forgotten that I have brought forth daughters who are mortal? Were they born for this end, that they should not die? The Son of God, the Mother of God, men who are most dear to God, all die, and am I angry that my daughters have ceased to live, who died, perhaps, on this account, that they might not fall a prey to sin! Why, therefore, do I weary God with my complaints, Who can will nothing that is evil? Why do I not rather end this foolish lamentation, and compose myself calmly in the bosom of the Divine Will and Providence?" Thus she spoke, and thus she acted. She separated herself entirely from worldly affairs, and shut herself up in a small house with one little waiting-maid, intending from that day forward to serve God with all her power. And that this change of life was pleasing to God miracles testified, for Monegundis healed many sick people without medicines, as Gregory of Tours affirms. (*De Glor. Confess.* 24.) So great a thing is it to commit oneself wholly to Divine Providence. S. Augustine has said, with the greatest truth,—"He who had a care for you before you were, how shall He not have a care for you when you are now that which He willed you to be?"

4. Robert, the first Abbot of Molesme, a man who was a most careful observer of Divine Providence, gave whatever he was able to the poor. Upon one occasion he ordered two loaves to be given to two beggars, who were waiting before the door; but the steward demurred, and said that there was not even enough for dinner. "What then," said Robert, "shall we dine upon?" "I do not know," said the steward. It occurred, however, to the holy man that something was being concealed, from a mistaken anxiety to provide what was needful. And so when the Divine Office was concluded, and the signal for the meal was given, the abbot asked whence the loaves had been brought. "I kept a few for ourselves," replied the steward. Robert, feeling justly indignant, ordered all the loaves to be collected in a basket, and to be immediately carried away to the poor; then turning to his brethren, he said,—"Lest the disobedience and want of faith of our House should proceed fur-

ther, fasting and hunger will teach us to trust in God." Robert wished that all who belonged to him should rest entirely on the most bounteous Providence of God, like an infant on its mother's breast. The very best remedy of ill-timed parsimony is hunger.

Dorotheus relates that a very devout old man felt a dislike for food for several days together, through weakness of stomach. A youth, who acted as his servant, in order to tempt his appetite, determined to cook a savoury morsel flavoured with honey. And so out of two jars he, in his haste, seized one in which rancid oil, made from flax, was kept, the resemblance between the vessels causing his error. In order, therefore, to do good to the old man, he poured in plentifully that which was not honey, but almost death itself, and cooked some pottage which could not have been offered even to a dog. The sick man scarcely tasted the disgusting food before he discovered that the hand of his cook had erred, still he said nothing, and ate beyond his strength. At length, when his stomach rejected any more, he put down the spoon, and not even by a single word did he complain of that loathsome dish. Whereupon his companion began to urge and press him to eat more heartily of the dainty food, saying that he had exhausted all his skill in its preparation, that it would work wonders upon his health, and that, in truth, he himself had wished to be the first to partake of this delicious feast. But the good old man so far restrained his loathing as not only not to be excited to use any harsh words, or even

thought, towards his companion, but made this single
excuse, that he had had enough of such delicate fare.
Scarcely, then, had his companion tasted the pottage
when he threw himself at the knees of the old man.
"I have killed you, father," he said, "and why did you
confirm my precipitate thoughtlessness by your silence?" Whereupon the old man replied,—"Do not
torment yourself, my son; for if God had willed that
I should eat honey, you would then have mingled
honey with my food." "Admirably," says Dorotheus,
"did the old man speak; for he knew, of a certainty,
that if God had willed that honey should be eaten by
him, He would not have permitted his attendant to
make a mistake, or, which is equally easy to God, He
would have turned that filthy oil into honey."

And thus does the man behave who recognizes Divine Providence in all things. He does not take everything for the worst, nor does he seek for some one to
whom he may ascribe his misfortune, but rather
refers the sins of men to the Providence of God.
Happen what may, he soothes the irritation by giving
it a kindly interpretation.

5. And here, good reader, I would wish that one
thing should be most thoroughly understood by you.
It is a saying of S. Jerome,—"All things are governed by the Providence of God, and oftentimes that
which is thought to be punishment is only medicine!"
And here this wonderful circumstance is to be observed, that Divine Providence allows things to be
borne onwards by their own impulse up to a certain

fixed time. For it is the custom of Divine Providence gradually, and by the passage of time, to lead all things to their destined ends; for it orders the smallest as well as the greatest. And for this reason Epictetus, that glorious sun among philosophers, said,— "Do not ask that whatever happens should happen according to your own will; but if you are really wise, desire that all things should happen as they do happen." It is a Christian and Divine saying,—*"Desire that all things should happen as they do happen."* S. Basil also (*Ad Eustach.*) speaks in the same way:— "Since things do not turn out as we wish, let us wish them to turn out as they do." And in the same way the Abbot Nilus says (*De Orat.* 29),—"Do not pray that what you wish should come to pass, but rather pray, as you have been taught to pray, that the Will of God be done in you."

Jacob, the Anchorite, answering the devil when he was threatening him with blows, said,—"If it is permitted you by God, strike me. Why do you delay? Strike me, and I shall receive the blows as willingly as if I were struck by Him Who permitted me to be struck. But if it is not permitted you, you will not strike me, even though ten thousand times you show your fury." Thus, too, the Empress Irene, when deposed by her own servant, exclaimed,—"I ascribe it to God that He elevated to the imperial dignity me an orphan, and utterly unworthy of it; but that He now permits me to be dethroned I ascribe to my sins; therefore blessed be the Name of the Lord!"

Well, then, does S. Augustine say,—"Constantly believe in God, and commit yourself entirely to Him with all your power; and so He will not cease to lift you up to Himself, and will permit nothing to befall you, but that which will be for your profit, even though you know it not."

CHAPTER IX

HOW GREAT IS THE PROVIDENCE OF GOD TOWARDS HIS ENEMIES AS WELL AS FRIENDS

G OD sees distinctly, and with a single glance, past, present, and future things. We are all of us present before His Eyes, Adam as well as Antichrist, the whole human race, all created things. "Wisdom reacheth therefore from end to end mightily, and ordereth all things sweetly." (*Wisd.* VIII. 1.) From the loftiest angels to the meanest worms the sleepless care of God extends, yea, and is never absent. Moses and Aaron, of old, proclaimed,—"In the evening you shall know that the Lord hath brought you forth out of the land of Egypt: and in the morning you shall see the Glory of the Lord." (*Exod.* XVI. 6, 7.) Of a truth we shall all of us know, *in the evening of death,* the marvellous Providence of God towards each one of us. "The steps of man are guided by the Lord; but who is the man that can understand his own way?" (*Prov.* XX. 24.) God, in the perfection of His Providence, leads us a long journey, and often through winding paths and inextricable labyrinths, but He knows by what way to guide us to the heavenly pastures. Why, therefore, do we murmur against this most watchful Leader? If anyone sets out on a journey with a companion who is thoroughly acquainted with the road, and when rough, difficult, and marshy parts come in sight begins to complain, and says,—"By what a round-about way you are leading me, my good friend? Unless I am much mistaken, we have long ago left the proper path,"—his guide will quickly reply,—"Do not be alarmed, good sir, but leave it all to me. I have led you by a circuitous path, I allow; but if we had kept a straight course we should have fallen into those quagmires, from which we should never have extricated ourselves. Trust yourself to me, and I will guide you in such a way that you shall not be sorry for having had me for a companion." And in this way, Divine Providence guides us. We must go, indeed, through many by-paths, and long circuitous windings of the road; why then are we angry with our most excellent Guide? Only let the road be *safe,* and what does it matter if it is *rough?*

2. It seems to me that Saul would have been the best of kings, if he had only finished his life as well as he began it. "There was not among the children of Israel a goodlier person than he." (1 *Kings* ix. 2.) While he was seeking his father's asses he found a kingdom. But let us examine a little more attentively God's providence towards him.

God had said to Samuel,—"Tomorrow about this same hour I will send thee a man of the land of Benjamin, and thou shalt anoint him to be ruler over my people Israel." (Ver. 16.) And the way in which he was sent was this:—"The asses of Cis, Saul's father, were lost:" whereupon he bade his son go and seek them. Saul therefore took one of the servants with him, "and when they had passed through Mount Ephraim, and through the land of Salisa, and had not found them, they passed also through the land of Salim, and they were not there: and through the land of Jemini, and found them not. And when they were come to the land of Suph, Saul said to the servant that was with him: Come, let us return, lest perhaps my father forget the asses, and be concerned for us. And he said to him: Behold there is a man of God in this city, a famous man; and all that he saith cometh certainly to pass. Perhaps he may tell us of our way." (Ver. 3-6.) Saul thought that the opportunity was not to be lost, and so after his long wanderings he came to Samuel, being entirely ignorant of what was to follow. Scarcely, however, had they seen one another's face, and began to speak together, when God said to Samuel, "Behold the man, of whom I spoke to thee, this man shall reign over My people." (Ver. 17.) And thus things fell out in their proper order. Saul both found the asses which he sought, and a kingdom which he had not so much as dreamt of. How vast is the depth of God's Providence! How great its hidden mystery! Saul was thinking of nothing less than a sceptre and royal crown when he was raised to a throne by Divine appointment! And so the asses were not lost by chance; neither was it by

chance that he did not immediately find them; nor
yet was it by chance that the plan of going to Samuel was suggested by the servant. All this was done
by the singular Providence of God, and for this special purpose, that the sceptre over Israel might be
conferred on Saul.

But perhaps you may inquire,—"Why did God
will that Saul should be anointed king, when He knew
that he would commit many wicked acts, and end his
life so miserably? And I, too, would ask,—"Why did
God, by His Grace, create angels, when He knew
that they would be tormented for all eternity in hell?
Why did he place Adam in that pleasant garden, from
which He knew that in a short time he would be expelled? Why did our Lord choose Judas Iscariot
to be an apostle, when He foreknew that he would be
a traitor? Why did he send his apostles into a certain city of the Samaritans, when He knew beforehand that they would not be received!" S. Jerome
(*Cont. Pelag.* III. 2.) replies to these questions. "Do
you desire," he says, "to know the reason? God
judges *present* things not *future,* neither does He by
His foreknowledge condemn anyone who He knows
will be such as hereafter to displease Him; but so
great is His goodness, and so ineffable is His mercy,
that He chooses one whom at the present He perceives
to be good, but knows will be wicked in the future,
giving to him the opportunity of conversion and repentance." Adam, therefore, did not sin because God
had foreknown that he would sin, but God foreknew

because Adam would hereafter determine to sin through his own will. "So that," as S. Ambrose says (*In Rom.* IX.), "Adam was not harmed because he received the command, nor Judas because he was elected to be an apostle, but God imposed neither on the former a necessity of transgressing, nor on the latter of becoming the traitor, and if each had preserved that which he had received, he might have refrained from sinning. Those who are foreknown to God as persevering in that which is good are often evil in the first instance, while others that are foreknown as determining to persevere in evil are sometimes good at the beginning." "Wherefore he that thinketh himself to stand, let him take heed lest he fall." (I *Cor.* X. 12.) The chief of the apostles fell, do you therefore watch. Judas fell; it was that you might stand. And here we have a remarkable proof, as Enthymius says, that neither human energy can effect anything without Divine Aid, nor Divine Aid profit at all without human energy. Peter and Judas are examples of this.

3. But to return to the history of Saul. Wonderful was the Providence of God towards him in all things! He who so often had wickedly designed to destroy David by the sword of the Philistines is himself enclosed by a vast army of those same Philistines, and being forsaken by God, and having consulted a sorceress as a crowning act of wickedness, he heard from Samuel the tidings of his coming ruin, which the miserable king could neither endure nor avoid. Alas,

how watchful was the Divine Vengeance! Nothing,
O my God, escapeth Thy Providence! This same
Saul also refusing utterly to destroy the Amalecites,
when God commanded him, is brought to such a depth
of misery that he would have esteemed it a kindness
to have been slain by an Amalecite! Truly "weight
and balance are judgments of the Lord." (*Prov.* xvi.
11.)

But Divine Providence is wont neither to punish
all acts of wickedness immediately, nor to leave them
altogether unpunished. If it were to punish none,
many would say that there was no such thing as
Providence; but if it were at once to inflict the penalty on all, they would believe that no state of reward
or punishment remained after this life. And so God
by punishing some displays His Providence, and by
leaving others unpunished reserves them for the punishment of a future life.

4. In such a way, then, does Divine Providence
lovingly embrace in its government all adverse things
which happen in this world, as that it disposes all the
ills of life, and orders them for our good, and permits sin also for deep and secret ends of its ordinance.
It is the same Providence which does good and permits evil. Of a truth God would never permit any
evil, unless He were so powerful as from every evil
to elicit good. What greater evils ever could have
happened than the sin of Adam, and the crucifixion
of our Lord? And yet the transgression of our first
parent drew down God from heaven to take upon

Himself the form of man; the death of Christ restored to us Heaven, and every blessing. God is such a skilful workman, that out of all forms of evil, just as if they were pieces of leaden coin, He is able to produce gold of the finest quality. "To them that love God, all things work together unto good." (*Rom.* VIII. 28.) The vileness of Magdalen has corrected many; the fall of Peter has raised up many; the doubtfulness of Thomas has confirmed many. The words "thou reapest that which thou didst not sow" (*Luke* XIX. 21) are in reality *commendation* for God, since He sows not sins, and yet from thence He gathers a harvest of many blessings. Of a truth God "sucks honey out of the rock, and oil out of the hardest stone" (*Deut.* XXXII. 13), when from great evils He produces greater blessings.

In such a. way, then, does Divine Providence watch around us and ours as that it has already decreed, to the smallest particular, all the sufferings even of the body. So that let every one at the beginning of sickness reason thus with himself:—This disease, from whatever cause it arises, whether from my own intemperance, or from the malice of another, or however it was contracted, is from Divine Providence, which so adjusts its violence to my strength that its commencement, increase, crisis, and cessation all depend entirely on the same. Thus the malady which now affects the head cannot fasten upon any other part, or increase in intensity, or last for a single hour more than God has decreed. The same Providence also disposes the effect of remedies and curative agents in such a way as that the physician either understands what mode of treatment is to be followed, or cannot keep pace with the progress of the disease and mistakes its character, and that medicines, suited or unsuited to the complaint, are administered opportunely or inopportunely. All the variations of disease, even their smallest fluctuations, are so directed by the ordinance of God, that whatever the Divine Will appoints comes to pass. And thus, in good truth, "Good things and evil, life and death, poverty and riches, are from God." (*Ecclus.* xi. 14.) "For all healing is from God." (Chap. xxxviii. 2.)

And precisely in the same way should we reason about Divine Providence, in reference to all adversities which befall either the mind or the body. Has an enemy slandered you? Reflect, then, that all his calumnies, all his words, yes, every syllable, were weighed out from all eternity in the balance of Divine Providence! As much as has been permitted him will he say against you, and not a single syllable more. Why, therefore, do you vainly struggle and chafe! Apply the same line of reasoning also to all your other sufferings, since their order, number, intensity, time of duration, and attendant circumstances are all most accurately arranged by Divine Providence. Submit yourself, then, to it, and say,—"I was dumb, and I opened not my mouth, because Thou hast done it." (*Ps.* xxxviii. 10.) Thou, O my God, hast done this. Thy Providence, Will, and Permission have sent this upon me. Since Thou, therefore, hast done all this, I should be impious if I were to murmur against Thee; I yield myself then, to Thy Will, and whatever proceeds from it I endure.

5. And this daily meditation on the Divine Will produces in the soul the deepest peace, entirely subjecting the will of man to the Divine in a sweet and delightful way. Whoever, then, yields himself absolutely to the guidance of Divine Providence is free from troubles of numberless kinds: he dwells "in the beauty of peace, and in the tabernacles of confidence and in wealthy rest." (*Isai.* xxxii. 18.) And so a holy Abbot used to say,—"Man will never have rest, unless he is able to say from his heart, 'I and God are alone in this world.'" And this S. Augustine confirms, when he says (*Conf.* iii. 11),—"O Thou Good Omnipotent One, Who so carest for every one of us as if Thou caredst for him only; and so for all as if they were but one!" And therefore, my good friend, God cares for you, and exercises His Providence towards you in such a way *as if He had nothing else to care for*. A great multitude does not disturb Divine Providence; it is the same whether it be one man or a thousand.

And here there is a thought full of comfort; God does not govern us as a prince does a province, or a king a kingdom, who stand in need of the help of so many others. There are viceroys, governors, councillors, and others among whom the cares of government are divided. But it is not in this way that God governs all men with such a Providence that He embraces each individual man with a peculiar care, and the whole of mankind with a general. "The eyes of the Lord in every place behold the good and the evil." (*Prov.* xv. 3.) "The Lord beholdeth the ways of man, and considereth all his steps." (*Prov.* v. 21.)

CHAPTER X

THERE was nothing which our Lord more frequently and more sharply rebuked in His disciples than want of Trust. Thus He often addressed them as "of little faith" (*Matt.* VI. 30); "slow of heart" (*Luke* XXIV. 25); "unbelieving and perverse generation." (*Matt.* XVII. 16.) In various ways He tried them, that they might unlearn their want of Trust in Him. For what was the object of that sleep of our Lord in the ship? (*Matt.* VIII. 24.) Or of that want of bread, and the question about providing food in the wilderness? (*John* VI. 5.) Or of the sinking of Peter in the waves? (*Matt.* XIV. 30.) Their want of Trust was set before them as a thing to be unlearnt.

Now want of Trust manifests itself under various forms. There are some who distrust God because they think that He is too indulgent to their enemies and holds them under no restraint. Others are distrustful about obtaining from God what they ask, especially if on account of sins formerly committed they are harassed with pains of conscience, and fear lest

He should have denied them forgiveness, even when
they sought it. Others distrust God, lest, perchance,
He should withdraw the necessaries of life. This
threefold kind of distrust separates many from God
by a course of deception which is most subtle in its
effect, and hurries them on to ruin. But this sin of
distrust is the more harmful in proportion as it is less
known. If, however, we search for the source of this
sin we shall discover that want of Trust in God arises
from the fact that man *trusts too much in himself.*
How common, then, but fatal, a sin this trust in self
is I must now explain before we proceed to consider
anything else.

1. Solomon rebukes with severity this trust in self,
when he says,—"He that trusteth in his own heart,
is a fool." (*Prov.* XXVIII. 26.) And therefore he admonishes us,—"Have confidence in the Lord with all
thy heart, and lean not upon thy own prudence. Be
not wise in thy own conceit." (*Prov.* III. 5, 7.) In
good truth the first elements of folly are to believe
oneself a wise man. But who is such a Phœnix as
not to have a high opinion of his own interests, but
think meanly of them, and not occasionally contemplate his personal graces, prowess, learning, or prudence with approving eyes, but regard them as his
loss? "He that trusteth in his own devices doth wickedly" (*Prov.* XII. 2), and therefore God, in order to
wrest this wickedness from us, often chastises us
with severity, or when we prove rebellious, altogether
cuts us off from Himself by His correction.

Goliath appears to me to have had such overweening trust in himself as if with his single breath he could scatter whole armies. And so when he saw David, the shepherd youth, advancing to meet him, he assailed so contemptible an adversary with a bitter taunt, and said,—"Come to me, and I will give thy flesh to the birds of the air, and to the beasts of the earth." (1 *Kings* XVII. 44.) But how soon was this self-confidence crushed! And who guided the stone so as with unerring aim to strike the forehead of Goliath but the Hand of God, which overthrew that haughty tower, not indeed with warlike engines, but with a single pebble?

Holofernes was equally confident in himself, and yet he was not of such estimation in God's sight as to fall even by the hand of a man; for a woman trampled all his arrogance under foot. Nabuchodonosor as "he was walking in the palace of Babylon, answered and said: Is not this the great Babylon, which I have built to be the seat of the kingdom, by the strength of my power, and in the glory of my excellence?" (*Dan.* IV. 26, 27.) Alas, Nabuchodonosor! up to this time a hundred dishes were wont to be placed before you as a royal repast, but hereafter you shall be served with but one, and that a wondrous strange one, until you learn both to think and speak aright. But how will your breakfast taste to you? You shall eat grass as oxen, until you learn to be wise, and descend from your haughty pretensions. Your bath shall be the cold dew of heaven; your hair shall be to you instead of garments interwoven with gold, and in place of nails you shall have the claws of birds. "While the word was yet in the king's mouth, a voice came down from heaven: To thee, O king Nabuchodonosor, it is said: Thy kingdom shall pass from thee, and they shall cast thee out from among men, and thy dwelling shall be with cattle and wild beasts: thou shalt eat grass like an ox, and seven times shall pass over thee, till thou know that the most High ruleth in the kingdom of men, and giveth it to whomsoever He will." (Ver. 28, 29.) Thus, then, excessive self-confidence changed him from a man into a beast; but hear how he changed again from a beast into a man, and learnt to trust in God and not in himself:—"Now at the end of the days, I Nabuchodonosor lifted up my eyes to heaven, and my sense was restored to me; and I blessed the most High, and I praised and glorified Him that liveth for ever; for his power is an everlasting power, and His kingdom is to all generations. And all the inhabitants of the earth are reputed as nothing before Him: for He doth according to His Will, as well with the powers of heaven, as among the inhabitants of the earth: and there is none that can resist His Hand, and say to Him: why hast thou done it?" (Ver. 31, 32.)

A great evil was that confidence in self which impelled even the chief of the apostles to his fall! Why, O Peter, do you weep now that the cock crows? It would have beseemed you to have wept before, when the Lord was uttering His parting words, when after supper was ended He made sad mention of His death, here indeed tears would have been well timed: but self-confidence then altogether quenched tears; and instead of weeping words of high promise were heard, —"Although all shall be scandalized in Thee, I will never be scandalized." (*Matt.* xxvi. 33.) But is it so? Will you *never* be offended? Only a few hours will pass by, and all this promise, arising from nothing but confidence in self, will collapse. S. Basil thinks that no one is overcome by any temptation unless he trusts in himself more than is right. He, on the other hand, who really distrusts himself never thinks of undertaking anything until he has previously invoked the Divine Aid. Let no one, then, trust in his strength, or skill, or in a crown and riches, or in learning and wisdom. The occasion comes when all these collapse before a gentle breeze. "Thus saith the Lord: Let not the wise man glory in his wisdom, and let not the strong man glory in his strength, and let not the rich man glory in his riches." (*Jer.* ix. 23.)

2. And not merely let not one place his hope and trust in himself, but neither in any other. Jeremias the prophet exclaims,—"Cursed be the man that trusteth in man, and maketh flesh his arm, and whose heart departeth from the Lord." (Chap. xvii. 5.) And here Origen says, when explaining the words, "Cursed is every one that hangeth on a tree" (*Gal.* iii. 13)—"I think that the meaning is the same as, 'Cursed be the man that trusteth in man.' For to hang on a tree is the same as to have one's hope sus-

pended from a man, who is, as it were, the frail trunk of a tree."

It is the practice of hunters, when they wish to take an elephant, to set a snare of this kind. They cut through the centre of a tree against which the elephant usually rests when sleeping, but they leave it still standing, as if it were sound and untouched. When the elephant comes, according to his custom, to take repose, he leans against the part which has been cut in sunder, and thus the tree and the beast fall together with great violence. And numberless are the people who choose trees for themselves against which to rest. One person tries with the utmost pains to please a prince; another courts the favour of a rich prelate; a third insinuates himself into friendship with a great man; some try to obtain the goodwill of others by presents, while others try to acquire favour in various ways. O miserable ones that you are! you are only deceiving yourselves, and preparing all this for your own destruction! The trees against which you think that you will lean have long ago been sapped by a secret wound, when you little thought it, and soon they will fall, and with them all your hopes.

Jonas made for himself a booth, and sat under the shadow of it, and he "was exceeding glad of the ivy." (*Jonas* IV. 6.) Alas! for his short and empty joy; for his twining plant had two enemies, the sun and a worm, and thus in a single day all the pleasure of its shadow passed away. And now behold the world, I pray you, and you will find it full of shadowing plants like this; they flourish, indeed, for a short time, but destruction is ever being threatened by worms of various kinds. What a common error it is to rest on human favour! and would that even Religious persons would here forbear to be so forgetful of their dignity, and with hidden practices seek for favour! These are but shading booths which the various worms of envy, detraction, calumny, and death itself, gnaw, and scatter, and devour. Take the case of a household which reposes the utmost trust in its master; in a short time death hurries away that master, and where now is the shade of all the family? Another relies on a patron who is rich and powerful; the patron dies, or his riches and power are diminished, and so this man's ivy also withers away.

And thus Aman, who was the eye of King Assuerus, recounted to his friends and his wife, with great self-congratulation, "the greatness of his riches, and the multitude of his children, and with how great glory the king had advanced him above all his princes and servants." (*Esth.* v. 11.) Oh! splendid shade. But full soon must it be ignominiously destroyed by the sun and worms. Aman himself was hanged (chap. VII. 10), and his ten sons were put to death. (Chap. IX. 14.)

3. We must rely, good friends, on the bounty, favour, and power of God, and not on that of men. David exclaims,—"Put not your trust in princes: in the children of men." (*Ps.* CXLV. 2, 3.) And why, I pray, must we not trust in those who are possessed

of the greatest power amongst us? The Psalmist immediately adds the reason, "in whom there is no salvation." And for this reason must trust be reposed in none, even of the most powerful of kings, not even in the invincible Cæsars themselves, since they also are only men. For why, O man, do you trust in a man, in whom *there is no salvation?*" "His spirit shall go forth and he shall return into his earth: in that day all their thoughts shall perish;" but "blessed is he who hath the God of Jacob for his helper, whose hope is in the Lord his God." (*Ps.* CXLV. 4, 5.) The Holy Scriptures declare that trust in man is but *a shadow;* "trusting in the shadow of Egypt." (*Isai* XXX. 2.) What can be more fleeting, or more inconstant and deceptive than a shadow? And such is trust reposed in man. "Many seek the face of the prince: but the judgment of every one cometh forth from the Lord." (*Prov.* XXIX. 26.)

When Jacob was returning from Mesopotamia into Chanaan, and was about to meet his brother Esau attended with four hundred men, he was afraid, and earnestly besought Divine help. God listened to his prayer, and promised him the fullest assistance, and yet He sent him away lame. (*Gen.* XXXII. 25.) And what sort of help or Providence is this, you may ask? Jacob implores aid, and he is dismissed with his thigh out of joint! Is this the way to help, to make a man lame? Yes, this was in truth the very way to help him; for there is a time when wounds cause health, and temporary loss is gain; and there are many occasions in which we are overcome for our own good. And therefore God sent away Jacob with his thigh thus out of joint that he might learn, and we through him, not to trust in ourselves or our own strength, nor yet in that of others, but to rely on the power and goodness of God alone. But because the sound man trusts in his health, the strong in his strength, the learned in his learning, the rich in his gold, the wise in his wisdom, and because the poor man hopes to be supported by the rich, and the weak by the powerful, therefore God, in the perfection of His wisdom, frequently removes all these, that, when the props on which we used to rest are gone, we may learn to rest on God alone.

Gedeon dismissed from his standard twenty-two thousand men (*Judges* VII. 3), keeping with him only three hundred (Ver. 6), for so God had commanded him, "lest Israel should glory against Me, and say: I was delivered by my own strength." (Ver. 2.) Benadad, king of Syria, reproaching Achab, king of Israel, with his weakness, threatened to destroy him utterly. (3 *Kings* XX. 1 and foll.) But these threats were vain, for although Benadad had brought with him to the war thirty-two kings, and an incredible number of horsemen and chariots with scythes, he was nevertheless routed in the very first battle, and a hundred-thousand of the Syrians fell in one day. And "they that remained fled to Aphec, into the city: and the wall fell upon seven and twenty thousand men, that were left." (Ver. 30.) This is how Benadad fared; let him now go and trust in himself and his own strength!

That excellent King Asa, whom we can never mention without sorrow, exhibited great Trust in God, if it had only been constant. And this God most signally rewarded when he routed an army of ten hundred thousand men which Zara the Ethiopian had led out against him. (2 *Par.* xiv. 9.) But alas! after passing so many years of his life in such an illustrious way, trust in human strength proved his ruin. And thus the prophet said plainly to him,—"Because thou hast relied on the king of Syria, and not relied on the Lord thy God, therefore is the host of the king of Syria escaped out of thine hand." (2 *Par.* xvi. 7.) And then followed a long series of reverses.

Admirably does S. Augustine say (*In Ps.* xxx. Exp. 2),"Thou hatest them that hold to vanity uselessly. But I, who do not hold to vanity, have trusted in the Lord. Thou trustest in money, thou holdest to vanity : thou trustest in honour, and in some eminence of human power, thou holdest to vanity : thou trustest in some principal friend, thou holdest to vanity. When thou trustest in all these things, either thou diest and leavest them here, or in thy life-time they all perish, and thou failest in thy trust."

4. Moses was most beloved by God, but, because he twice sinned through want of Trust, he expiated his sin by death, and was only permitted to see that fruitful Land of Promise afar off. The first display of want of Trust was when, like a master of a household who is filled with anxiety about feeding his

family, he began to argue and say,—"There are six hundred thousand footmen of this people, and sayest Thou, I will give them flesh to eat a whole month? Shall then a multitude of sheep and oxen be killed, that it may suffice for their food? or shall the fishes of the sea be gathered together to fill them?" (*Numb.* XI. 21, 22.) But this, O Moses, is to reason with your want of Trust, and not with Divine Providence. Is the Hand of the Lord shortened? (*Isai,* L. 2.) And this should have made Moses more careful for the future; but his want of Trust returned, and displayed itself just as on the former occasion, for when all the congregation were gathered together at the rock he exclaimed,—"Hear, ye rebellious and incredulous: Can we bring you forth water out of this rock? And the Lord said to Moses and Aaron: "Because you have not believed Me, to sanctify Me before the children of Israel, you shall not bring these people into the land, which I will give them." (*Numb.* XX. 10, 12.) And therefore God showed to Moses, when he was about to die, that land afar off from the top of a mountain, saying,—"Thou hast seen it with thy eyes, and shalt not pass over to it." (*Deut.* XXXIV. 4.) Of so great consequence is it entirely to expel from the soul this plague of want of Trust, against which, as being so thoroughly opposed to God's glory, He exacts the severest penalties!

The children of Israel also sinned most grievously, and upon many occasions, through exhibiting afresh their want of Trust. Nor did any wonders or miracles avail for their correction; if they could not at once perceive anything with their eyes, or feel it with their hands, they immediately relapsed into their former want of Trust, and affirmed that it could not be done. To such a pitch did this at length arrive that with continual murmurings they accused God, either of forgetting them, or caring not for them. And how wicked were those exclamations,—"Would God that we had died in Egypt: and would God we may die in this vast wilderness, and that the Lord may not bring us into this land, lest we fall by the sword, and our wives and children be led away captives. Is it not better to return into Egypt? And they said one to another: Let us appoint a captain, and let us return into Egypt." (*Numb.* XIV. 3-4.) And is it come to this, ye wicked ones? Just as if there were not everywhere a place for dying! But some may wonder, perhaps, why God not merely gave no wine to His Own chosen people, but permitted them also to want water! In this way their want of Trust was to be expiated. Why did he send fiery serpents against this same people, which not only bit so many, but also slew them? On account of their want of Trust. Why did He sometimes permit twenty or thirty thousand men to be slain in a single battle? On account of this same want of Trust. Why did He set before them warlike enemies, who were never entirely subdued? On account of the same want of Trust, which He could not extinguish in this murmuring people by any punishments, but it was ever bursting out afresh. At length,—"The Lord said to Moses: How long will this people detract Me? How long will they not believe Me for all the signs that I have wrought before them? I will strike them, therefore, with pestilence, and will consume them: but thee I will make a ruler over a great nation, and a mightier than this is." (*Numb.* xiv. 11, 12.) Upon this Moses pleaded with God on their behalf, and still the Divine Decree was,—"According as you have spoken in my hearing, so will I do to you. In the wilderness shall your carcasses lie. But your children, of whom you said that they should be a prey to the enemies, will I bring in: that they may see the land which you have despised." (*Numb.* xiv. 28, 29, 31.) And so the Divine threatenings were executed, for out of so many hundred thousand men whom God had brought up out of Egypt, not one so much as saw the fruitful land, for they all perished in the wilderness. Only Caleb and Josue, who had never cast away their hope of possessing that land, were allowed to enter it. In such a way were they to pay the penalty for their want of Trust! And yet after all this they ceased not from this sin, but repeated it afresh even at the very passage of the Jordan!

5. When the city of Siceleg had been burnt with fire by the Amalecites, and all the women and children had been taken captive, matters had come to such a dreadful pass that the people spoke of stoning David. But the greater was the want of Trust in the rest, the loftier was the confidence of David. He "took cour-

age in the Lord his God." (1 *Kings* xxx. 6.) Thus, then, conceiving the most confident hope, he pursued the enemy with four hundred men, and having found them "spread upon all the ground, eating and drinking," he "slew them from the evening unto the evening of the next day. So David recovered all that the Amalecites had taken." (Ver. 16-18.)

Eliseus predicted, at a time of the utmost scarcity, that there would shortly be great plenty of corn. A certain nobleman of Samaria heard his words, and, mocking them through want of Trust, exclaimed,—"If the Lord should make flood-gates in heaven, can that possibly be which thou sayest?" To whom Eliseus replied,—"Thou shalt see it with thy eyes, but shalt not eat thereof." (4 *Kings* vii. 2.) And it turned out as the prophet had said, for that lord was trodden under foot of the people in the gate, and died. A worthy reward for his want of Trust! Of a truth "the thoughts of mortal men are fearful, and our counsels uncertain." (*Wisd.* ix. 14.) But God knows all things alike, as well future as present and past. And yet because this abyss of Divine Providence is utterly secret, many people, when they perceive so many acts of wickedness remaining unpunished, and unseen, as it were, by God, and when also they see good men sorely scourged with troubles, precipitate themselves into the whirlpool of want of Trust, just as if God had no care for human affairs, since oftentimes no difference appears between the just and unjust. "All things," says the Preacher (*Eccles.* ix. 2.), "equally happen to the just and to the wicked, to the good and to the evil, to the clean and to the unclean, to him that offereth victims, and to him that despiseth sacrifices. As the good is, so also is the sinner: as the perjured, so he also that sweareth truth." These things seem to us to happen at random, and by chance. And thus we are like a man who looks at a clock in a tower; he sees its face indeed, and the hands by which the time is told, but the clock itself, and its skilfully-constructed mechanism of wheels he cannot see. A child or an idiot might believe that the hands of the clock move by themselves, and not according to any fixed design, but by chance. The people, however, who live in that town know full well that this is not the case, but that behind the wall the works of the clock are concealed. And just in the same way the government of God is secret, but conducted on principles of most perfect order. We perceive outward indications of its presence in everything, but the marvellous mechanism we cannot see.

And this Horologe of Divine Providence has inscribed on its dial the hours of all men, even to the smallest seconds. Baltasar, king of Babylon, when drinking wine at his most sumptuous banquet, saw a man's handwriting upon the opposite wall. "Then was the king's countenance changed, and his thoughts troubled him; and the joints of his loins were loosed, and his knees struck one against the other." (*Dan.* v. 6.) But what do you see, O king? Why are you troubled? Whose is this hand? If you know it, how

is it that you do not also know the writer? But if
you recognize neither one nor the other, why do you
fear so exceedingly? The wretched king consulted
all the wise men of the city about this mysterious
writing, but none could understand it; all could see
the face of the horologe, but none its interior works.
Yet who could doubt that the hands were made to
revolve by Divine Providence? Then came Daniel
and proclaimed,—"This is the interpretation of the
word. Mane: God hath numbered thy kingdom,
and hath finished it." (Ver. 26.) The last hour of
your life, O king, is come, it is even now hastening to
its end. Therefore, make haste to live; the last moment of the clock is passing away. And how did
Daniel know this? He saw it on the Horologe of
Divine Providence.

6. Hence it appears that all the affairs of men,
whether they be adverse or prosperous, are most accurately and exactly inscribed on this Horologe of
Divine Providence, which cannot be so deceived in
even the minutest point as not to cause all things to
be directed to the end which is most expedient. "One
jot or one tittle shall not pass." (*Matt.* v. 18.)
"Neither will I leave thee, till I shall have accomplished all that I have said." (*Gen.* xxviii. 15.) But
if we trust a clock which has a most skilful workman
to attend to its mechanism, what folly and madness
it is sometimes to find fault with that Horologe of the
universe, which cannot err, and wherein all events are
most admirably ordered? "But Thy Providence, O

Father, governeth it: for Thou hast made a way even in the sea, and a most sure path among the waves. Shewing that Thou art able to save out of all things, yea though a man went to sea without art." (*Wisd.* XIV. 3, 4.) When excellent men, however, are oppressed and afflicted, while the wicked flourish, and bring all their undertakings to a prosperous issue, Divine Providence seems to sleep, or to wink at this. And this thought has sometimes disquieted even the saintliest of men; but their disquietude is our instruction and confirmation. David says of himself,—"But my feet were almost moved; my steps had wellnigh slipped. Because I had a zeal on occasion of the wicked, seeing the prosperity of sinners. They are not in the labour of men: neither shall they be scourged like other men. And I said: Then have I in vain justified my heart, and washed my hands among the innocent." (*Ps.* LXXII, 2, 3, 5, 13.) David evidently thought that he could discover the reason for this, for he says,—"I studied that I might know this thing, it is a labour in my sight: until I go into the sanctuary of God, and understand concerning their last ends." (Ver. 16, 17.) We shall one day know all this in heaven, but now we must not attempt to find it out. "Thou indeed, O Lord, art just, if I plead with Thee, but yet I will speak what is just to Thee: Why doth the way of the wicked prosper: Why is it well with all them that transgress, and do wickedly? Thou hast planted them, and they have taken root: they prosper and bring forth fruit: Thou art near in their mouth, and far from their reins." (*Jer.* XII. 1, 2.) And in the same way Habacuc complains (chap. I. 13, 14),—"Why lookest Thou upon them that do unjust things, and holdest Thy peace when the wicked devoureth the man that is more just than himself? And thou wilt make men as the fishes of the sea, and as the creeping things that have no ruler." But all such complaints arise from our seeing *only one part* of Divine Providence; the other is entirely hidden from our eyes, and yet, when the manifestation of an event should be waited for until the day of judgment, we nevertheless pass a rash judgment before that day. And therefore S. Paul says (1 *Cor.* IV. 5):—"Therefore judge not before the time, until the Lord come, Who both will bring to light the hidden things of darkness, and will make manifest the counsels of the hearts."

Hereafter, when we shall see not merely the face of that great Horologe, but the very works themselves of Divine Providence, and it will be permitted to us to inspect them all, then each person will behold most clearly the courses of all ages, and the events of his own life, and then will be seen with what wonderful Providence God has governed all men, individually and collectively, and with what fatherly care He has ordered every moment of each person's life for their good and salvation, and has never allowed anything to happen to any one which might not help towards this end. Then it will be seen why God permitted the angels to be cast down from heaven, and the first Pair to fall. Why He chose the Jews, a stubborn nation, to be His Own people, while he rejected the rest of mankind. Why He has decreed that some should be born of Christian parents, while He has permitted others to be born among idolaters. Why He has early delivered one person from all kinds of sorrows, while He has allowed another to grow old in calamity and die in it. Then whatever has been patiently endured for love of Christ will be of priceless value. Whoever seriously reflects on this, salutes with a reverent kiss the sceptre of Assuerus (*Esth.* v. 2); that is to say, every chastisement of God.

CHAPTER XI

JUST as in a golden chain link hangs from link, so from knowledge of Divine Providence springs Trust in God; and from this there very naturally arises conformity of the human will with the Divine. Show me a man who in all things recognizes the Providence of God, and trusts in Him, and I will also show you one who most absolutely yields himself to the Divine Will. In this way God instructs us,—"That He might make known unto us the mystery of His Will, according to His Good-pleasure which He hath purposed in Him." (*Eph.* i. 9); "That we may be filled with the knowledge of His Will in all Wisdom and spiritual understanding." (*Col.* i. 9.) We may see this very clearly in the case of Noe.

1. Noe at first needed to be instructed concerning the infinite Providence of God, and therefore He explained to him most circumstantially for what purpose the ark was to be made, as well as its length, and breadth, and height; in what way living creatures of

every kind were to be collected together in it, how the proper food for each was to be procured; and how he was at last to enter the ark when it was completed, together with seven human beings, his nearest relations, since God had determined to drown all that lived in the waters of the flood. From this Noe learnt the marvellous Providence of God, and on the knowledge of this Providence he reposed such entire Trust as to be fully persuaded that he and his would be preserved amidst the destruction of the world. And when this Trust had been conceived it was very easy for him to cause his own will to rest on the Divine Will, and to do everything according to its rule. Thus, therefore, he earned the distinguished praise,— "And Noe did all things which God commanded him." (*Gen.* VI. 22.) And here it is very worthy to be noted that when Noe and those who belonged to him had entered the ark, "the Lord shut him in" (chap. VII. 16); and thus He may be said to have taken away with Him the key for opening the ark. But you may perhaps inquire, would it not have been better to have delivered that key to Noe, so that, when the waters of the deluge abated, he himself might open the door and go out? For this reason God willed to entrust this key to no one, but to keep it for Himself, that those who were enclosed in the ark might be let out by the same Hand by which they had been let in, and might not place their Trust in any other than the Author of their liberty and salvation.

And in the same way Joseph, the governor of

Egypt, needed to be instructed by such marvellous changes of fortune, in order that he might recognize the Providence of God; and when he had learnt how ever-watchful Divine Providence was, he then needed to be inspired with Trust. On this account God permitted that the butler of Pharao should for two whole years forget the interpreter of his dream, though so earnestly asked to remember him (*Gen.* XL. 23, and XLI. 1), in order that Joseph might learn not to rely on the favour of men, but on that of God alone, to Whom alone he ought to refer the recovery of his liberty. S. Chrysostom (*Hom.* LXIII. *in Gen.*) admirably remarks upon this,—"Consider how that after the butler was restored to favour two years passed away. Joseph must wait for a fitting time, in order that he may be brought out with more distinguished honour. For if the chief butler had remembered him before the dreams of Pharao, and had obtained his liberation through his influence, Joseph's virtue would not perhaps have been so conspicuous to others. But now the Almighty and wise God knowing, like a skilful workman, how long the gold ought to be kept in the fire, and then withdrawn from it, permitted the chief butler to forget Joseph for the space of two years, in order that both the time for Pharao's dream might come, and that through the very force of necessity that just man should become known through the whole of Pharao's kingdom." And hence the devotion of Joseph to the Divine Will was so great that all the ills which befell him he ascribed to this alone.

Hence arose that noble speech of his to his brethren, when unfolding the mystery of the Divine Will he said,—"You thought *evil* against me: but God turned it into *good,* that He might exalt me, as at present you see, and might save many people." (*Gen.* L. 20.) If Joseph had not so thoroughly learnt the mystery of the Divine Will, he would have ordered his brethren to be slain, and would not have loaded them with so many acts of kindness. And the same zeal for the Divine Will which was manifested by Noe and Joseph may be seen also in all men of saintly life. Concerning each one of them it may be affirmed, they *"gave their own selves first to the Lord,* then to us by the Will of God." (2 *Cor.* VIII. 5.)

2. In the year 1095, when Pope Urban the Second had made a public address at the Council of Clermont in France, about the recovery of the Holy Land, the minds of all present were inflamed towards this sacred war, and they cried out,—"God wills, God wills." This was afterwards used by the entire army of three hundred thousand men as a watch-word, and particularly when the conflict was beginning, and the hostile lines were closing, the Christian soldier used nobly to cry out,—"God wills, God wills!"

And as many of us, in truth, as are called by the name of Christ are marching to the Holy Land, even to the land of the living. Let us, therefore, excite our courage, and especially when dangers press on us, and when secret foes harass us, let us cry out with joy,—"God wills! Let us, then, play the man, let us labour, fight, and conquer: God so wills!"

S. Aldegundis, a most holy virgin, having made wonderful advance in virtue, was often refreshed with heavenly visitations. In the course of these a strange damsel, who seemed to have come from foreign parts to visit her, bade her ask what she would from God, for that she would without difficulty obtain her petition. Aldegundis immediately replied,—"This one thing I ask, that God's will may be done. My sole pleasure is the Will of God."

3. And what need is there of multiplying words? This was the absorbing study of all the saints, to know Divine Providence, and to rise upwards from this knowledge to Trust in God, and from Trust to pass into sweetest union with the Divine Will; to act, in one word, in such a way as that their own will should esteem it a delight to be absorbed in God's Will. And he, in truth, who ever desires that the Will of God should be done is at the same time gratifying his own in all things. For what can withstand the man who, in place of his own will, recognizes the Divine? And hence arose that most laudable custom of the old fathers, in accordance with which they ascribed all things, however they happened, to the Providence and Will of God alone. The brethren of Joseph, who in other respects were rugged in disposition and wicked also, were nevertheless so far deserving of commendation that when they had found the money which they had brought for buying corn

safely laid up in every man's sack, they were filled with wonder, "and said to one another: What is this *that God hath done unto us?*" (*Gen.* XLII. 28.) The words "that God hath done unto us" are worthy of all observation. Which of us would not have said?— "It is a manifest act of deception. The Egyptians are seeking occasion to ruin us; this is done in order to furnish a false charge against us; unless the steward forgot the money through carelessness, by some chance or other, he must have hidden it in the sacks of corn. But what if he intended to return our money to us as an act of charity? What if in this way he designed to attract more buyers?" But they said nothing of the kind, but wisely exclaimed,—*"What is this that God hath done unto us?"* Whatever error or fraud occurred, God caused it, and for us He caused it; the reason of all this is the Will of God, without Whose Permission not even a grain can fall from a mountain, a hair from the head, a leaf from the tree, a sparrow from the air.

4. Christ our Lord, being hurried away to the thought of the eternal Providence of His Father by an ardour of most perfect sweetness, exclaimed,— "Yea, Father: for so hath it seemed good in Thy sight." (*Matt.* XI. 26.) Yea, Father; Thou hast done all things well, nor can any mortal find fault with anything in Thy Providence and Thy Judgments, for so hath it seemed good in Thy sight. And behold how sweetly are we instructed not to assign a limit to the Divine Power, not to pry into the Judgments of

God, and not to examine His Decrees, but to acquiesce for this single reason, *since thus it seems good to God.* Our Saviour declares that THUS it seemed good to the Father; but *why* it so seemed good to Him He does not explain, since a reason is neither to be assigned to the Divine Will, nor to be inquired for. It stands for a thousand reasons that GOD SO WILLED. And therefore in all things which you either do or do not, which you either shrink from or endure, ever say, my Christian friend, after the example of our Lord,—"Yea, Father. Yea, Father." Continue to say, even though it be repeated thousands of times a day,—"Yea, Father." Utter this when waking or sleeping, in sickness or health, and even in death itself; just as if you were to say,—"I can deny Thee nothing, O Lord, Thou knowest. As therefore Thou willest, disposest, ordainest, and permittest all things to be done, even so be they done, O my Father, and so be they done in me, and may nothing be done in me which in even the smallest particular is contrary to Thy most just and holy Will. Yea, Father; so be it done now, and always, and for all eternity."

And in this way one of the early Fathers was wont to pray,—"O Son of God, as Thou knowest, and as Thou willest, have mercy on me." And in the same way that writer, who was so devoted to the Divine Will (THOMAS À KEMPIS, *de Imit. Christi,* III. 17), exclaims,—"So that my will may remain right, and firmly fixed on Thee, O Lord, do to me whatever shall seem good in Thy sight. If Thou willest that I should be in darkness, blessed be Thou! If Thou willest that I should be in light, still blessed be Thou! If Thou deignest to comfort me, blessed be Thou! And if Thou willest that I should be troubled, equally blessed be Thou forever! I will willingly suffer for Thee, O Lord, whatever Thou willest should come upon me. I am ready to receive alike from Thy Hand good and evil, sweet and bitter, joy and sadness, and to give thanks for everything that befalls me." This, my Christian friends, is really to pray with DEVOTION, and to act with DEVOTION.

Nor does the following prayer differ from the preceding:—"O good JESU, Thou didst so love me as to surrender Thyself wholly to the fury of murderers to be nailed to the cross; and what great thing is it if I yield myself wholly to Thy Hands, not indeed like the hands of those cruel men, but those which truly belong to a Father. I am sure that all things tend to my profit. Deal, therefore, with me, O Lord, according as it seems good in Thine Eyes; for all things are Thine, neither is there any one who can resist Thy Will, 'for Thou, O Lord, hast done as it pleased Thee!'" (*Jonas* I. 14.) Such were the prayers of the saints under the elder covenant. In this way Tobias prayed,—"Now, O Lord, do with me according to Thy will." (Chap. III. 6.) And thus too Judith prayed,—"Let us ask the Lord with tears, that according to His will so He would shew His mercy to us." (Chap. VIII. 17.)

5. And here you may perhaps object:—"If God

wills that my parents should die, in what way can I will their death? And supposing that God should will that I or they should be damned, could I also will the same?" God wills that your father and mother should die, my good friend, not merely that their enjoyment of life should be closed, but that satisfaction may be made to His Justice, or that the order of nature should be preserved; and thus it is most fitting that you yourself should also will. And, in the same way, if God wills that you should be damned, He does not will it in order to bring evil upon you, but to punish evil, and maintain His Justice; so that it is right that you also should will that sin should be punished, even in yourself.

Why, therefore, do we hesitate and adopt so many shifts? All created things obey the Divine Will, and man alone refuses. God regards the end which He has proposed to Himself and attains it; and we, too, shall attain our end if we recognize His Providence, and ever unite our own will to His. But, alas! how delicate we are, and how grievously do we mourn over calamities of all kinds! If God sends anything upon us which causes severer trouble than we are accustomed to, and from which the lower facilities of our soul recoil, then let us reflect that this is a most noble opportunity for imitating our Lord, and let us say with Him,—"Not my will, but Thine be done." This is the way to commit one's self wholly to God's Providence and Will, that He should decree for us what, how much, and when He wills, and that we should make no reservations, nor give way to any contradictions.

And here let Ludovicus Blosius confirm this with his own words:—"Let man," he says, "everywhere forsake his own will and resign it to God, transfusing it wholly into Him, and uniting it perfectly to His Will. Never let him say with his mouth, or even with his heart, such words as, 'I will this; I will that not: I choose this; I reject that.' Neither in time nor eternity let him seek *anything of his own;* but rejecting everything that belongs to self, let him spoil, as it were, and deprive himself of self, and die to himself, and all created things, in such a way as if he had never been created. But let him seek God everywhere, and His Honour and Will, in such a way as that even to his prayers and holy intentions he may unite denial and resignation of self; seeking not that his own will should be done, but the Will of God. Let him ascribe all that happens to him to that same Divine Will, and receive it purely from the Hand of the Lord, without Whose Providence not so much as a single leaf falls to the ground. Let him patiently and cheerfully submit to and praise God's Permission and Ordinance alike in prosperity and adversity, in losses, injuries, calumnies, reproaches, mockings, and contempt of self; in sufferings of body, in pangs of heart, in griefs, in desolation and internal woe, and in afflictions of every kind, believing that GOD BOTH WILLS AND IS ABLE TO PROMOTE HIS SALVATION BY ALL THINGS."

Caius Popilius was sent as an ambassador from the

Roman Senate to Antiochus, king of Syria, to demand that he should abstain from hostilities against Ptolemy, king of Egypt. The king received him with great kindness, and offered him his right hand with every sign of friendship; but Popilius refused to hold out his hand in turn, and, assuming a look of dignity, replied,—"Let us lay aside our private feelings of friendship; business of the state now claims our attention, for the senate has passed a decree, according to which King Antiochus must either abstain from invading Egypt, or commence hostilities with the Roman people." As soon as Antiochus had read the letter of the senate, he said that he would confer with his friends; upon which Popilius replied,—"The business admits not of delay; there must be no procrastination." And at the same time, with a stick which he held in his hand he made a circle round the king in the sand, exclaiming,—"Before you go beyond this circle give me an answer which I may carry back to the senate." You would not have thought it was an ambassador who spoke, but that the senate itself was arrayed before his eyes, for the king immediately declared that Ptolemy should have no further cause of complaint against him. Then at last Popilius grasped his hand as that of a friend; and at the same moment overawed the King of Syria, and protected the King of Egypt. And that which befell Antiochus happens in our case; we wish to be friends with God, but we are not ready to transport ourselves into conformity with His Will. Therefore the Son was sent into the world as an

Ambassador by the Father, and, drawing the circle of the Divine Will around us, said,—"Not every one that saith to Me, Lord, Lord, shall enter into the kingdom of heaven; but he that doth the Will of My Father Who is in heaven." (*Matt.* VII. 21.) Behold, then, O man, in this circle you are enclosed, nor can you pass beyond it till you have declared whether you are willing to surrender yourself to the Will of God, or to live according to your own pleasure! If you love peace, if you desire not to be an enemy of God, if you hate impious war with God, you will immediately give your answer. But why, my Christian friend, do you try to avoid the question? Why do you deliberate? Why do you delay? This business admits of no hesitation. If you are really wise, you will imitate that king, and will reply with the utmost readiness,—"O my God, I deliver my whole self absolutely to Thy most holy Will, and bind myself firmly to it, being ready both to do and suffer all things, to live and die as Thou willest. In all afflictions, however grievous they may be, Thy most just Will will be my chief consolation. This I set before myself as the one and only rule both of living and dying, *The Will of the Lord be done!* Let the universe be disturbed by tempests from every quarter, let armed battalions close in deadly fray, let fleets be crippled and destroyed by fleets, let the law courts ring with endless litigation, and still this is my chief business in life, to conform myself entirely to the one and only Will of God. And now I embrace and store in my inmost heart that most holy and Divine saying,—'The world passeth away, and the concupiscence thereof: BUT HE THAT DOTH THE WILL OF GOD ABIDETH FOR EVER.' " (I *John* II. 17.)

DEO GRATIAS.

SUPPLEMENT

May God's Holy Will Be Done

O Lord, do to me whatever shall seem good in Thy sight. If Thou willest that I should be in darkness, blessed be Thou! If Thou willest that I should be in light, still blessed be Thou! If Thou deignest to comfort me, blessed be Thou! And if Thou willest that I should be afflicted, equally blessed be Thou forever! I will willingly suffer for Thee, O Lord, whatever Thou willest should come upon me. I am ready to receive alike from Thy hand good and evil, sweet and bitter, joy and sadness, and to give thanks for everything that befalls me. Keep me only from all sin and I will fear neither death nor Hell. Cast me not off forever, nor blot me out of the Book of Life, and whatsoever tribulation befalleth me shall not hurt me.

(Imitation of Christ, Bk. III, *Ch.* 17)

Prayer Of Job

The Lord hath given, and the Lord hath taken away. Blessed be the Name of the Lord!

(Job 1:21)

Prayer Of St. Alphonsus

My Jesus, grant that I may love Thee always, and then do with me what Thou wilt.

(St. Alphonsus Liguori)

Words Of Our Lord Jesus Christ

Not my will, but Thine be done.

(Luke 22:42)

Prayer To Do The Will Of God

Grant me, Most Kind Jesus, Thy grace, that it may abide with me, and labor with me, and persevere with me, to the end.

Grant me ever to will and to desire that which is most acceptable to Thee, and which pleaseth Thee best.

May Thy will be mine, and let my will always follow Thine, and agree perfectly with it.

Let me always will, and not will, the same with Thee, and let me not be able to will or not will otherwise than as Thou willest or willest not.

(Imitation of Christ, Bk. III, *Ch.* 15)

An Aspiration

May the most just, the most high, the most lovable Will of God be in all things accomplished, praised, and magnified forever!

Acceptance Of Death

O Lord, my God, even now I accept from Thy hand, willingly and with submission, the kind of death it may please Thee to send me, with all its sorrows, pains and anguish.

Prayer From The Psalms

Teach me to do Thy will, for Thou art my God.
(*Psalm* 142:10)

Act Of Surrender To God's Holy Will

O good Jesus, Thou didst so love me as to surrender Thyself wholly to the fury of murderers to be nailed to the cross; and what great thing is it if I yield myself wholly to Thy hands, not indeed like the hands of those cruel men, but hands which truly belong to a Father. I am sure that all things tend to my profit. Deal, therefore, with me, O Lord, according as it seems good in Thine eyes; for all things are Thine, neither is there anyone who can resist Thy will, "for Thou, O Lord, hast done as it pleased Thee!"

(*Heliotropium*, p. 394)

Act Of Confidence In God

O sweet and tender Providence of my God, into Thy hands I commend my spirit; to Thee I abandon my hopes and fears, my desires and repugnances, my temporal and eternal prospects. To Thee I commit the wants of my perishable body; to Thee I commit the more precious interests of my immortal soul. Though my faults are many, my misery great, my spiritual poverty extreme, my hope in Thee surpasses all.

Though temptations should assail me, I will hope in Thee; though I should break my resolutions, I will look to Thee confidently for grace to keep them at last. Though Thou shouldst kill me, even then I will trust in Thee; for Thou art my Father, my God, the support of my salvation. Thou art my kind, my tender and indulgent Parent, and I am Thy loving child. I put my trust in Thee, and so trusting, shall not be confounded. Amen.

(Blessed Claude de la Colombiere)

Prayer for Conformity To The Will Of God

O Lord Almighty, who permittest evil in order to draw good therefrom, hear our humble prayers, and grant that we remain faithful to Thee unto death. Grant us also, through the intercession of Most Holy Mary, the strength ever to conform ourselves to Thy Most Holy Will.

Prayer Of Trust

Most Sacred and Adorable Heart of Jesus, I know not what trials may come to me this day, but I am certain that nothing will happen to me which Thou hast not foreseen and decreed. I trust Thy love for me in all and through all and in spite of all.

In all my trials and crosses, *O Sacred Heart of Jesus, I place my trust in Thee.*

In dangers and difficulties, *O Sacred Heart of Jesus, I place my trust in Thee.*

In doubts and anxieties, *O Sacred Heart of Jesus, I place my trust in Thee.*

In failure and disappointment, *O Sacred Heart of Jesus, I place my trust in Thee.*

In unemployment, *O Sacred Heart of Jesus, I place my trust in Thee.*

In spite of my past, *O Sacred Heart of Jesus, I place my trust in Thee.*

In spite of my sins and evil habits, *O Sacred Heart of Jesus, I place my trust in Thee.*

When I cannot pray, *O Sacred Heart of Jesus, I place my trust in Thee.*

When my prayers are unanswered, *O Sacred Heart of Jesus, I place my trust in Thee.*

When temptations are strongest, *O Sacred Heart of Jesus, I place my trust in Thee.*

When my dear ones are in danger, *O Sacred Heart of Jesus, I place my trust in Thee.*

In sickness and suffering, *O Sacred Heart of Jesus, I place my trust in Thee.*

At the hour of my death, *O Sacred Heart of Jesus, I place my trust in Thee.*

A Prayer Of Confidence In God

Jesus of the loving Heart, I believe You care for me more than You care for the birds of the air or the lilies of the field.

I believe that You care for me more than a mother cares for the child in her arms.

I believe that even though a mother may forget the child of her womb, yet will You not forget me.

And, therefore, I trust in Thee in all and through all and in spite of all. Amen.

> Strong Heart of Jesus,
>   my God and my Friend,
> In life and in death,
>   on Thee I depend.
> *(Rev. James O'Brien, S.J.)*

Conformity To God's Holy Will

My Jesus, I accept any sorrow or suffering Thy Providence sees fit to send me. My wish is in all things to conform myself to Thy Holy Will. Whenever I kiss the crucifix, it is to show Thee that I am willing to carry my cross.

(St. Margaret Mary)

Welcome Be The Holy Will Of God!

O Lord, Thou knowest what is best for me. Give what Thou wilt and how much Thou wilt, and when Thou wilt. Deal with me as Thou thinkest good and as it best pleaseth Thee and is for Thy honor. Set me where Thou wilt and deal with me in all things as Thou wilt.

Help me to bear my sufferings for Thy sake, and to say in all sincerity: Welcome be the Holy Will of God!

When sorrow darkens my life, *Welcome be the Holy Will of God!*

When sickness strikes me down, *Welcome be the Holy Will of God!*

When hunger and unemployment threaten, *Welcome be the Holy Will of God!*

When hunger and unemployment are my lot, *Welcome be the Holy Will of God!*

When my hopes are unfulfilled, *Welcome be the Holy Will of God!*

When my friends forsake me, *Welcome be the Holy Will of God!*

When I am unhappy, *Welcome be the Holy Will of God!*

When enemies injure me, *Welcome be the Holy Will of God!*

When men calumniate me and speak that which is evil against me, *Welcome be the Holy Will of God!*

When my undertakings fail, *Welcome be the Holy Will of God!*

When the cross presses heavily upon me, *Welcome be the Holy Will of God!*

[407]

When my last hour comes, *Welcome be the Holy Will of God!*

Short Acts Of Trust

Sacred Heart of Jesus, I believe in Thy love for me. Sacred Heart of Jesus, I trust in Thee!

Act Of Faith And Trust

Most loving Heart of my God,
  I believe in Thy power,
  I believe in Thy knowledge,
  I believe in Thy personal love for me;
And therefore, O Sacred Heart of Jesus,
  I place all my trust in Thee;
  Welcome be Thy Holy Will!

Prayer To Imitate The Example Of Christ

My King and My Saviour, teach me
  to see things as Thou dost see them,
  to feel things as Thou dost feel them,
  to value things as Thou dost value them, and
    consequently
  to be what Thou wouldst have me to be.

(Archbishop Goodier, S.J.)

A Psalm Of David

The Lord ruleth me: and I shall want nothing. He hath set me in a place of pasture.

He hath brought me up, on the water of refreshment: He hath converted my soul.

He hath led me on the paths of justice, for His own name's sake.

For though I should walk in the midst of the shadow of death, I will fear no evils, for Thou art with me.

Thy rod and Thy staff, they have comforted me.

Thou hast prepared a table before me against them that afflict me.

Thou hast anointed my head with oil; and my chalice which inebriateth *me*, how goodly is it!

And Thy mercy will follow me all the days of my life.

And that I may dwell in the house of the Lord unto length of days.

(*Psalm* 22:1-6)

Hymn To The Will Of God

'Tis Thy good pleasure, not my own,
In Thee, my God, I love alone;
And nothing I desire of Thee
But what Thy goodness wills for me.
O Will of God! O Will divine!
All, all our love be ever Thine.

[409]

In love no rival canst Thou bear,
But Thou art full of tenderest care;
And fire and sweetness all divine
To hearts which once are wholly Thine.
O Will of God! O Will divine!
All, all our love be ever Thine.

In Thee all pure affections live,
To love Thou dost perfection give;
While ever burning with desires
The loving soul to Thee aspires.
O Will of God! O Will divine!
All, all our love be ever Thine.

Thou makest crosses soft and light
And death itself seem sweet and bright.
No cross nor fear that soul dismays
Whose will to Thee united stays.
O Will of God! O Will divine!
All, all our love be ever Thine.

To all the glorious choirs of Heaven
Their very bliss by Thee is given;
And Heaven itself deprived of Thee
Would be a land of misery.
O Will of God! O Will divine!
All, all our love be ever Thine.

Yea, to the lost who burn in Hell
If in their souls Thy love could dwell,
The very flames and torments there
Would seem but sweet and light to bear.
O Will of God! O Will divine!
All, all our love be ever Thine.

Oh! That one day my life may end
In closest bonds to Thee enchained!
For thus to die is not to die,
But live, and live eternally.
>O Will of God! O Will divine!
>All, all our love be ever Thine.

To Thee I consecrate and give
My heart and being while I live;
Jesus, Thy heart alone shall be
My love for all eternity.
>O Will of God! O Will divine!
>All, all our love be ever Thine.

Alike in pleasure and in pain
To please Thee is my joy and gain;
That, O my Love, which pleases Thee
Shall ever more seem best to me.
>May Heaven and earth with love fulfill,
>My God, Thy ever-blessed Will!
>>(*St. Alphonsus Liguori*)

Prayer For Myself

My Lord and my God, Thou hast created me for Thyself: grant that I may realize that my true happiness lies in doing Thy Holy Will. Grant, too, that I may labor unto the end for Thy greater honor and glory. I beseech Thee also to allow no one to be damned through any word or act of mine. Jesus meek and humble of heart, make my heart like unto Thine.

The Great Request

One special grace I ask of Thee, dear Heart of Jesus: the grace of a happy death. If Thou dost give me this grace I shall be indifferent as to what Thou dost with me. Send me trials, disappointments, failure, misfortune, ill health, the loss of my dearest friend, but in return give me the grace of a happy death, and I shall be well content. Amen.

Act Of Trust In The
Sacred Heart Of Jesus

My Lord and my God, I believe all that Thou hast ever taught . . . There is nothing harder for me to believe than Thy personal love for one so sinful and so worthless as I am; but I do believe it, Lord, and therefore, *O Sacred Heart of Jesus, I place all my trust in Thee.*

I believe that Thy love for me is not an affair of yesterday: "Thou hast loved me with an everlasting love," and therefore, *O Sacred Heart of Jesus, I place all my trust in Thee.*

I believe Thy love for me is as tender as a mother's love, and therefore, *O Sacred Heart of Jesus, I place all my trust in Thee.*

I believe Thou hast planned everything that shall ever happen to me, lovingly and wisely, and therefore, *O Sacred Heart of Jesus, I place all my trust in Thee.*

I will never seek pleasure forbidden by Thee, because Thou knowest what is bad for me and what is good, and I trust in Thee, *O Sacred Heart of Jesus.*

I will always pray: "May Thy Holy Will be done in all things," because I trust in Thee, *O Sacred Heart of Jesus."*

I will accept the crosses of life, as I accept the joys, with a grateful heart, because I trust in Thee, *O Sacred Heart of Jesus.*

I will not be worried or anxious about anything, because I trust in Thee, *O Sacred Heart of Jesus.*

I will never lose heart in my efforts to be good, because I trust in Thee, *O Sacred Heart of Jesus.*

However weak or sinful I may be, I will never doubt Thy mercy, because I trust in Thee, *O Sacred Heart of Jesus.*

In all my temptations, *O Sacred Heart of Jesus, I place my trust in Thee.*

In all my weaknesses, *O Sacred Heart of Jesus, I place my trust in Thee.*

In all my difficulties, *O Sacred Heart of Jesus, I place my trust in Thee.*

In all my trials, *O Sacred Heart of Jesus, I place my trust in Thee.*

In all my sorrows, *O Sacred Heart of Jesus, I place my trust in Thee.*

In every failure, *O Sacred Heart of Jesus, I place my trust in Thee.*

In every discouragement, *O Sacred Heart of Jesus, I place my trust in Thee.*

In all my undertakings, *O Sacred Heart of Jesus, I place my trust in Thee.*

In life and in death, *O Sacred Heart of Jesus, I place my trust in Thee.*

In time and in eternity, *O Sacred Heart of Jesus, I place my trust in Thee.*

The Answer Is Assured!

The time may be delayed, the manner be unexpected, but the answer to prayer is sure to come. Not a tear of sacred sorrow, not a breath of holy desire, poured out in prayer to God, will ever be lost.

Deo Gratias